Skating Engineers
Hockey at RPI

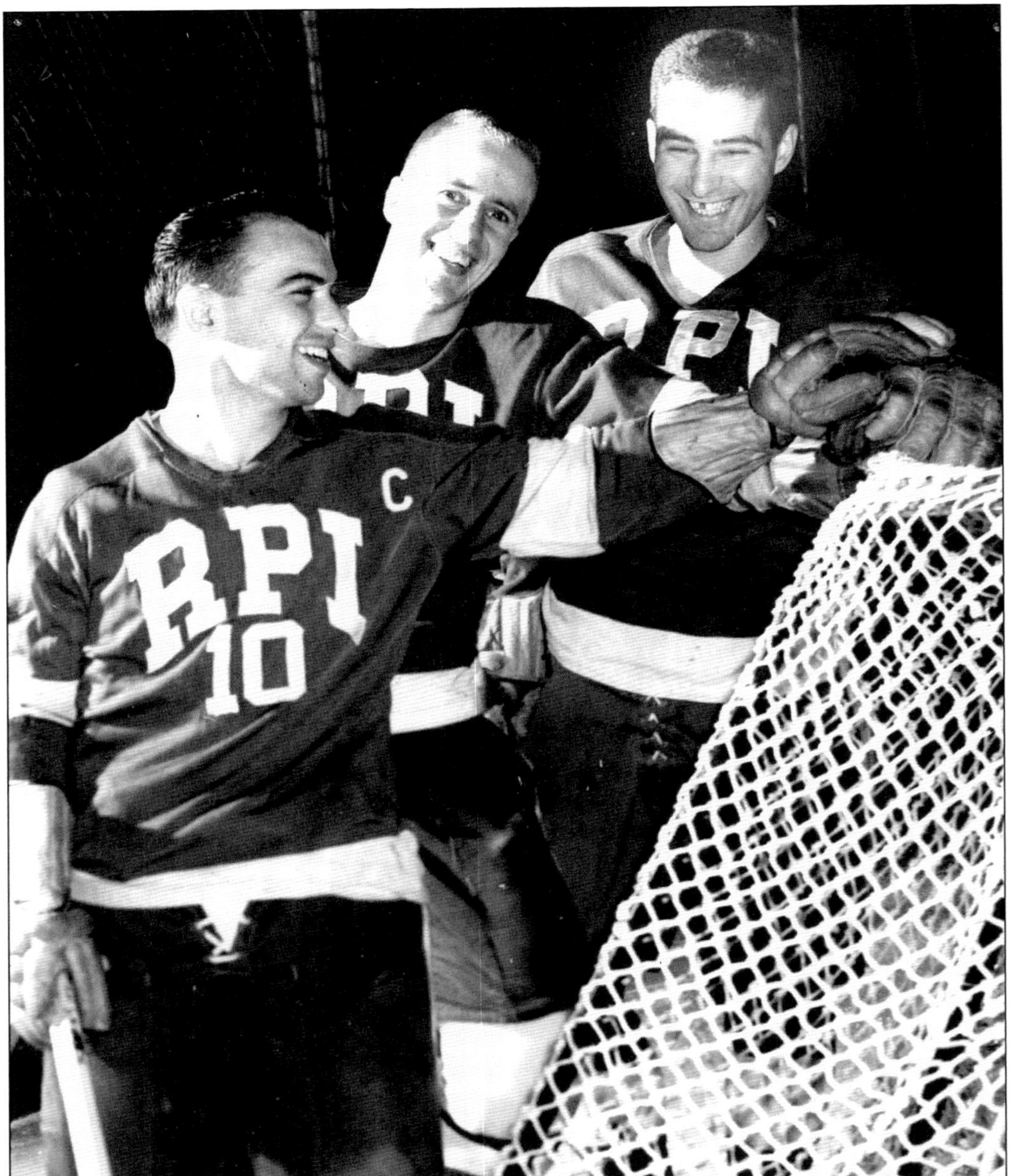

GARRY KEARNS '58, RON PALMER '58, AND PAUL MIDGHALL '59. The top three scorers of the 1957–1958 season stand around the net. These three combined to score 173 points while leading the Engineers to a 14-6-1 record.

SKATING ENGINEERS
HOCKEY AT RPI

Kurt Stutt

ARCADIA
PUBLISHING

ISBN 978-0-7385-3692-7

Published by Arcadia Publishing,
Charleston, South Carolina

Printed in the United States of America

Library of Congress Catalog Card Number: 2004110294

For all general information, contact Arcadia Publishing:
Telephone 843-853-2070
Fax 843-853-0044
E-mail sales@arcadiapublishing.com
For customer service and orders:
Toll-free 1-888-313-2665

Visit us on the Internet at www.arcadiapublishing.com

Contents

Acknowledgments

The author would like to thank Kevin Beattie, sports information director at RPI, for allowing access to the athletic department's picture archives, and Rensselaer Polytechnic Institute for allowing the use of the photographs in this book. Information and statistics for post-collegiate careers have been taken from the Internet Hockey Database (www.hockeydb.com), run by Ralph Slate '91.

INTRODUCTION

Students at Rensselaer Polytechnic Institute (RPI) are not the type of people to sit by idly when innovations occur—not just science and technological advancements, but athletic ones as well. Hockey was in its infancy at the beginning of the 20th century. Johns Hopkins University and Yale University had only played the first documented collegiate hockey game on February 3, 1896. Some students at RPI were interested in this new game, and in those days, all a team needed was a few people. Therefore, a hockey club at RPI was born.

They took to the ice competitively for the first time on January 25, 1902, at the Cohoes Ice Rink against Williams College. The lineup for RPI was unspectacular: W. A. Reeves, goalie; N. A. Taylor, point; E. A. Bonney, cover-point; H. A. Harcourt, rover; H. Clark, center; C. E. Brown, wing; and W. Reichard, wing. It is doubtful any of those players thought this would become anything more than a way to have some fun during the school year. Certainly, it could never surpass the popularity of football; RPI's gridiron team played in front of thousands. RPI lost to Williams that day, but in time, the outcome was not as important as the fact the game was played at all.

The sport grew slowly at the institute. The team played one game per year against collegiate opponents for the first three years. Then, they had no opponents for two years and only played practice games against local athletic clubs. In the winter of 1906–1907, the team managed to play three games, including two in Pittsburgh and one at West Point. Without their own rink, the players had to travel to Albany to host games, assuming the weather cooperated and there was ice. Without a coach, the team organized practices on their own. Hockey was considered a minor sport at the school, and it received less attention as a result.

Things started to improve in 1912, when the school built a rink on campus. In 1917, the team received a coach, Leroy Clark '06, assistant professor of Rational and Technical Mechanics and the composer of "Loyal to Rensselaer," a rousing song seemingly inspired by the football team. The team scheduled approximately 10 games each season, but generally, half were cancelled because there was no ice. The team never played more than six times a season in these years, and even then, slush was a common description for the ice conditions.

Clark left his coaching position in 1923, and the team led themselves for a season. W. J. Cook came aboard for one year, and in 1925, Marvin Callan was hired by the athletic department to coach the team. Still, the program never really evolved. By this time, college teams in Boston were playing in front of thousands of fans, but RPI's rink had no seating. Clarkson College of Technology was playing lengthy schedules, due to the colder weather north of the Adirondacks, but RPI was still canceling games when it was too warm to play. The program was dropped in 1931, revived for the winter of 1936, and then dropped again in 1937. When World War II began, everyone lost interest in hockey.

Hockey was reborn at the institute through the efforts of two men: Livingston W. Houston '13, the school's president, and Ned Harkness, a veteran of the Royal Canadian Air Force who was hired to coach the lacrosse team. The two discussed reinstating the hockey program, but the first obstacle was a facility. Enter the federal government, which had surplus facilities left over from World War II. The Veterans Education Facilities Program was disposing of excess property, and RPI applied to have a navy warehouse moved from Davisville, Rhode Island, to Troy. The move was free, but RPI had to pay $500,000 to renovate the interior for athletics. In 1949, the new facility opened on campus, and hockey began again in January 1950. Houston provided the facility, and now the school needed a team.

Harkness was building the program from scratch, and growing pains were expected until he could recruit for the team. The 4-6 record in the first season was followed by a 5-10 record in the second season, in which RPI went 1-5 in the new Tri-State League. By the third year, things were clicking, and the Engineers (or the Bachelors, as some called them) went 15-3, followed by a 15-4-1 season, a Tri-State League Championship, and a trip to Colorado for the NCAA Tournament, where they finished third. Then, everything came together in the 1953–1954 season. RPI won the Tri-State League Championship again, returned to the NCAA Tournament, and upset the University of Michigan and the University of Minnesota to claim the title as the best college hockey team in the nation.

The team continued to excel during the 1950s, with only one losing season (1954–1955) and another Tri-State League title (1956–1957), but they were unable to break into the NCAA Tournament again in that decade. In the 1960–1961 season, RPI was once more on the hunt for a national championship, but the team lost to both St. Lawrence University and the University of Minnesota in Denver and finished fourth. Harkness remained at RPI for two more seasons. He then took a job offer at Cornell University, having previously turned down an opportunity to coach at Yale. He was succeeded by Rube Bjorkman, who took a Harkness-recruited team back to the NCAA Tournament, where RPI lost to the University of Denver in Denver and beat Providence College to finish third.

The mid-1960s proved to be the worst period for the hockey program. The change in coaches and Bjorkman's short tenure, combined with the always difficult task of recruiting for a niche school like RPI, left the team severely depleted. In 1964, the Eastern Collegiate Athletic Conference (ECAC) split its hockey playing schools in two, after grouping more than 25 schools in one division when it was founded in 1961. RPI opted for the higher classification. Suddenly, the Engineers were no longer competitive. The 3-19 season in 1965–1966 featured a number of out-of-hand games, including a 9-0 loss against Boston University during which Dick Greenlaw '68 made 78 saves to prevent a greater rout. It is possibly the best performance by a goaltender who gave up nine goals. At this point, there was serious discussion about dropping the hockey program to a lower classification.

That talk disappeared when RPI defeated Cornell in December 1968 and made the ECAC playoffs in the spring of 1969, for the first time in five years. A new coach, Garry Kearns, had put the program on track. The coaches who succeeded him, Leon Abbott and then Jim Salfi, maintained the program at a competitive level. Even still, it was a 50-50 proposition as to whether RPI would make the playoffs. In a 20-year span, they won only one playoff game, a 7-6 overtime shocker against the University of New Hampshire. The college hockey world was also changing. Don Cutts '74 drew national attention and was drafted by two professional leagues. Students at RPI who played hockey had been expected to use their degrees as their livelihood after graduation, but it was slowly becoming more common for students to be hockey players first. Some anticipated a professional career, the way college football players had for decades. A greater commitment from the school was required in order to compete at this level.

In the early 1980s, there were two noticeable changes to the program. Under the leadership of George Low '48, president, and Bob Ducatte, director of athletics, a $1.5 million upgrade was made to the Houston Field House and full athletic scholarships were offered to play hockey. RPI was now offering scholarship money to play hockey in a modern facility. The results occurred quickly. A program that had been more-or-less average for two decades suddenly became the power of the east in the 1983–1984 season, winning the ECAC Tournament and reaching the NCAA Tournament for the first time in 20 years. A tough loss in the NCAA quarterfinals did not stop the momentum. The next year, the team was even better. They went 35-2-1, became the ECAC Champions again, and won the school's second NCAA Championship with thrilling victories over the University of Minnesota–Duluth and Providence College. Head coach Mike Addesa used all the tools available to make RPI's hockey team the best in the nation.

A number of players left school early after the national title was won, and the team fell back to being a good, not great, team for the remainder of the 1980s. In 1989, the only controversial period for the program, Addesa's use of a racial epithet in the locker room became public, and it ultimately led to his resignation. His successor, Buddy Powers, brought the Engineers back to the ECAC title game in 1990, where they lost to national runner-up Colgate. He then returned the Engineers to the NCAA Tournament in 1994, where they lost to the University of New Hampshire. After his departure in 1994, Dan Fridgen took over, and the team won the ECAC Championship for the third time in March 1995. Another trip to the NCAA Tournament followed, where RPI lost at Madison, Wisconsin, to the University of Minnesota. The program faced a mini-crisis during the 2003–2004 season when an NCAA reform package, aimed at changing the already complicated association rules, threatened to remove RPI's ability to offer scholarships to Division I athletes. This was defeated in a vote in 2004 and the scholarships remained.

Things change, but the hockey team remains. Some traditions are still strong, such as the Big Red Freakout, a super-spirit event during the spring semester where everyone is encouraged to wear red and cheer the team on. Some have faded, for example Hockey Line, which occurs when students wait for weeks (or months) on line outside the student union for the right to pick the best seats. Originally created when the field house had numerous posts that obstructed spectator's views, Hockey Line survived the field house renovation, but slowly students have lost interest in getting the best seats. There are also new events, such as Black Friday, when the team wears black uniforms in November. Many fans also enjoy tracking the progress of former players as they make their way through the professional ranks, with most everyone following the long career of Adam Oates '86 in the NHL.

Women's hockey is on the rise at RPI, as well. Started as a club team in the 1970s, it gained varsity status in 1995 at the NCAA Division III level. On January 12, 2004, after RPI and its allies were victorious in defeating the NCAA reform legislation, Dr. Shirley Ann Jackson, president of Rensselaer, and Ken Ralph, director of athletics, announced plans to elevate the women's program to Division I, effective in the 2005–2006 season. This includes a full slate of scholarships and the additional coaching and support staff required, all to be instituted by 2008. This puts the women's team on par with the men's team, continuing the long tradition of hockey at RPI.

One

The Early Years

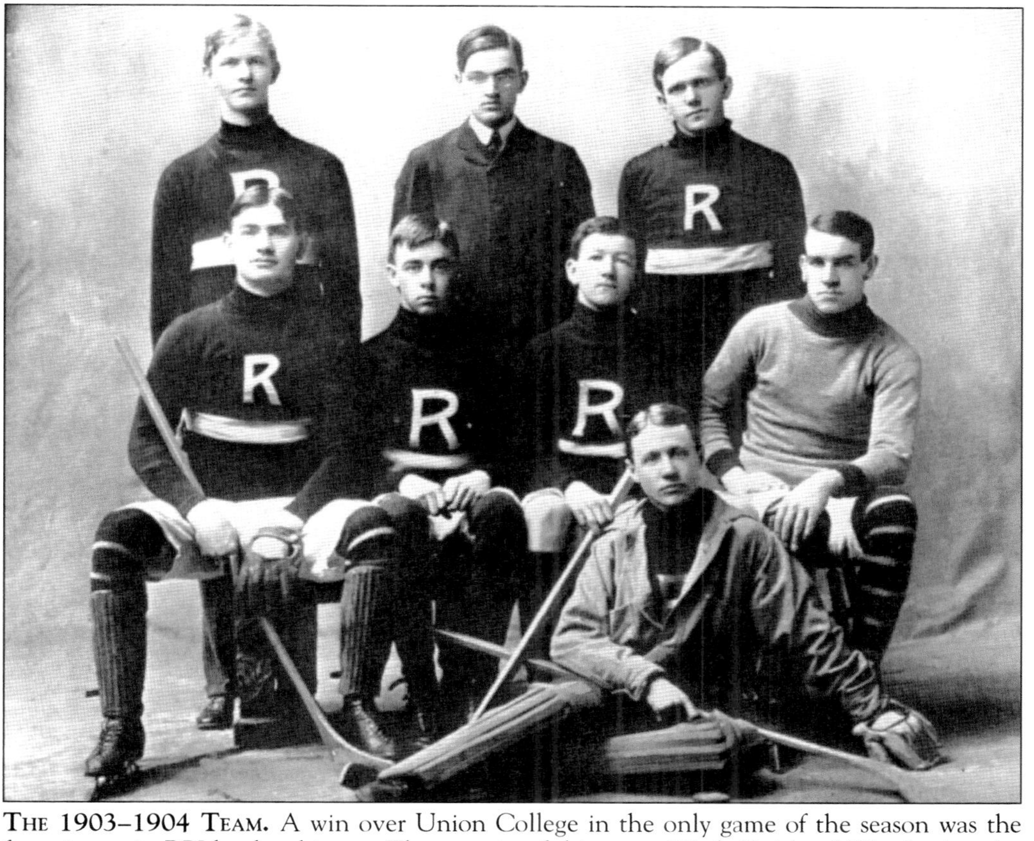

The 1903–1904 Team. A win over Union College in the only game of the season was the first victory in RPI hockey history. The captain of this team, Wade Reichard '05, also has the distinction of scoring the first goal for the hockey team in a 4-1 loss to Williams College on January 25, 1902. That game, played in Cohoes, was the first ever for the school.

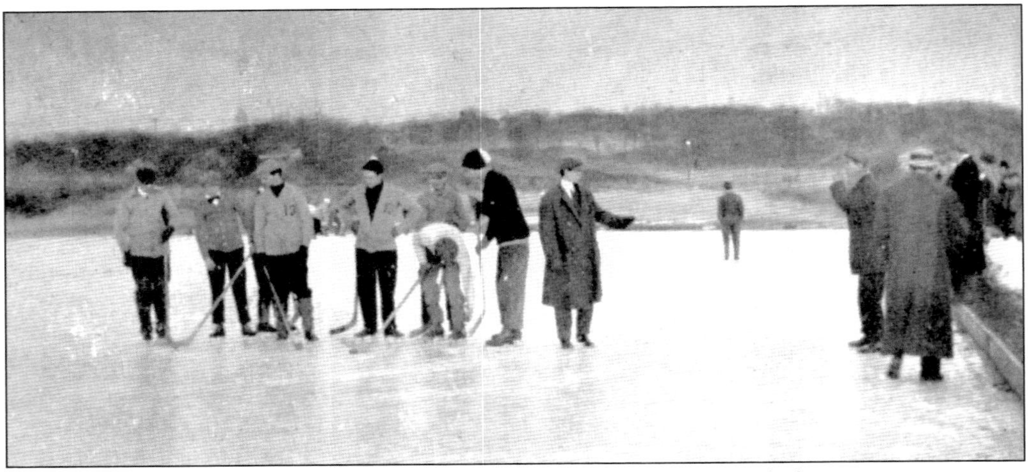

PRACTICE, C. 1910. Players are dressed in street clothes and shin pads for a practice session. The rink is likely in Albany, and there appears to be another group practicing in the background. Early hockey was different, lacking boards, using seven skaters per side, and relying on natural ice. The snow off to the side indicates it was cold enough to maintain the rink this day.

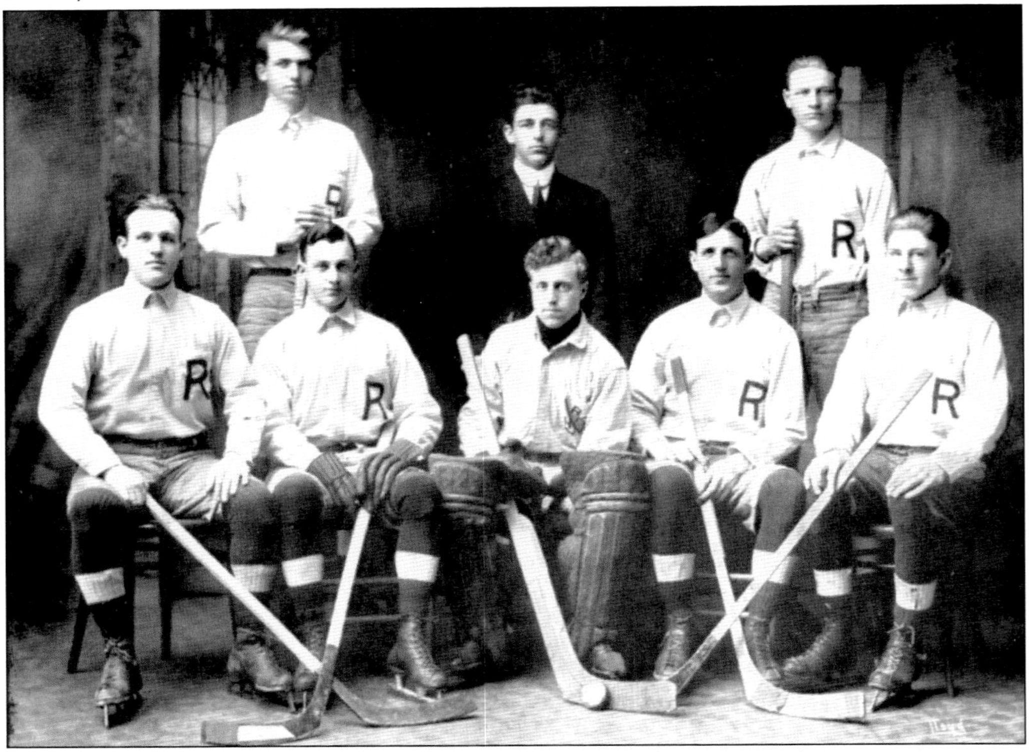

THE 1911–1912 TEAM. This is the first squad to play its home games on the institute's campus. Prior to this season, the team played all but one game in Albany, usually at the Empire Curling Rink but also the Yates Street Rink or the Albany Academy Rink. They had a 1-3-1 record this season, with the only victory against Syracuse University. William Coughtry '15 picked up the win in the net.

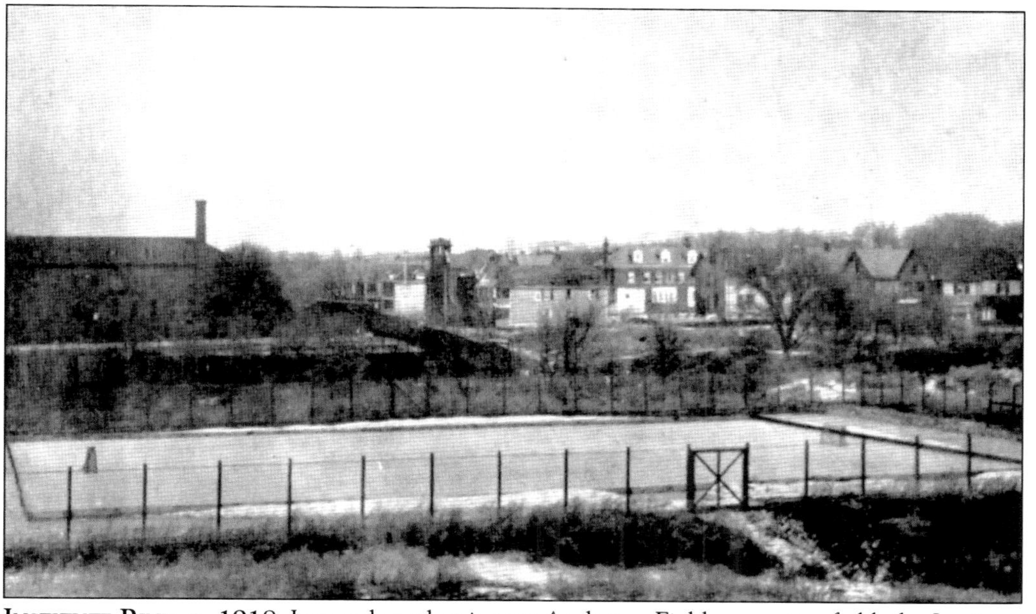

INSTITUTE RINK, C. 1918. Located at what is now Anderson Field, a practice field, the Institute Rink was constructed in the winter of 1912. It was also known as the Avenue B Rink, Sage Rink, and the North Field Rink during its existence. (Sage Avenue was formerly Avenue B.) The houses pictured are on 15th Street. Note the right-angle corners of the rink.

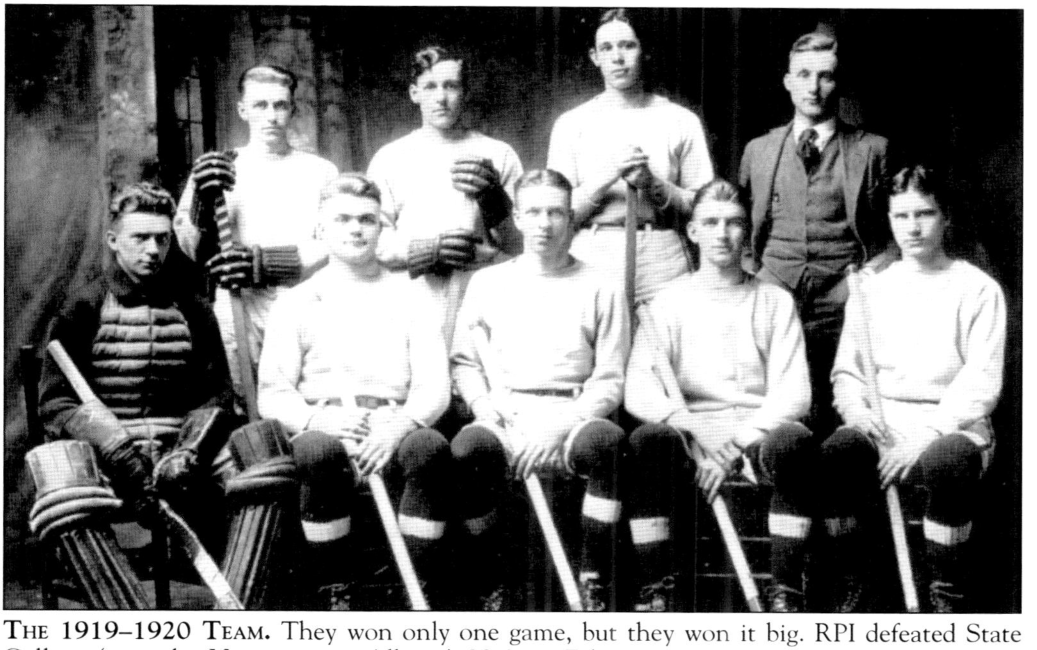

THE 1919–1920 TEAM. They won only one game, but they won it big. RPI defeated State College (now the University at Albany) 23-0 on February 14, 1920, the biggest margin of victory in school history. Richard Cook '21, team captain, scored seven goals, a single-game school record that still stands. Marshall Barker '21, John Morgan '21, and William Tierney '22 also had hat tricks. Wade Reichard '05 refereed this game.

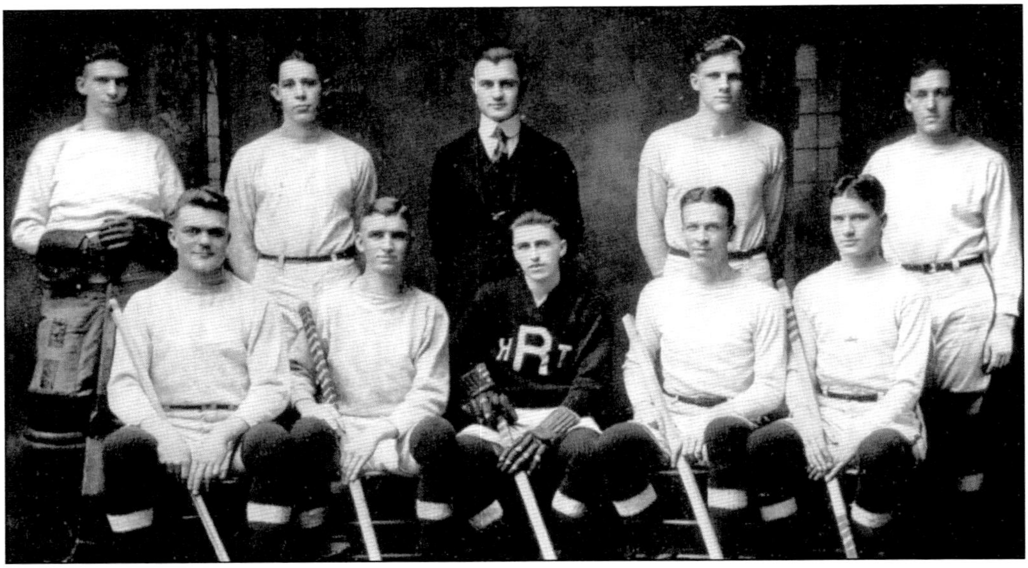

THE 1920–1921 TEAM. This is the first squad to play six-per-side hockey. In the seven-per-side game, the defensemen were called "point" and "cover-point," and there was an additional player called a "rover." Colgate University arrived for a January game short a man, so the rover was eliminated and the teams played six-per-side. In February against Hamilton College, half the game was played with seven players, half with six. The next season, RPI switched to a six-player lineup permanently.

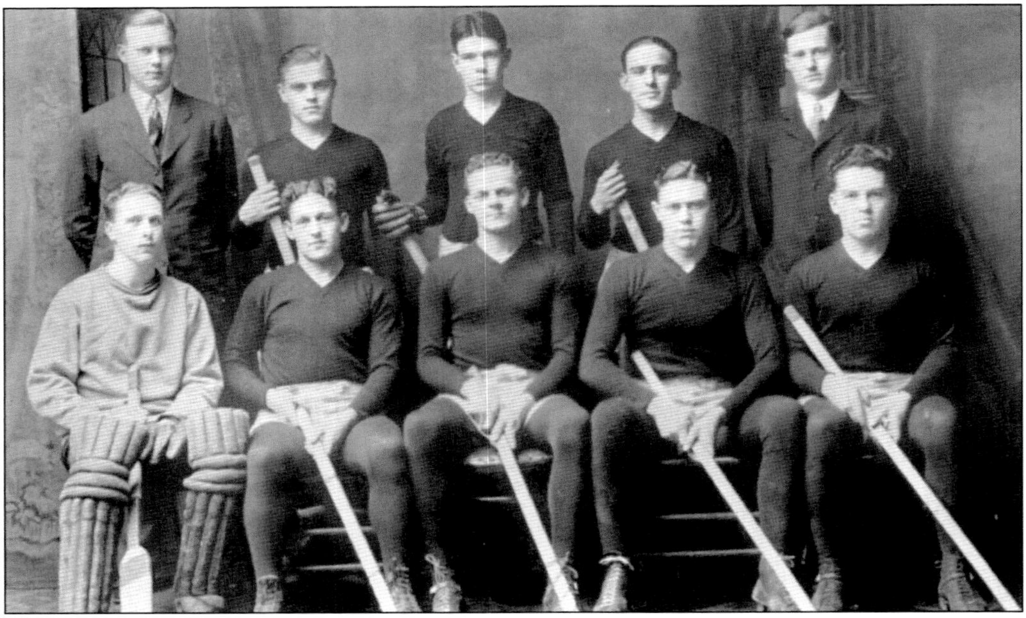

THE 1924–1925 TEAM. The longstanding rivalry against Clarkson University (Clarkson College of Technology back then) started this season with a 14-1 RPI victory. In that game, John Reuther '26 scored four goals and Cliff Reuther '28 scored three, making this the only game in which brothers have notched hat tricks for RPI. John also holds the school's football record for the longest field goal, a 49-yard drop kick against Rochester in 1924.

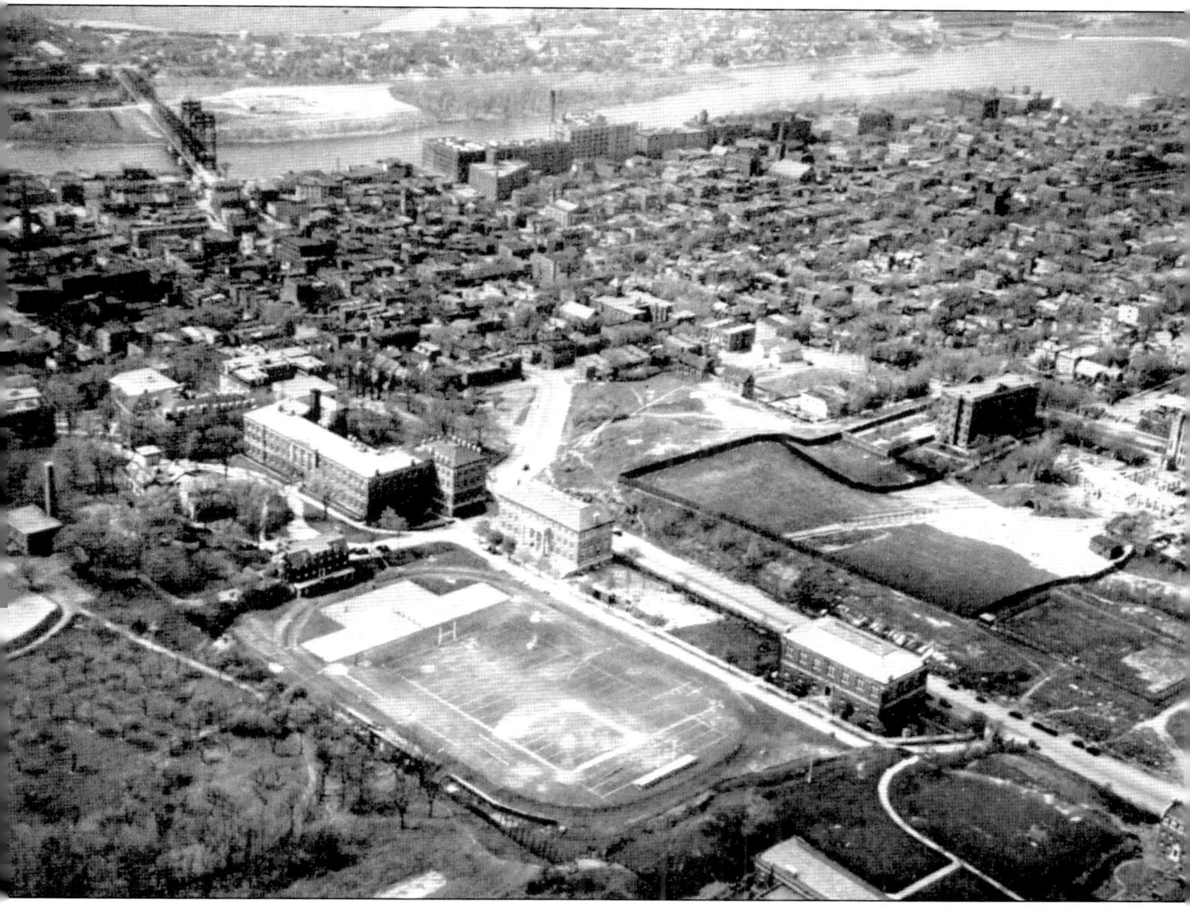

A CAMPUS VIEW IN THE MID-1920S. Sage Avenue runs from the lower right to the middle of this picture. Institute Rink (lower right) was across the street from the campus. It is spring or summer, so the ice is not present. The football field, known as '86 Field, has a baseball field laid out, as it was used for almost all outdoor sports prior to World War II. The tennis courts to the west of '86 Field, in front of the Troy Building, were used to construct a hockey rink for the winter of 1936. The hockey team played one home game at that location before the rink was reconstructed once more on the opposite side of the street for the next season. In the ensuing years, '86 Field was shifted westward. As a result, the current football team plays on space that was once a hockey rink. This picture is from no later than 1927, as the football goal posts are located on the goal line. For the 1927 season, they were moved to the end line.

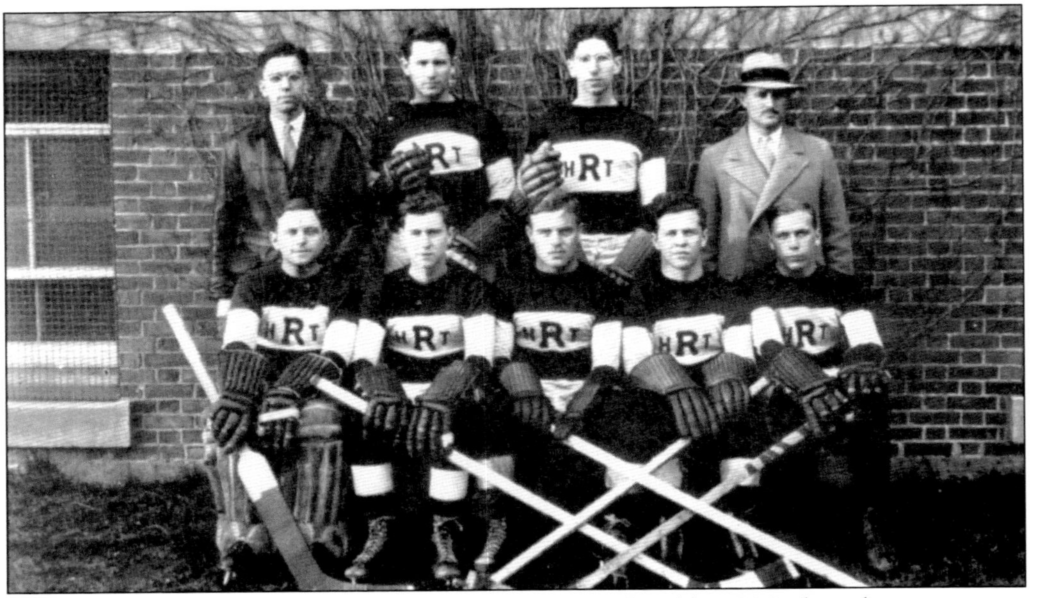

THE 1929–1930 TEAM. Hockey was almost three decades old at RPI when this picture was taken. Marvin Callan, the third head coach in team history, appears wearing the hat. The equipment looks more modern, but the program was only active for one more year before it went on hiatus. This year's captain was A. J. Magadini '30, father of future player John Magadini '55.

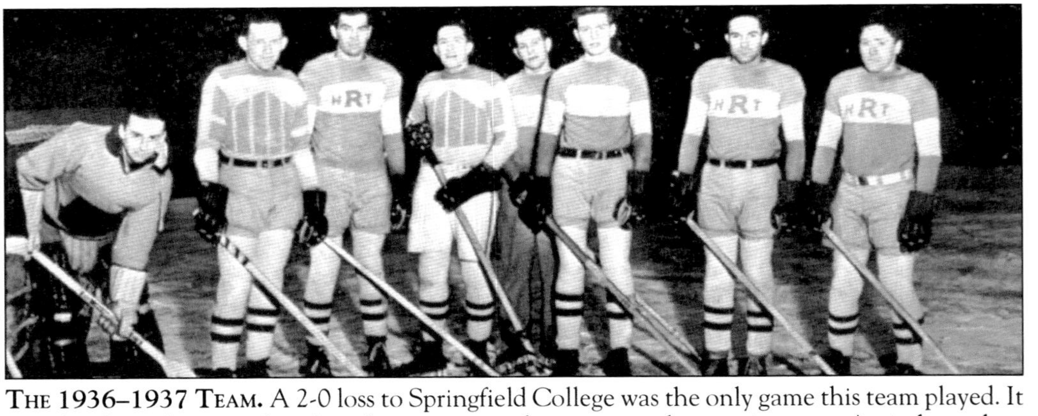

THE 1936–1937 TEAM. A 2-0 loss to Springfield College was the only game this team played. It was also the only game played on the main part of campus, on the tennis courts. An independent team of RPI students played Union College in 1936, prompting the school to revive the hockey program. After 1938, the program was abandoned once more; the problems of maintaining ice were not solved until the field house was built.

Two

The Harkness Era

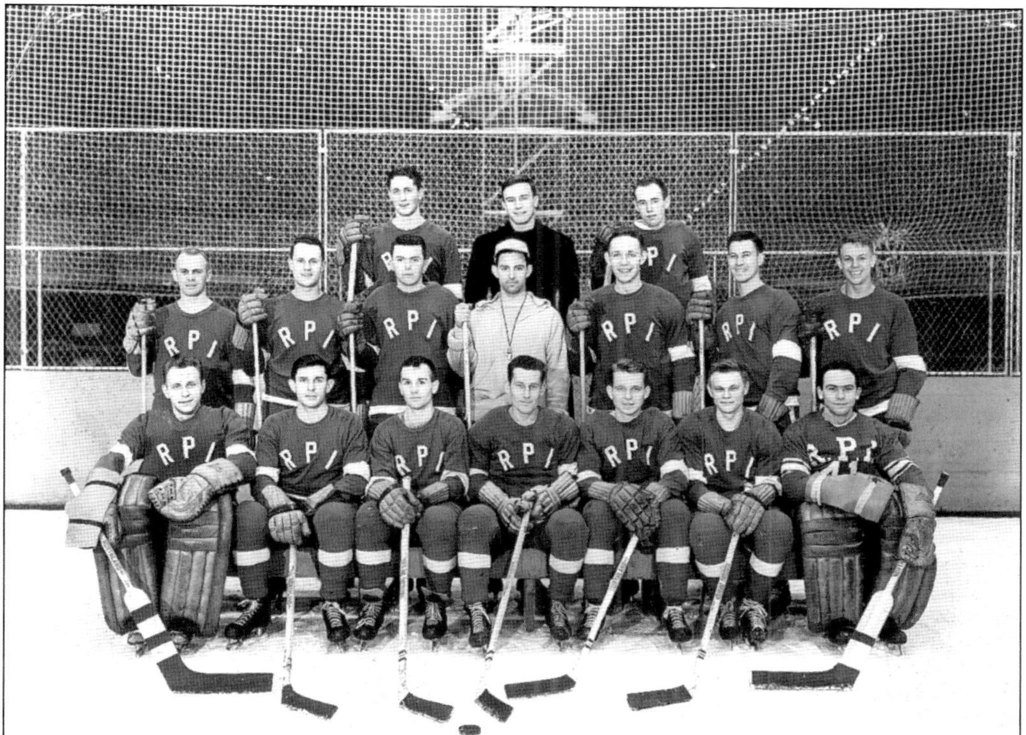

Hockey Returns to RPI. Ned Harkness, the lacrosse coach, assembled a new squad of players to take the ice in the recently constructed RPI Field House. The new program started slowly, with a 4-6 record in the 1949–1950 season and a 5-10 record in the 1950–1951 season; but after that, Harkness's teams were among the best in the east and in the country.

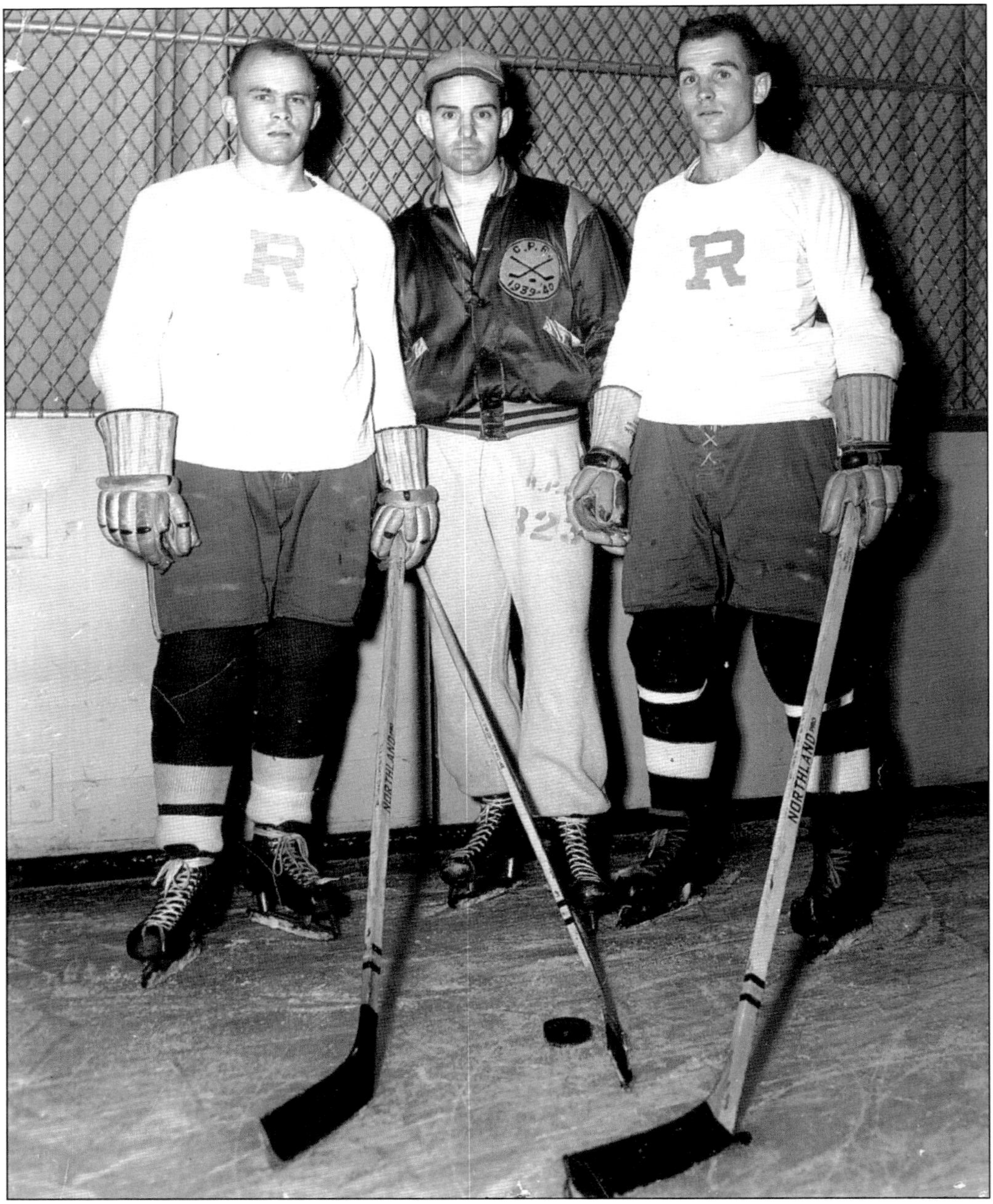

BILL MOODY '51, NED HARKNESS, AND TOM BELLATY '51. Moody and Bellaty were co-captains during the 1950–1951 season. Bellaty played up front at right wing, and he led the team in scoring with 26 points. Moody was a defenseman, but he only played seven games. He broke his nose and had to wear a mask for the season. They were among the first group of players to encounter Harkness's style of coaching hockey, which stressed physical fitness to an extent seldom seen at that time. It was common for RPI to play undermanned but defeat teams due to superior conditioning. The fact that the ice in the field house was only 185 feet long, instead of the common 200 feet, helped as well. Harkness's motivation and preparation techniques contributed to his teams' success, at RPI as well as Cornell and Union College.

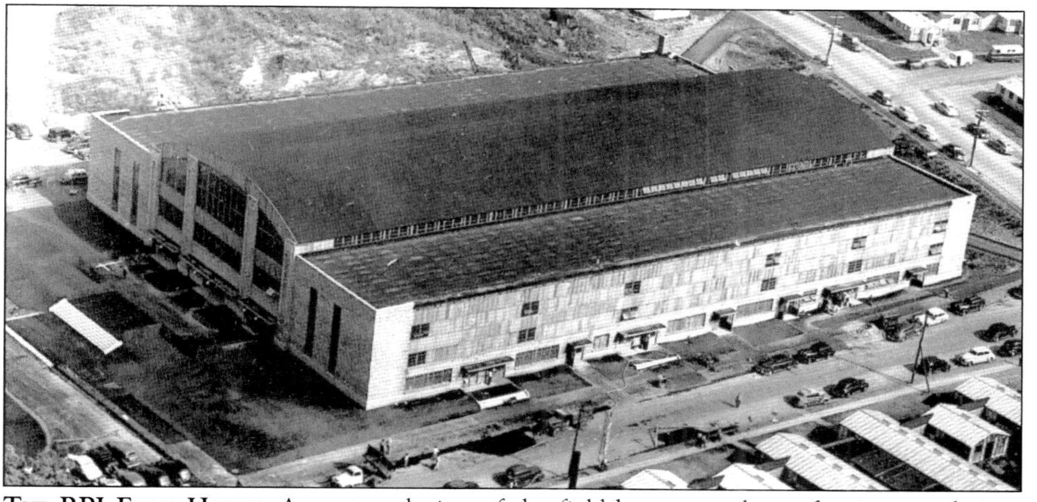

The RPI Field House. An external view of the field house, not long after its completion, shows the old curved roof of the structure and lacks the ticket office and lobby later built on the front. The building's windows are visible; currently, these have been removed or painted over. The temporary housing seen was built to handle the increase in enrollment following World War II and now is a parking lot.

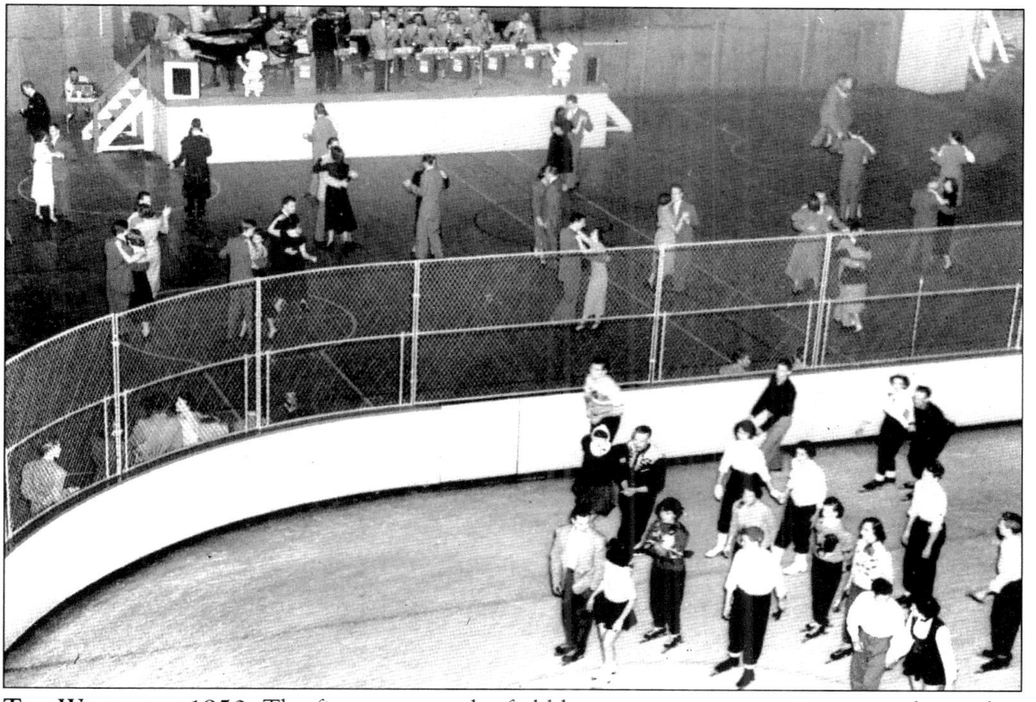

The Winter of 1950. The first event at the field house was not a sporting event, but rather the Interfraternity Ball on November 12, 1949. Music was performed by Elliot Lawrence and his orchestra. This photograph shows a combined skating and dancing event from 1950. In the early years, the field house was used for numerous on-campus activities, many of which no longer exist or have moved to other facilities. It has been quite some time since a skate-dance was held at the arena, much less a dance with live music.

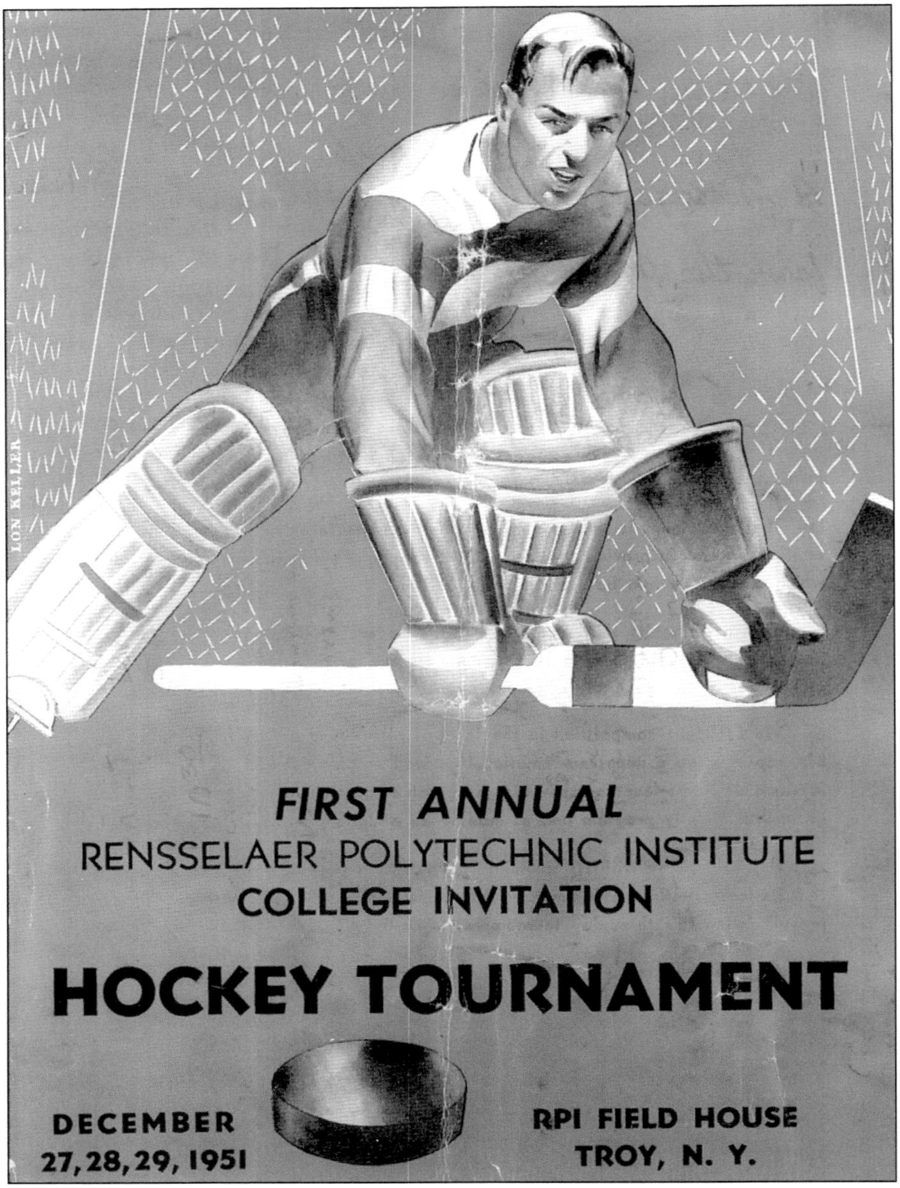

The RPI Invitational Tournament. This is the longest-running college hockey tournament in the country (the Beanpot Hockey Tournament is one year younger). Conceived by Harkness and others as an activity for the hockey team during the winter break, it began as an eight-team tournament in 1951. Brown defeated Williams College, RPI, and St. Patrick's College en route to the title. The number of participants was reduced to four teams in subsequent years, and the tournament became a round-robin affair until 1981, when it became a two-day event. From 1985 to 1987, the tournament was played the weekend after Thanksgiving. Starting in 2004, it is played after Thanksgiving as well. RPI has managed to win the tournament 16 times. In a rare tournament moment in 1980, Maine's goaltender, Jim Tortorella, scored a goal when Väsby's goaltender misplayed the puck. Väsby was a Swedish club team that played in the tournament that year.

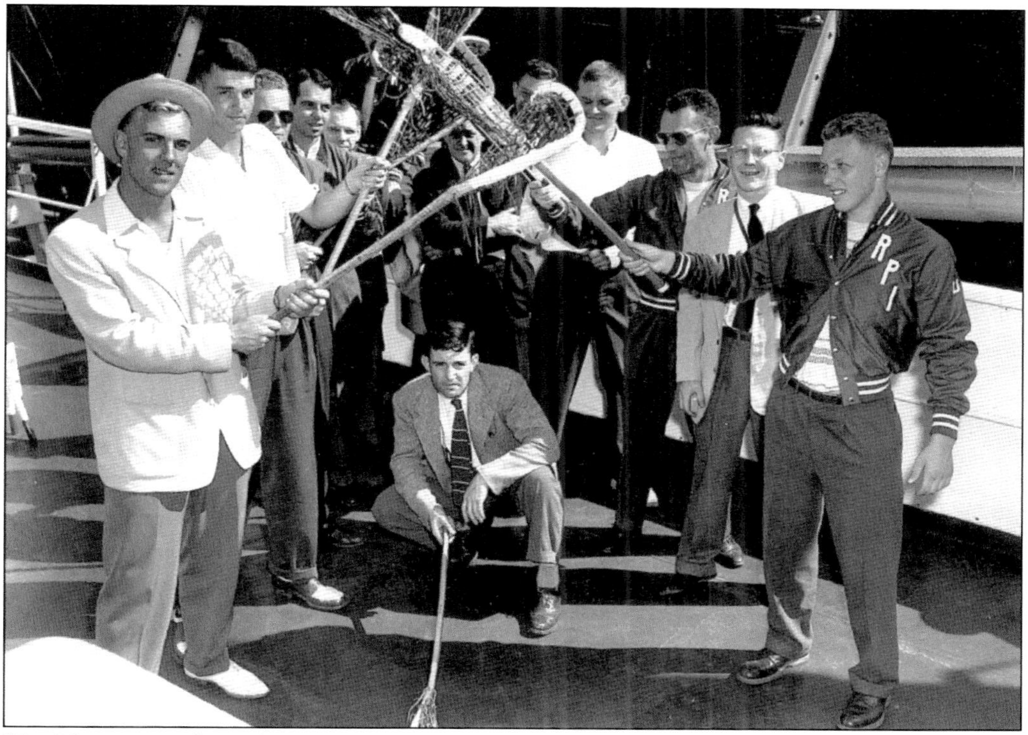

NED HARKNESS. Shown here on tour with the lacrosse team, Harkness first gained a national title when RPI's lacrosse team was named the U.S. Intercollegiate Lacrosse Association co-champions in 1952. The hockey team then won the NCAA title in 1954, making Harkness one of the rare coaches to win a national title in two sports. For his accomplishments, he is a member of the U.S. Hockey Hall of Fame and the U.S. Lacrosse Hall of Fame.

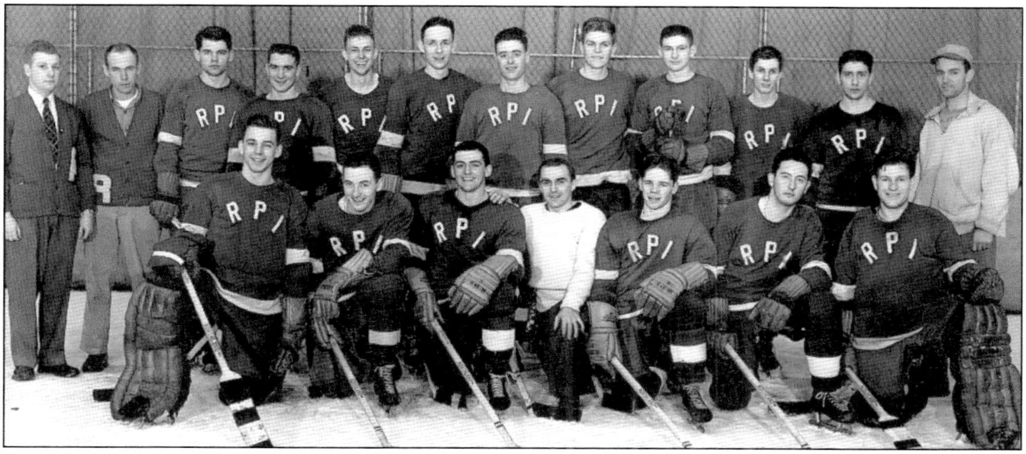

THE 1952–1953 TEAM. The first RPI hockey team to win a title and make the NCAA Tournament was the 1952–1953 team. After winning the Tri-State League championship, they lost a close game to the University of Minnesota 3-2 in the NCAA semifinals. Co-captain Herb LaFontaine '53 had a reputation for stamina. He was on the ice for the entire semifinal, except the three times he entered the penalty box. RPI bounced back to defeat Boston University 6-3 and finished the tournament in third place.

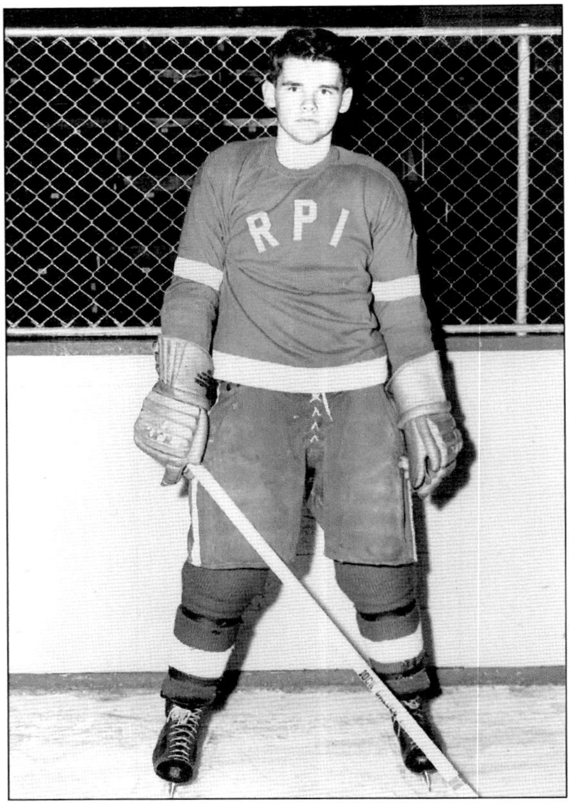

Don Shildneck '53. Don, the older of the two Shildneck brothers, played both defense and forward and was co-captain of the 1951–1952 squad. His best day on the offensive side was when he scored four goals against St. Anselm College in December 1950. The shift to defense saw his goal totals drop during his final season, but he was highly regarded for his team leadership.

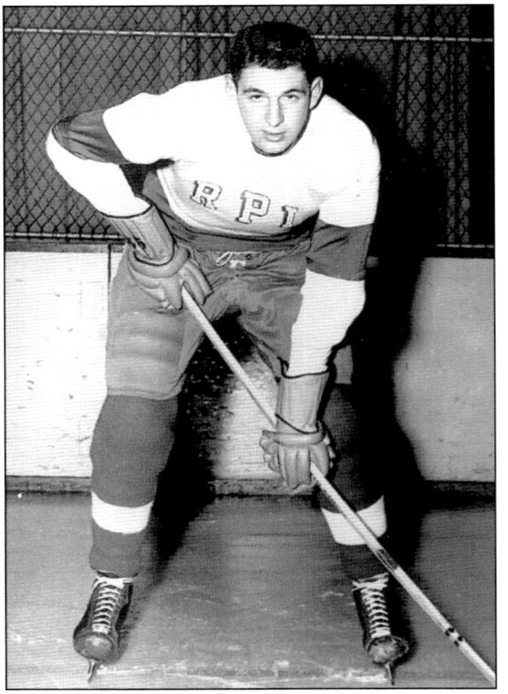

Jim Shildneck '54. Jim Shildneck was co-captain of the 1953–1954 NCAA Championship team. Injuries limited him to only seven games played in the championship season, but he played both tournament games in Colorado, where he was an All-Tournament team honorable mention. In an era when college hockey players were not large, Shildneck's six-foot two-inch 180-pound frame was imposing.

ABBIE MOORE '54. Moore was named Most Outstanding Player of the NCAA Tournament for his two-goal performance in the title game. He was also a second-team All-American that season and the Tri-State League's MVP. He finished his career with 102 goals and 104 assists, averaging more than 3.3 points per game. In the 1954 championship game, it was his goal in the third period that tied the score at 4 and forced the game into overtime.

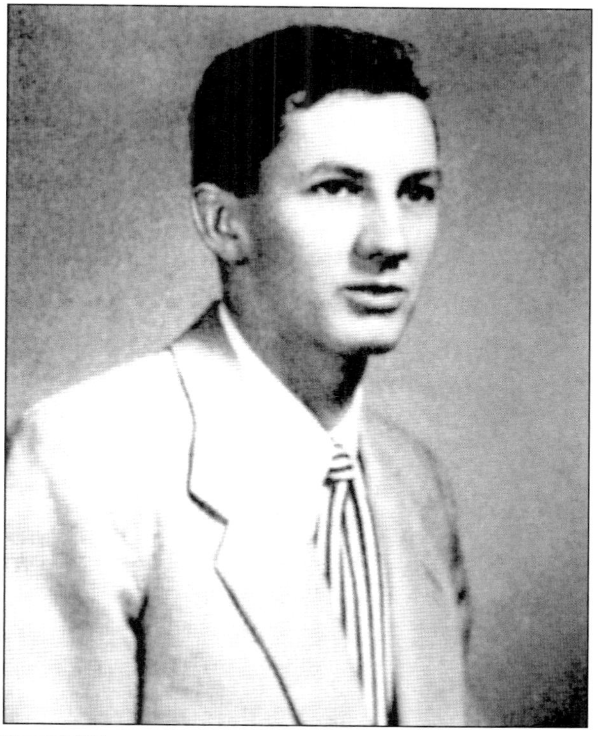

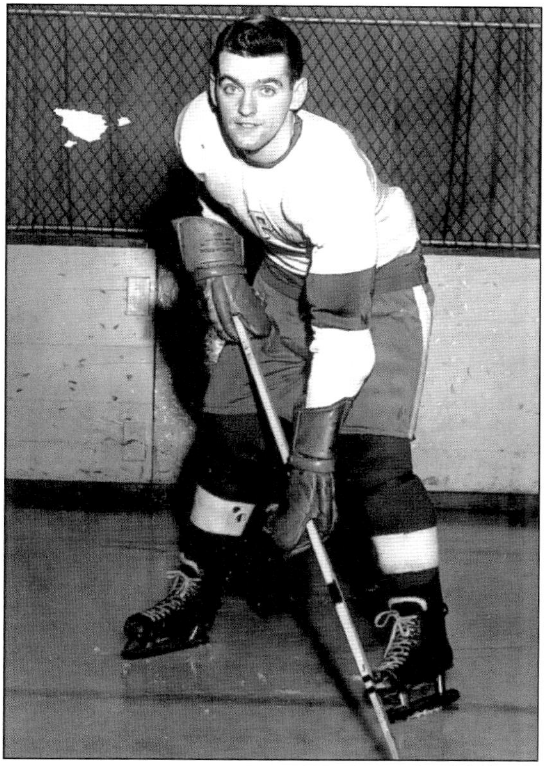

FRANK PARADISE '54. A forward with scoring ability, Paradise was overshadowed by some of his more prolific teammates. He accumulated 60 points in 61 games played over three seasons. He picked up a hat trick in RPI's 12-0 win over American International College in February 1954, for his best scoring outing. Paradise assisted on Frank Chiarelli's goal in the first period against the University of Minnesota in the championship game, giving RPI a 2-0 lead after one period.

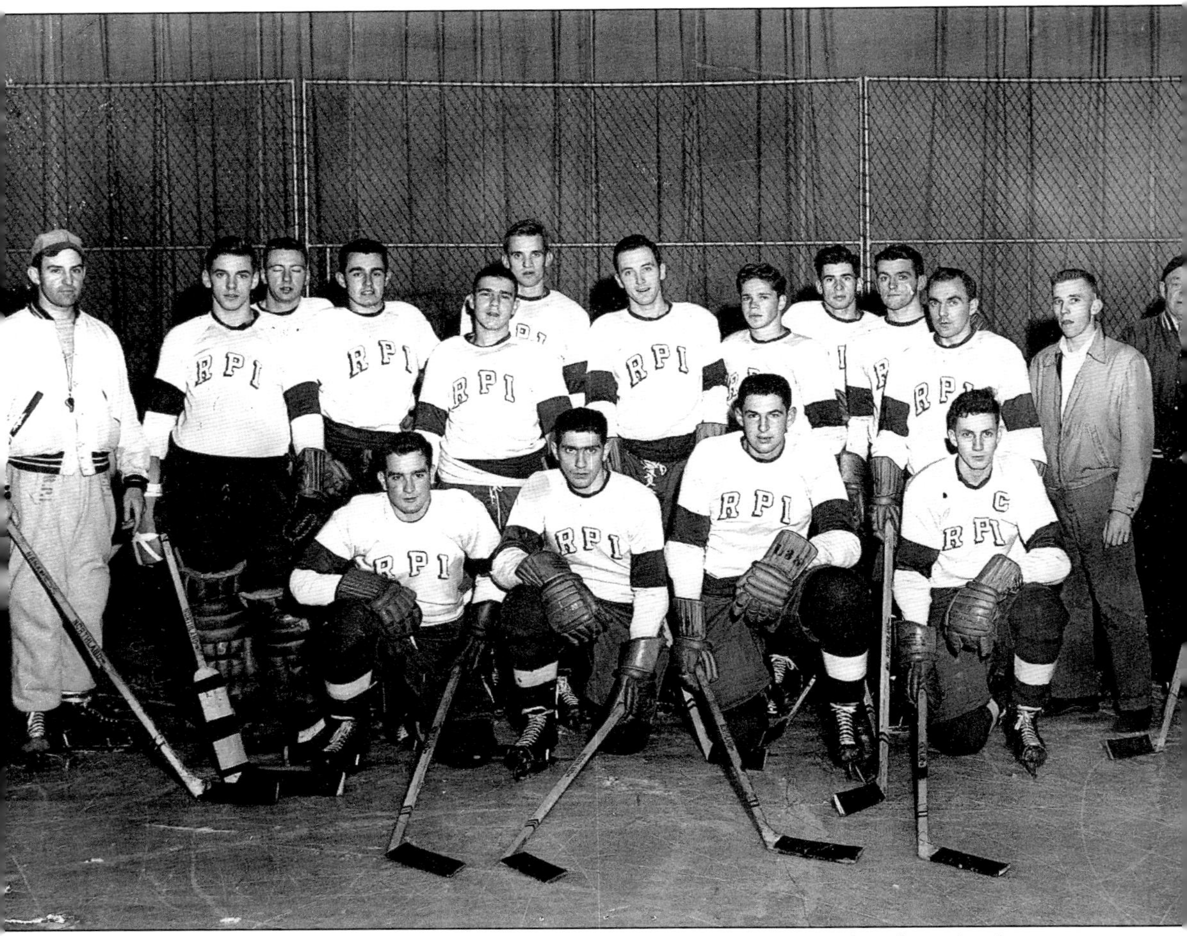

The 1954 National Champions. This small school in New York, whose hockey program was only five years old, stunned the college hockey world with victories over the University of Michigan and the University of Minnesota to claim the 1954 national title. Not many people apart from RPI gave this team a chance. On a trip to Colorado earlier in the season, RPI lost twice to the University of Denver and once to Colorado College by a combined score of 19-8. However, the second trip to Colorado counted for much more, and on March 12, RPI stunned Michigan with a 6-4 victory. The next night, they faced the University of Minnesota, which had a larger roster and an extra day to rest. The Engineers opened up a 3-0 lead on the Gophers early in the second period, but Minnesota roared back with two goals in both the second and third periods to lead 4-3. Moore scored from Chiarelli to tie the game late in the third and force overtime. Gordie Peterkin scored from John Magadini in overtime to secure the championship for RPI.

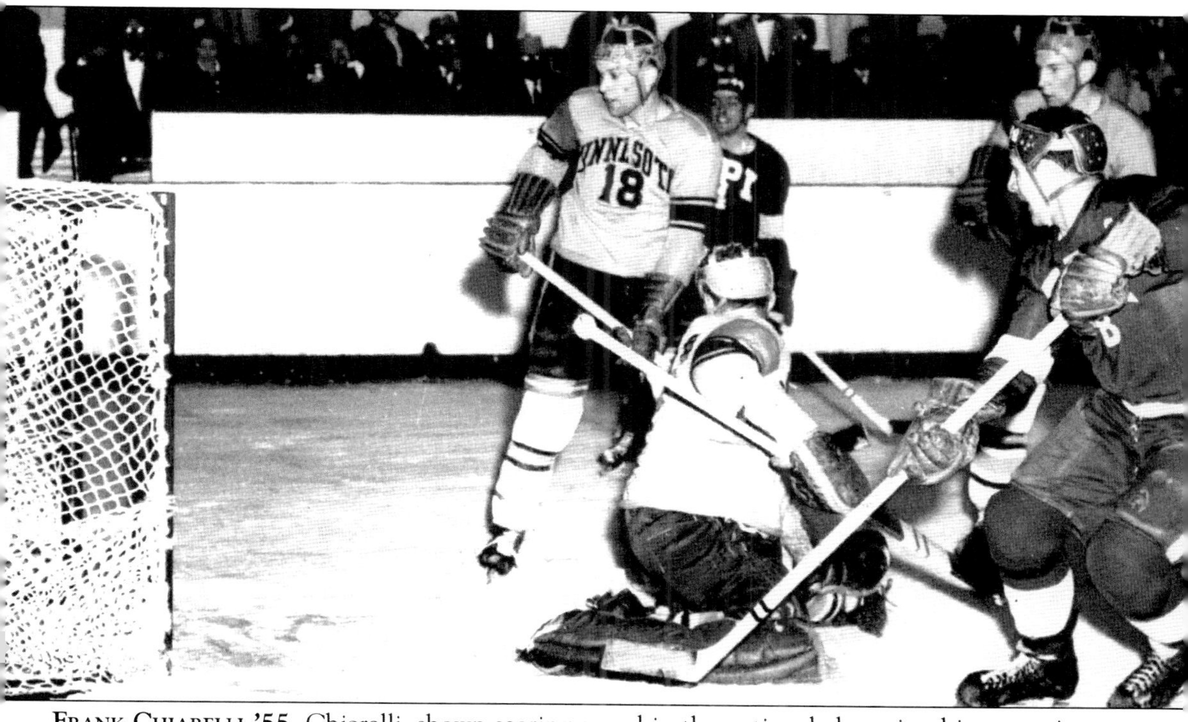

FRANK CHIARELLI '55. Chiarelli, shown scoring a goal in the national championship game, is still the record holder in many scoring categories at RPI, including the following: most goals in a season, 55 in 1951–1952; most hat tricks in a season, 9 in 1951–1952; most goals in a career, 155; most points in a career, 265; and most hat tricks in a career, 23. He was a first-team All-American in the 1952–1953 season, made the second team in the 1951–1952 and 1953–1954 seasons, and was the Tri-State League's Most Valuable Player in the 1952–1953 and 1954–1955 seasons. Including all the various tournament and eastern all-star teams, no player at RPI has been awarded more honors. Twice Chiarelli scored seven goals in a game—against Champlain College in December 1951 and Loyola College in January 1952, tying Richard Cook's school record. He was the first of three brothers to play for the institute and followed his career at RPI by playing senior amateur hockey in the Eastern Ontario Hockey League and later the Eastern Professional Hockey League, making him the first RPI alum to have a significant hockey career after graduation.

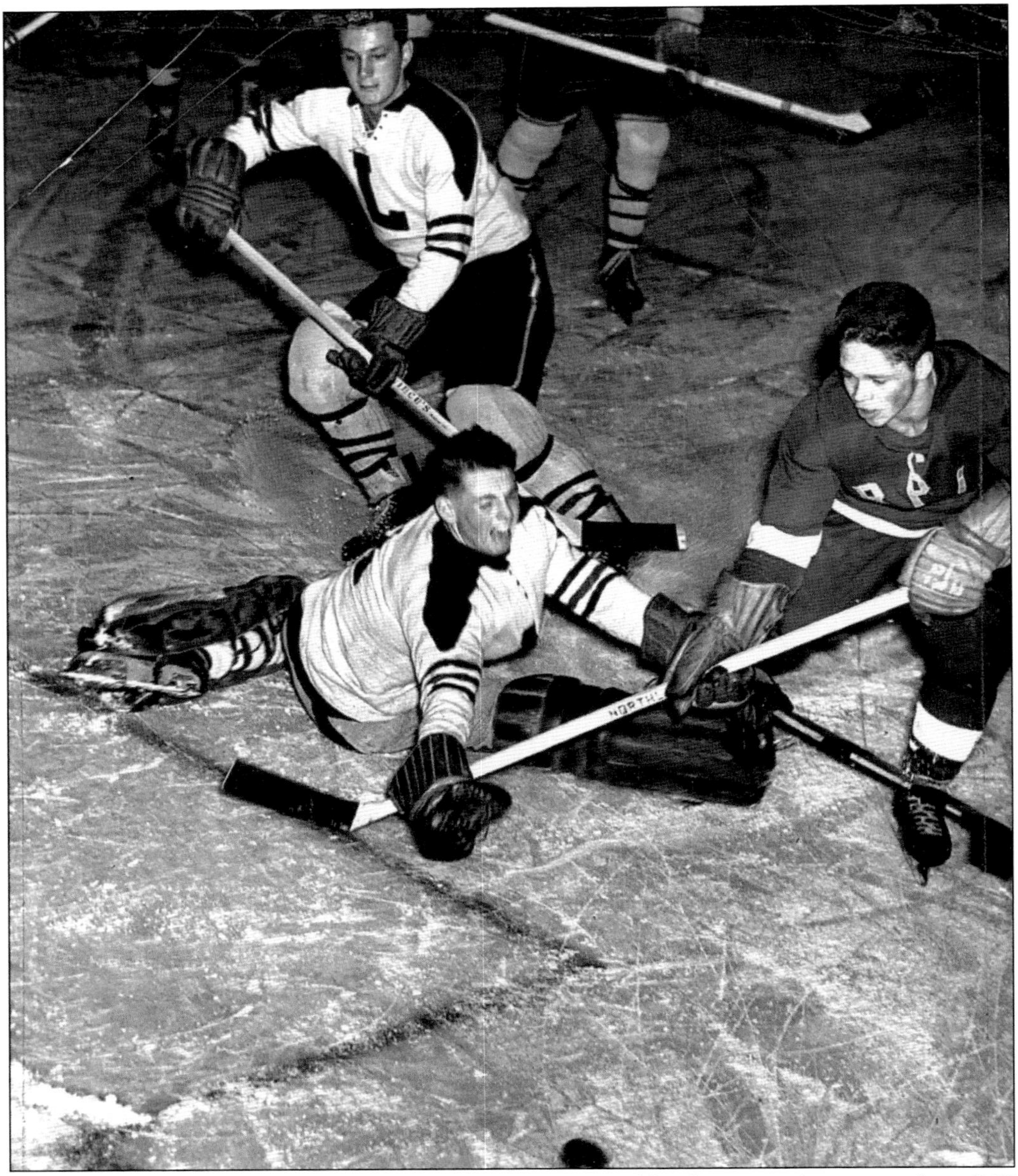

Gordie Peterkin '55. Peterkin scored what was arguably the most famous goal in RPI history, the overtime game winner against the University of Minnesota in the 1954 national championship game. In this picture, he struggles to reach the puck in front of the net in a game against St. Lawrence University at the field house. Peterkin accumulated five hat tricks during his career, but certainly the most important of these occurred against the University of Michigan in the NCAA semifinal when he scored three times and also assisted on another goal. That performance put RPI in the title game and led to Peterkin's overtime goal, where he was so close to the net he pushed the puck and goaltender into the net for the score. Following his graduation, Peterkin went to work for Bell Telephone in his native Canada until his retirement. When the team returned to Troy for the 50th anniversary celebration of the championship, Peterkin was the only player from that team to skate in the alumni game.

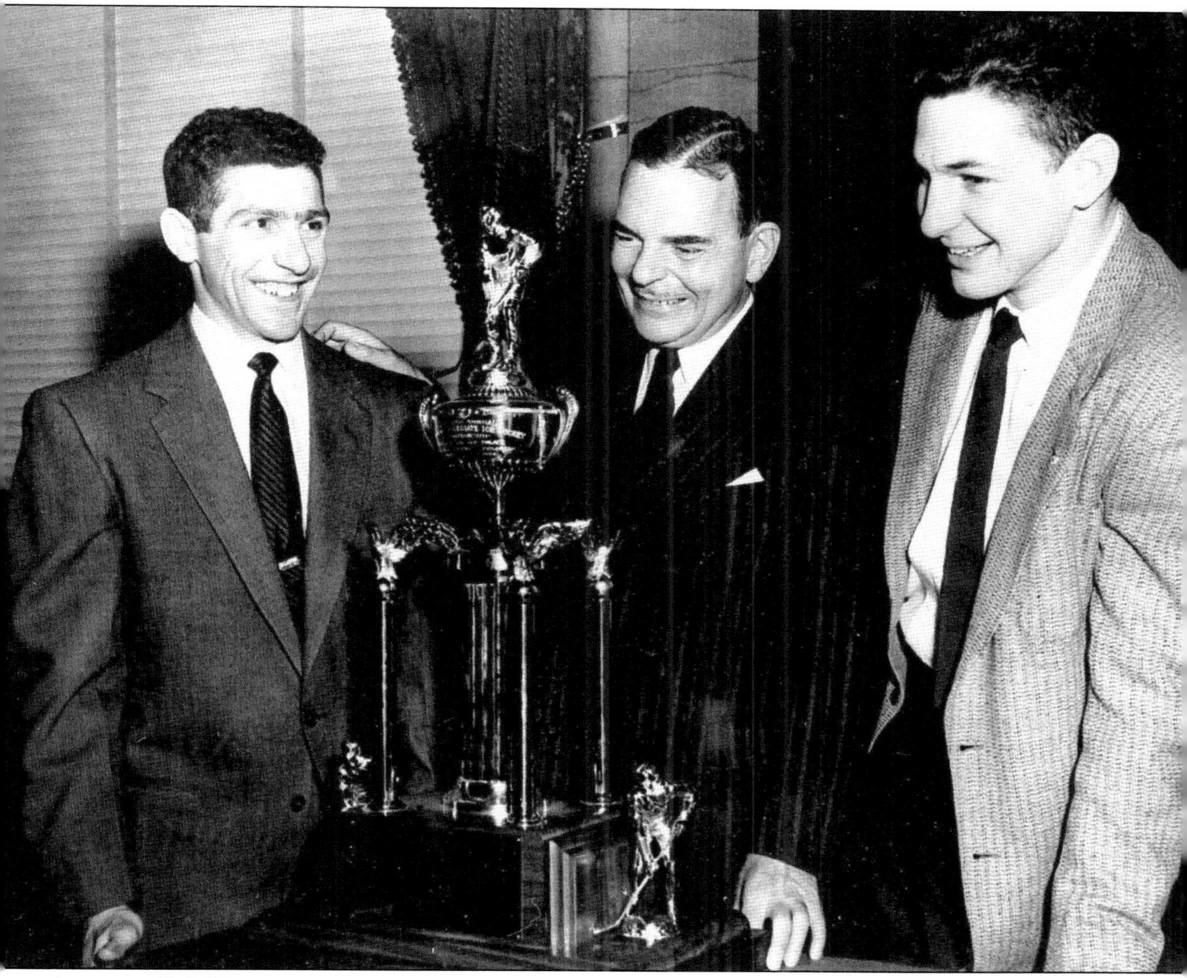

AMBROSE "MO" MOSCO '55, GOV. THOMAS E. DEWEY, AND JIM SHILDNECK '54. This was a time before championship teams visited the White House. Instead, the Engineers took the trophy a few miles down river to the governor's office. The trophy awarded at the Broadmoor Ice Palace that year was far more ornate than the plaque given by the NCAA in modern times. Mo Mosco frequently skated on a line with Moore and Chiarelli—the "Whiz Kids Line"—an all-Ontario group, which Harkness considered the best line he ever coached. Mosco finished his career with 137 points in 55 games and saw only limited action his senior year after being injured playing against Boston College in December 1954. He returned to play for the first minute against St. Lawrence University in March, the last game of the season for the Engineers. Governor Dewey is best remembered now as having the New York State Thruway named for him.

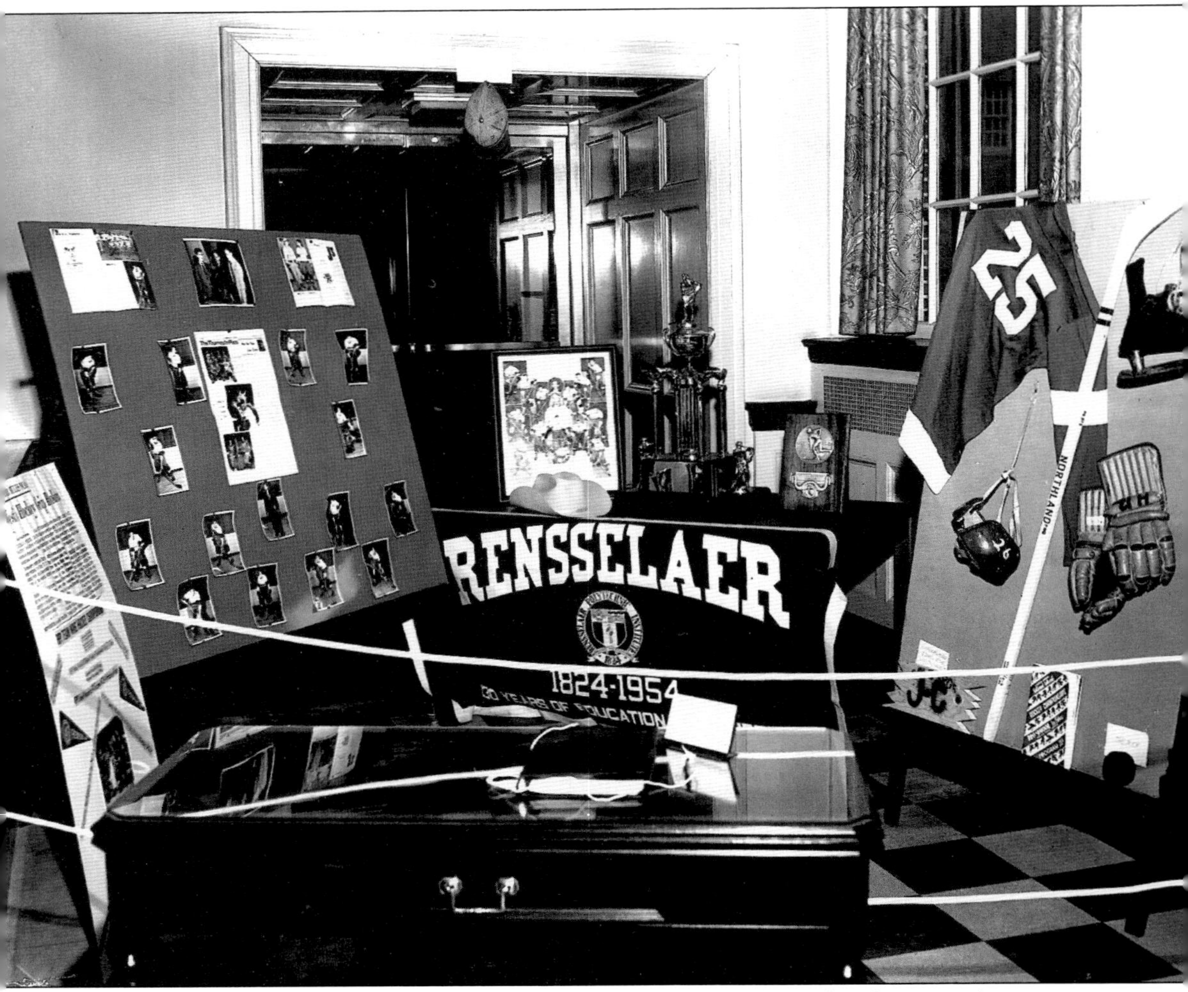

MANUFACTURERS NATIONAL BANK DISPLAY. Paraphernalia from the championship team is on display at the Manufacturers National Bank branch on Broadway in Troy. This is now the HSBC bank, still located on Broadway. The display on the right has a puck near the bottom and is labeled, "The Puck." Most likely, this is the game-winning puck. The No. 25 jersey was not worn by anyone that season. The trophy is visible in the middle, on the table. Many of the pictures on the display to the left appear in this book. Relations between the school and the city were much closer at this time. The field house, in addition to being a sports venue, was also a cultural venue, where concerts and plays were performed regularly. Interaction between the city and campus was natural in this day. As the decades have passed, this is less true.

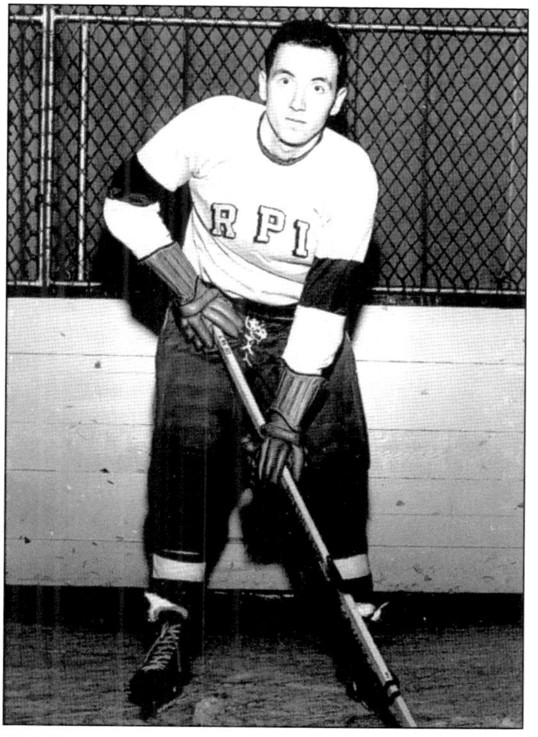

JIM POPE '55. A defenseman from Ottawa, where Harkness recruited a number of his players, Pope put up exceptional numbers for a pre–Bobby Orr defenseman. In his 62 games played, he accumulated 62 points, with a career-high 32 (17 of which were goals) in the 1954–1955 season. He was named to the All-Tournament first team at the 1954 championships.

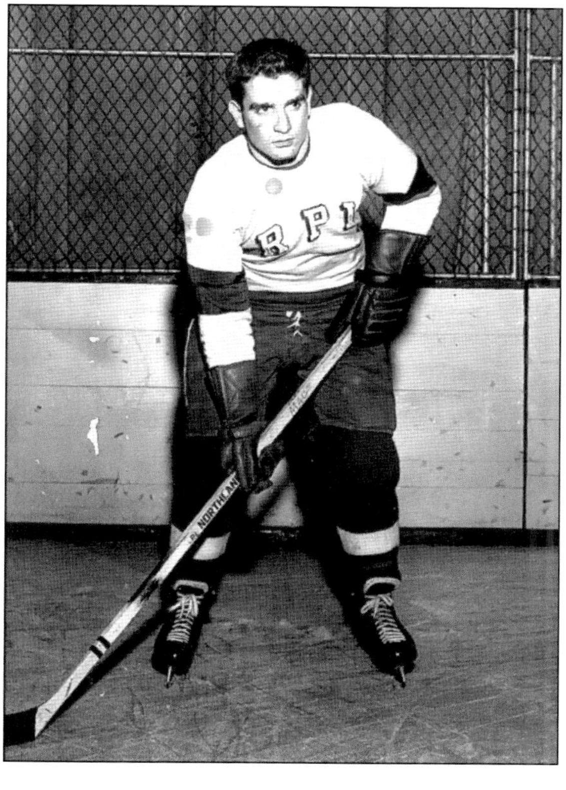

JOHN MAGADINI '55. Son of A. J. Magadini '30, captain of the 1929–1930 squad, Magadini was a forward who had a career season in 1953–1954. He picked up 24 points during the season, including a four-goal performance against Providence College in December 1953. He set up Peterkin for the overtime game winner versus the University of Minnesota, going in deep when Harkness had requested a soft fore-check by his line.

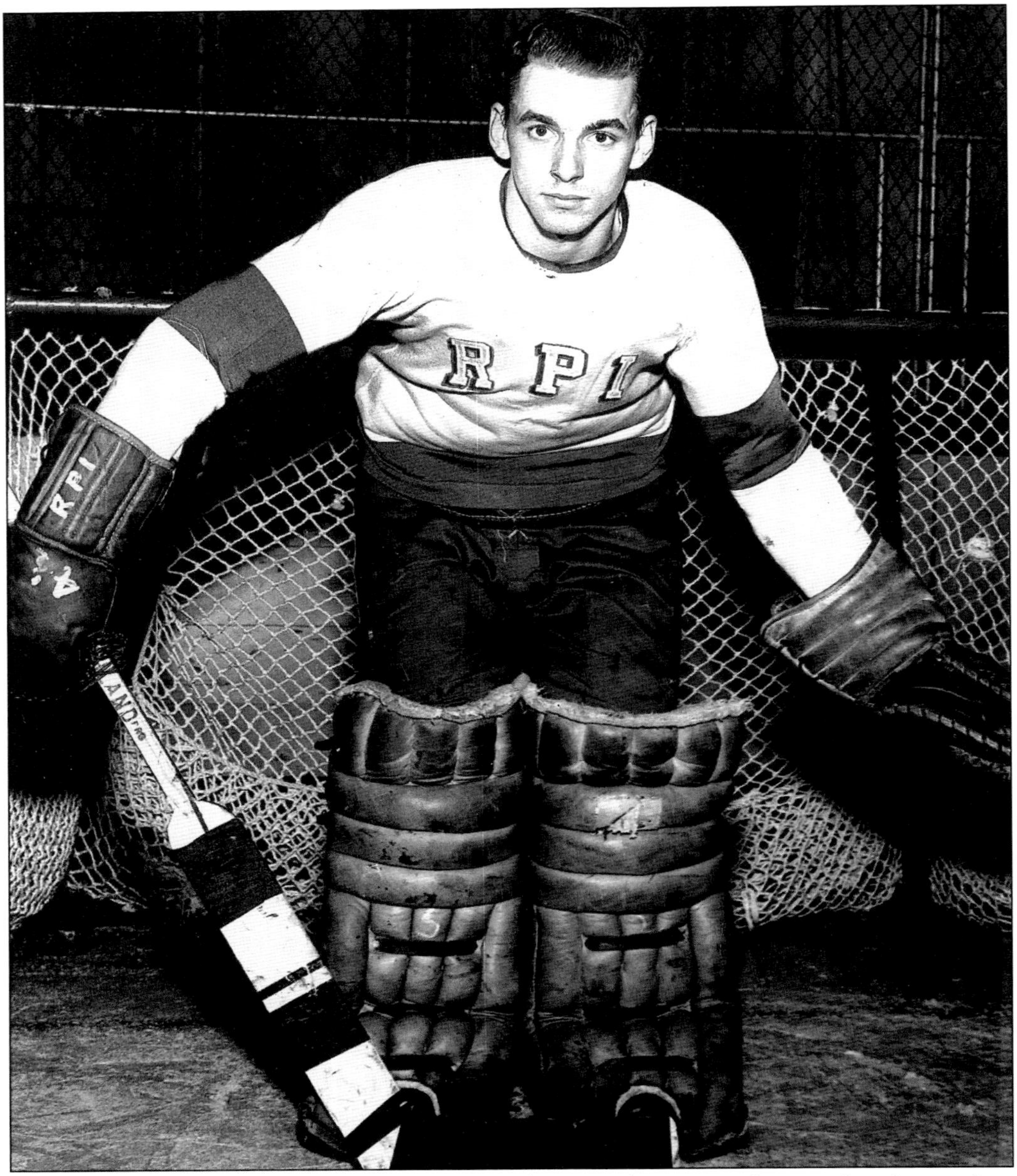

BOB FOX '55. Fox was a vital component of the championship team, whose goaltender numbers stand up to his modern counterparts, in spite of the greater offensive hockey of his day. A native of Verdun, Quebec, Fox took over the starting goaltending job in February 1952, making his first appearance against Amherst College and his first start in the next game versus Army. During each of his final three seasons, he was named to the All Tri-State League teams. He set school records that were not broken until 2000 for most shutouts in a season and in a career—with 5 in both the 1953–1954 and 1954–1955 seasons, leading the nation each time, and 12 in his career. He is fifth on the career school list for games started and minutes played, third for lowest goals-against average (2.71), and fifth for most wins (47). He is the only RPI goaltender to shut out Clarkson University and was the grand marshall at RPI his senior year. Following graduation, he earned a doctorate and became a member of the faculty at Purdue University.

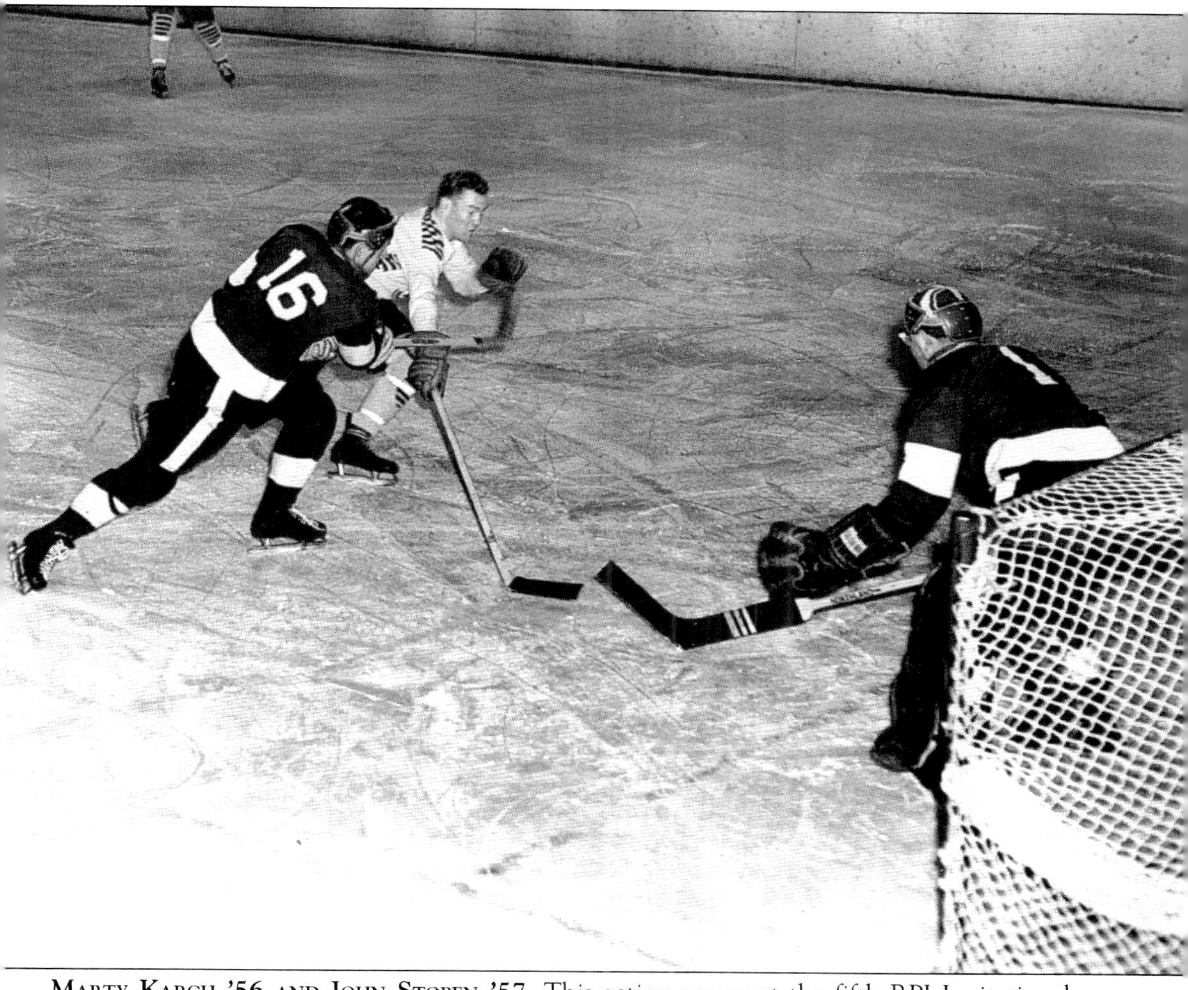

Marty Karch '56 and John Stopen '57. This action occurs at the fifth RPI Invitational Tournament, as Karch defends while Stopen plays goalie against Loyola College. RPI defeated Loyola in this game 6-4 but lost to the University of Minnesota the next night and finished second in the tournament. The Engineers did not win their own tournament until the seventh installment in January 1958. It was common for powerhouse teams like the University of Michigan, the University of Minnesota, and the University of North Dakota to come to Troy in the tournament's early days, making the competition fierce for RPI and the other teams. Karch was a defenseman on the national championship team and co-captain of the squad for the 1955–1956 season, picking up 10 points, a respectable total for a blue-liner. After receiving his degree in electrical engineering, Karch did a stint in the army and later worked for General Electric in New Jersey.

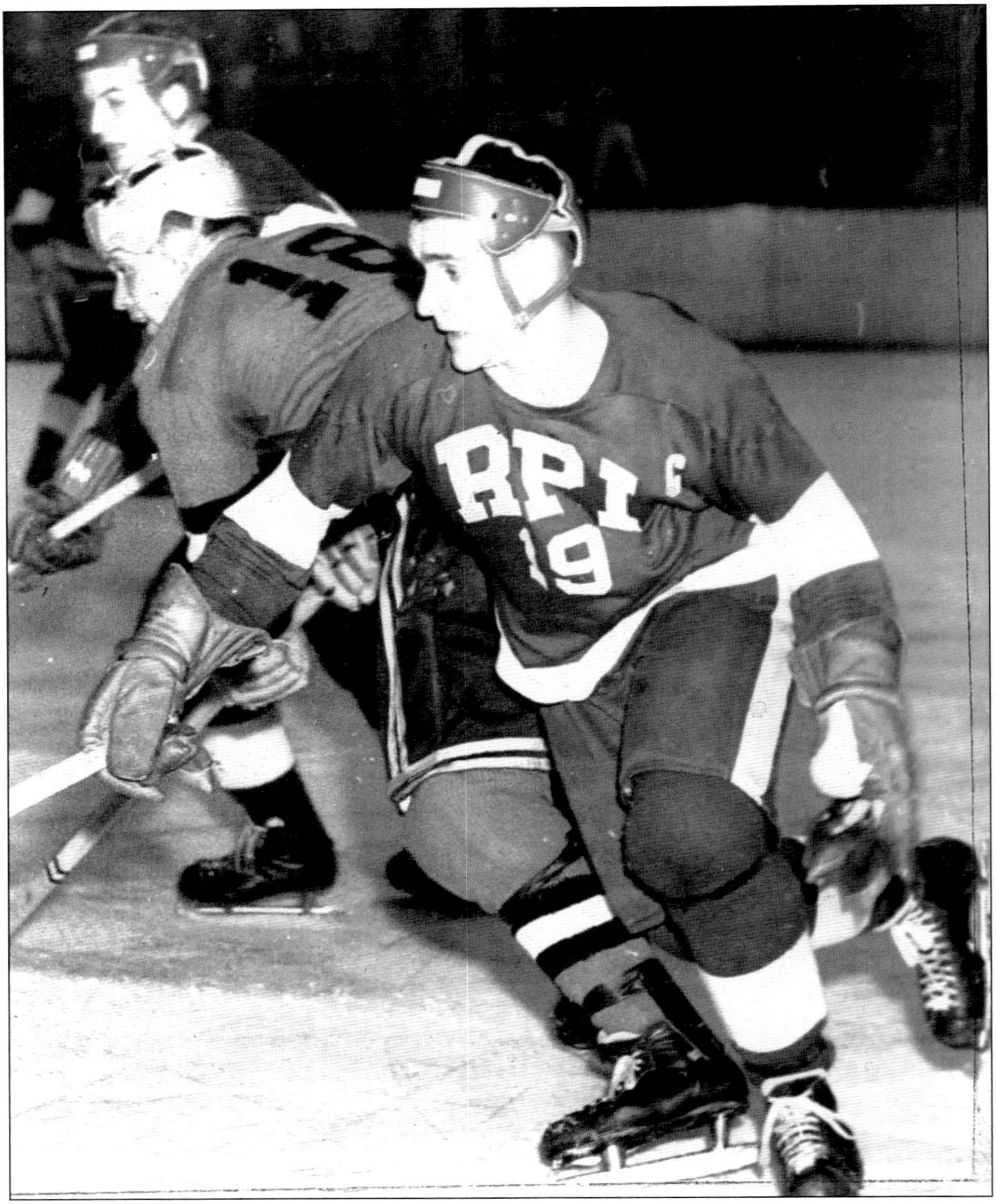

DICK CHIARELLI '57. Second of three brothers and four family members to play hockey at RPI, Chiarelli was a prolific scorer who amassed 138 points in 61 games over three years. The first year, he played alongside his brother Frank, and in the last, he was co-captain. Against Northeastern University in January 1956, he scored 7 goals, tying the school record, as RPI routed the Huskies 13-2. After graduation, he returned to the Ottawa area, ultimately running his own company, Chiarelli Engineering. He was followed in the cherry and white by the third brother, Pat Chiarelli '61, who played defense for two seasons (1958–1959 and 1959–1960). A cousin of the brothers, John Chiarelli '62, was another forward who played 65 games in his three seasons and scored 111 points.

SLOAN SARGEANT '57. A big defenseman from Toronto, Sargeant helped anchor the blue line for the 1956–1957 team that won the Tri-State League title. One of his 12 assists his senior year came in overtime versus St. Lawrence University, as he set up Jim Wadley '58 for the game winner while shutting down St. Lawrence University's top-scoring line for the game.

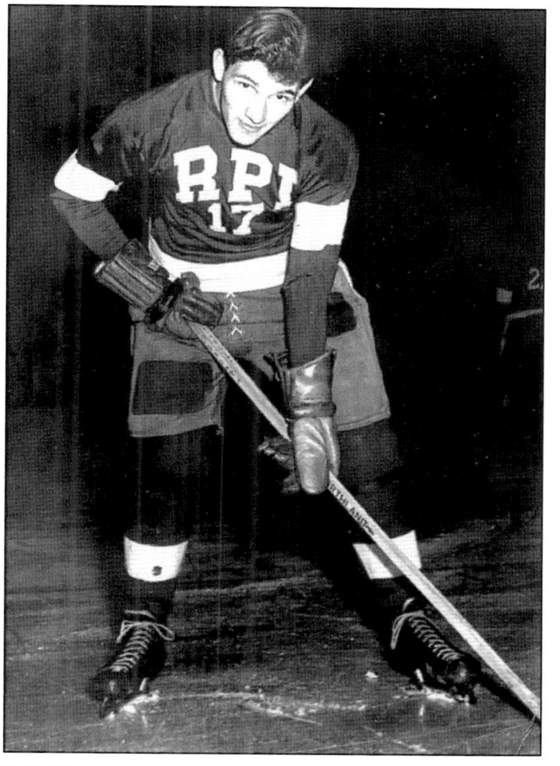

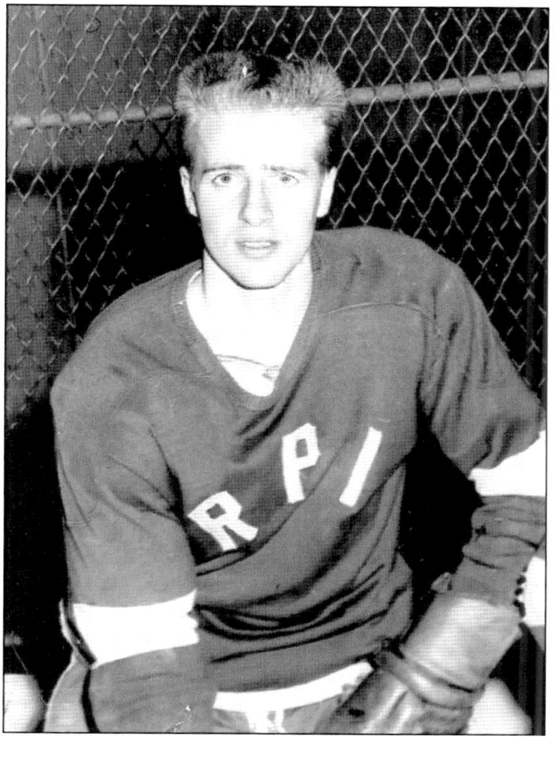

RON PALMER '58. Palmer, a Toronto native, scored 102 points over the course of three seasons. He was named to the All-Tournament first team as a forward in the RPI Invitational Tournament in 1958, the first championship for RPI in the tournament. During that tournament, Palmer picked up 2 goals and 1 assist as RPI went 2-0-1.

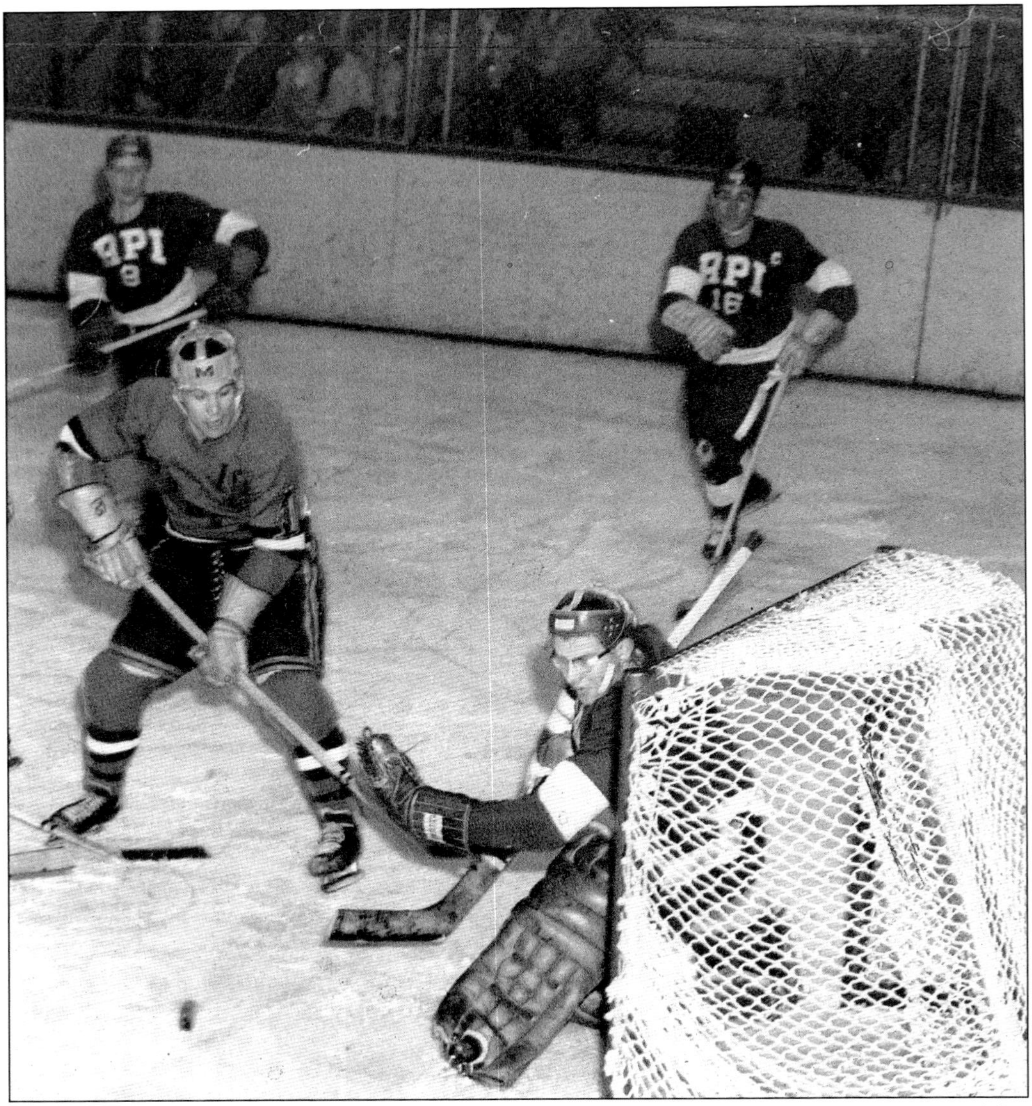

JOHN STOPEN '57. Stopen was the successor to Bob Fox in net for the Engineers, and his introduction to college hockey was perfect. He shut out Springfield College 13-0 during his first game in goal in February 1955. He compiled a 24-12-1 record in 37 starts, with three shutouts. He is shown here playing against the University of Minnesota during an RPI Invitational Tournament game in January 1956, which RPI lost 5-3. Jim Wadley '58 and Garry Kearns '58 are in front as the puck moves to the left of Stopen. Marty Karch '56 and Ron Palmer '58 are out of the play to the right. Note the primitive leather helmets worn by all the players, especially Stopen in goal, along with goggles that look like the kind used in a chemistry lab. In the background, above the boards, is the chain-link fence that once surrounded the rink, in the days before Plexiglas was the norm.

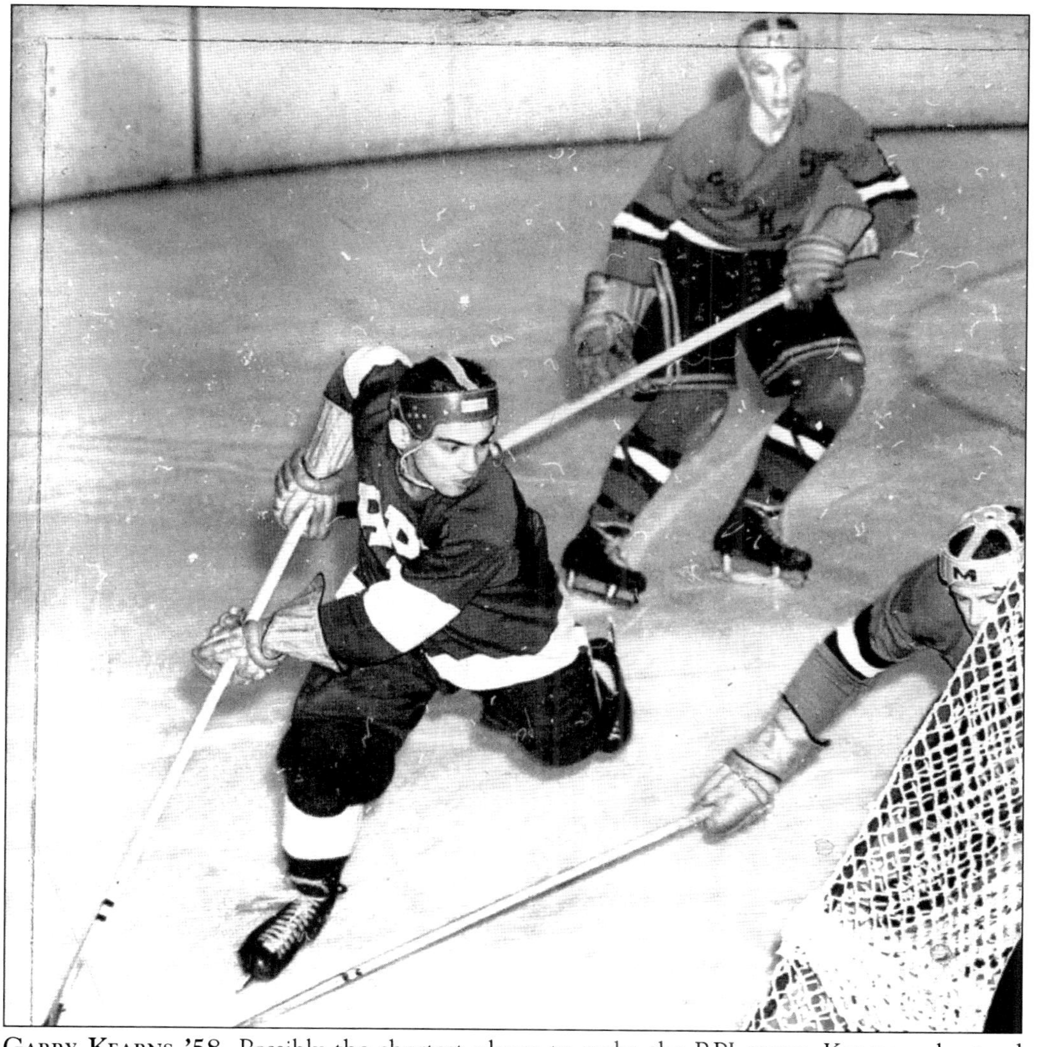

Garry Kearns '58. Possibly the shortest player to make the RPI roster, Kearns only stood five feet two inches tall but made up for it as a speedy and quick forward who could score. He amassed 144 points in three seasons—averaging more than 2.5 points per game—and was a first-team All-American in the 1955–1956 season. After graduation, Kearns remained in the area as an architect, but circumstances called him back to the institute after Harkness's successor, Rube Bjorkman, left the head coaching job and another candidate backed out. Therefore, in 1964, Kearns was named head coach of the team, which was hurt by a lack of recruits during Bjorkman's tenure. That problem caused the team to cease being competitive. They went 3-19 during the 1965–1966 season, resulting in discussions about dropping the program to a lower classification. Kearns squelched that idea and recruited heavily around his hometown of Peterborough, Ontario. By the time he returned to architecture in 1969, RPI had a winning program again.

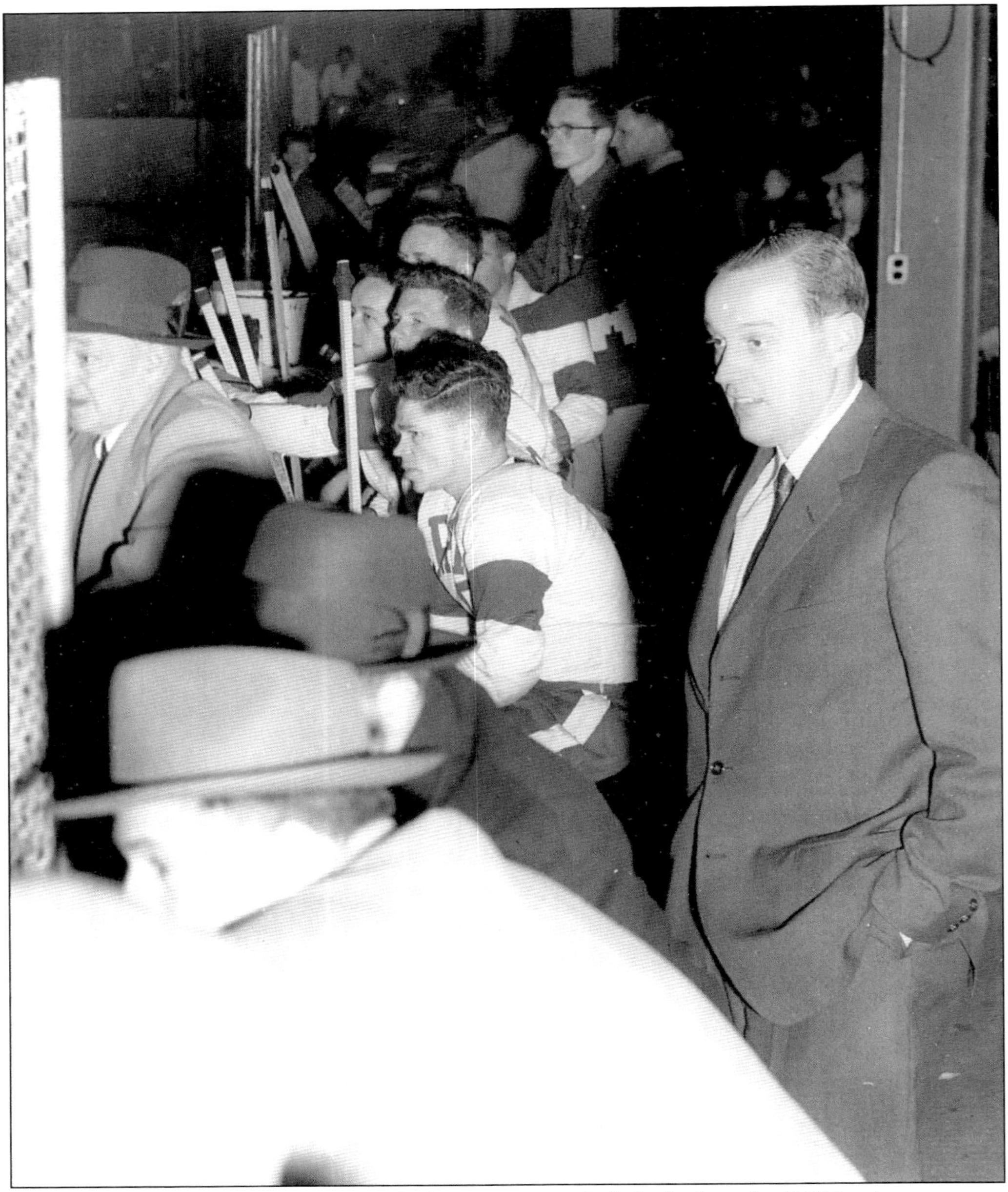

DON BIRKMAYER '49. For 50 years, Birkmayer was tightly linked to the RPI hockey program as a supervisor of officials and the public address announcer at the field house. His deep, commanding voice could penetrate all corners of the building. He was also deeply involved with college hockey as the editor and publisher of the *Intercollegiate Hockey Newsletter*, which for many decades was the authoritative source for information about the college hockey scene. Birkmayer is pictured here behind the bench at an alumni game, which is why the players are not wearing helmets; it is not an official game. Behind him are the posts that obstructed fans' views of the game in the original building configuration. Note that there is no glass or fence separating the fans from the players or protecting the fans from loose pucks, a situation that would be unacceptable today.

CHUCK URMSON '59. A rare, but not the last, hockey player who majored in aeronautical engineering, Urmson followed it with a master's in mechanical engineering in 1961. He exploded on offense his senior year, scoring 39 points (his previous season best was 9) to finish third behind Ray Belasky and Paul Midghall. A disciplined player, he rarely took penalties and followed with a career as a structural design engineer.

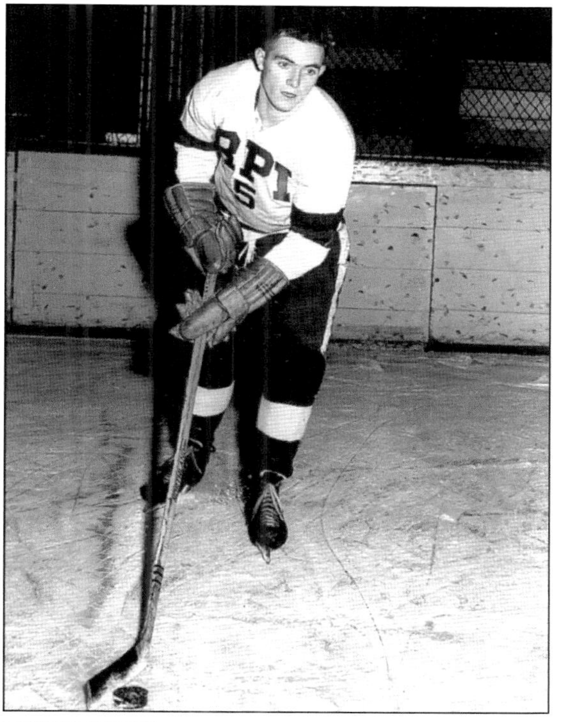

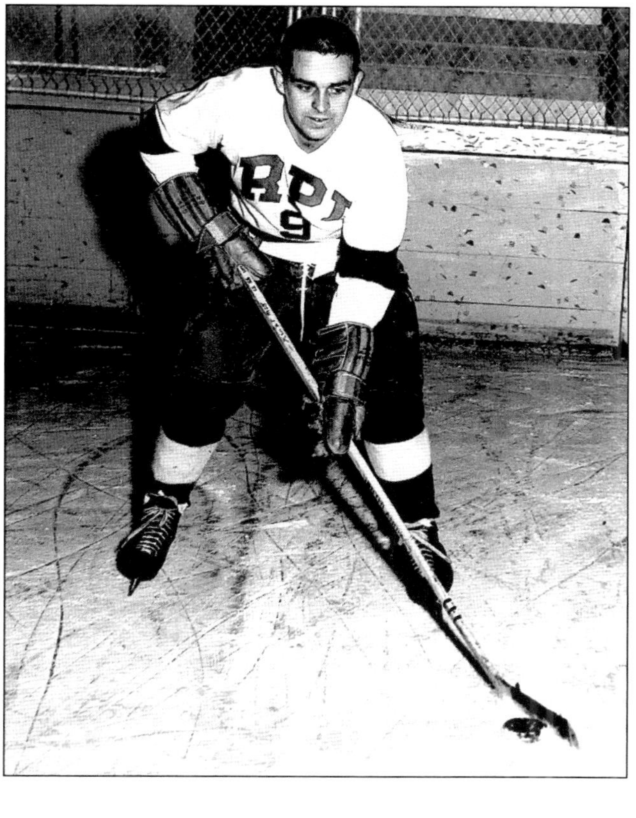

RAY BELASKY '60. Belasky was a forward from Hull, Quebec, who scored prodigiously. His 37 goals in the 1958–1959 season is the fifth-best mark in school history. That season, he also notched six hat tricks. He played only eight games in his sophomore year and managed 26 points, a sign of things to come. He captained the 1959–1960 squad, which he led in scoring with 46 points.

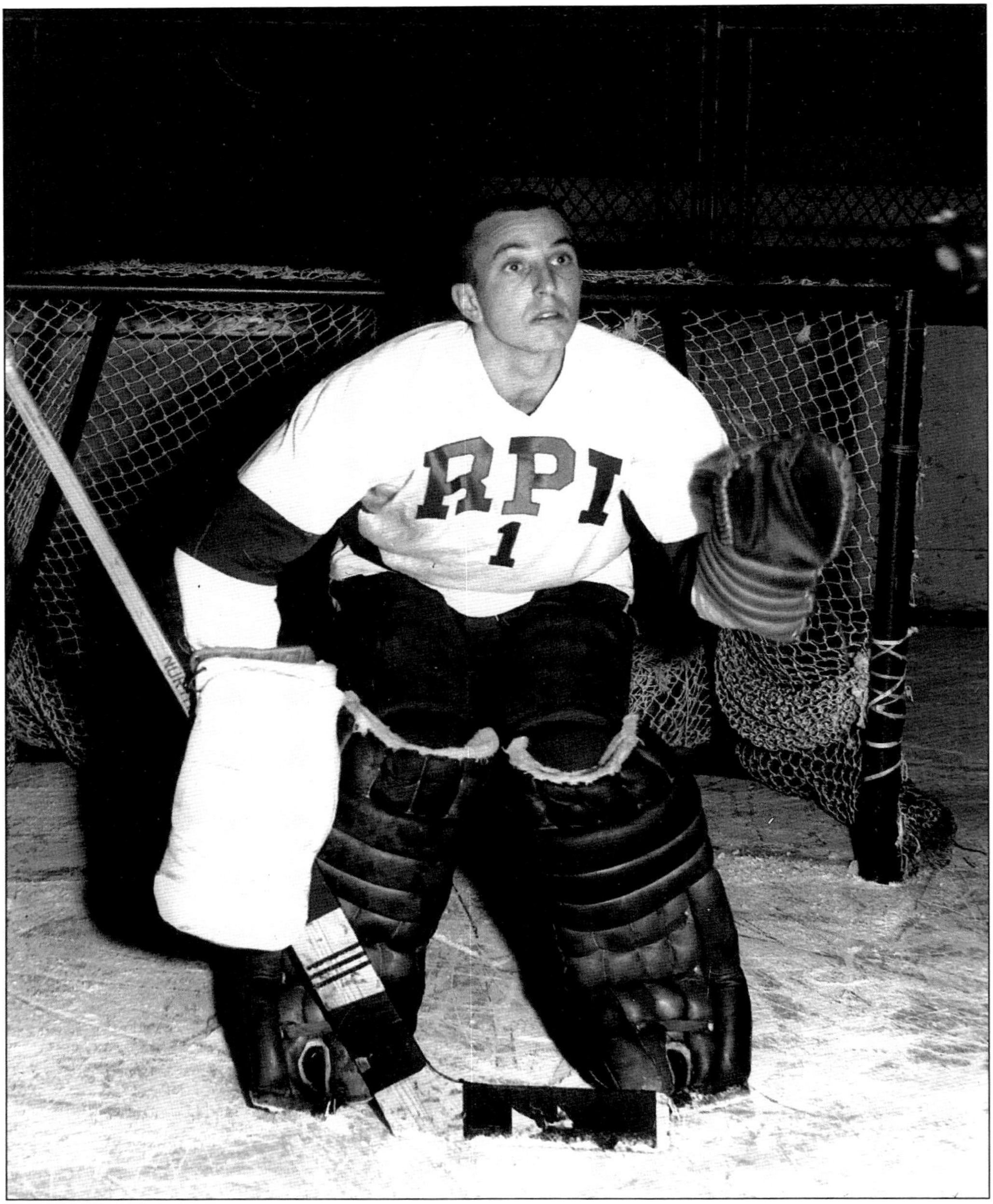

Bob Ottone '59. The successor to Johnny Stopen in goal, Ottone was a mechanical engineering major from Springfield, Massachusetts. He compiled a 30-14-1 record during his three seasons between the pipes. Ottone and others in the late 1950s had the misfortune of skating for very good teams that could not break into the NCAA Tournament, restricted at that time to only four teams, two teams selected from both the east and west. Since the east had substantially more teams, good teams were left home. From 1955 through 1960 (five seasons), RPI's winning percentage never dropped lower than .619, but no bids to the tournament were forthcoming. The NCAA did not expand the tournament until the late 1970s, too late for those quality RPI squads.

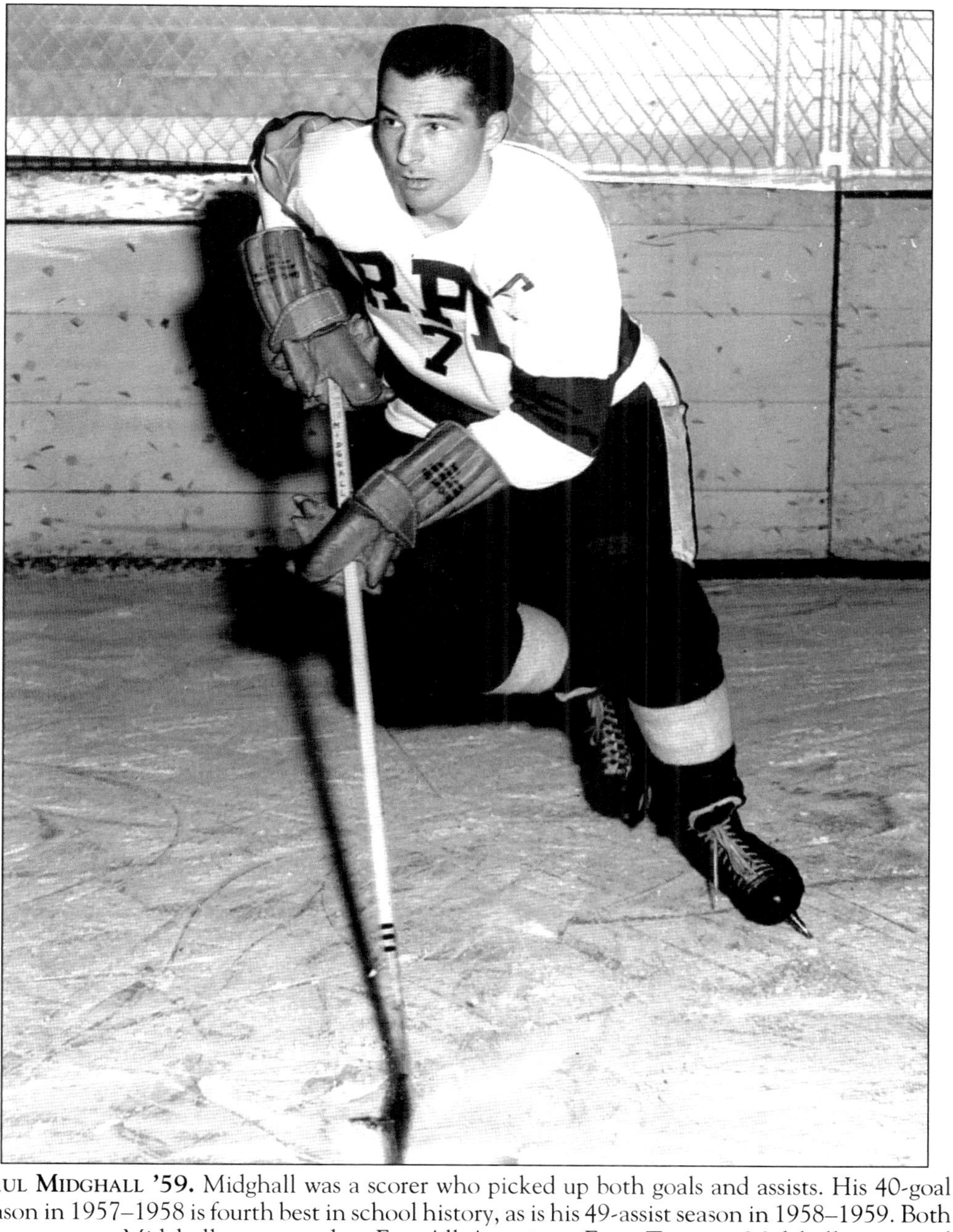

PAUL MIDGHALL '59. Midghall was a scorer who picked up both goals and assists. His 40-goal season in 1957–1958 is fourth best in school history, as is his 49-assist season in 1958–1959. Both those seasons, Midghall was named an East All-American. From Toronto, Midghall continued in the long line of hockey talent that Harkness recruited from his native Ontario. He led the team in scoring in each of his three seasons and co-captained the 1958–1959 squad with Karl Balland '59. His 118 career assists are good for third on the school list, and his 3.35 points-per-game average is second to only Abbie Moore. At times, the points came in important bunches. For example, he either scored or assisted on all the goals versus Boston College in a 4-1 win in February 1959, and he assisted on four of five goals against Clarkson College of Technology one week later. Later, he worked as a hockey official.

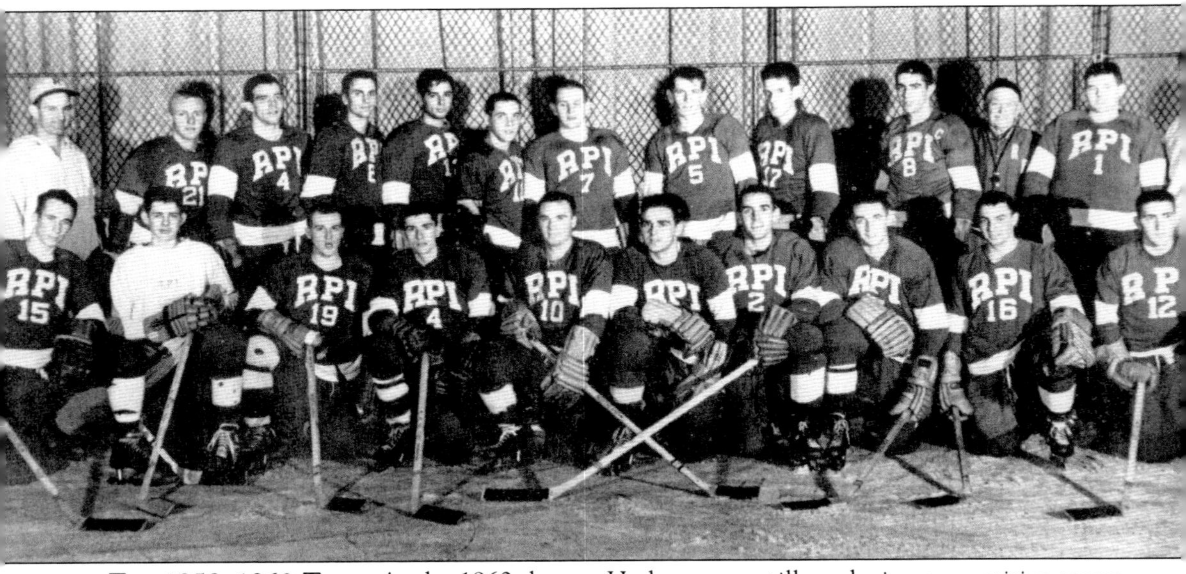

The 1959–1960 Team. As the 1960s began, Harkness was still producing competitive teams. This squad started out with seven straight wins, before dropping two in the Invitational Tournament, and they ended with a 15-7 record and a second-place finish in the Tri-State League. This was the first season for two outstanding forwards. Jim Josephson '62 finished second in scoring. For his career, he had 148 points and was always in the top three for team points. He also co-captained the team in his junior and senior seasons. He followed up his time at RPI by playing in the Eastern Hockey League and the International Hockey League as one of the first RPI alums to have a significant minor-league professional career. The other great forward of this time was Trevor Kaye '62, a small forward in the mold of Garry Kearns. He accumulated 135 points during his time at RPI and, like Paul Midghall, worked as a college hockey official. They contributed greatly the next season, when RPI returned to the NCAA Tournament for the first time since 1954.

Bryan Pryce '63. Co-captain with Ken Astill of the 1962–1963 team, Pryce was a hard-hitting defenseman who saw limited duty his first two seasons. He came on strong with 23 points his senior year, when he was named to the All-ECAC second team. He even managed a hat trick against American International College in February 1962, the first game he played that season.

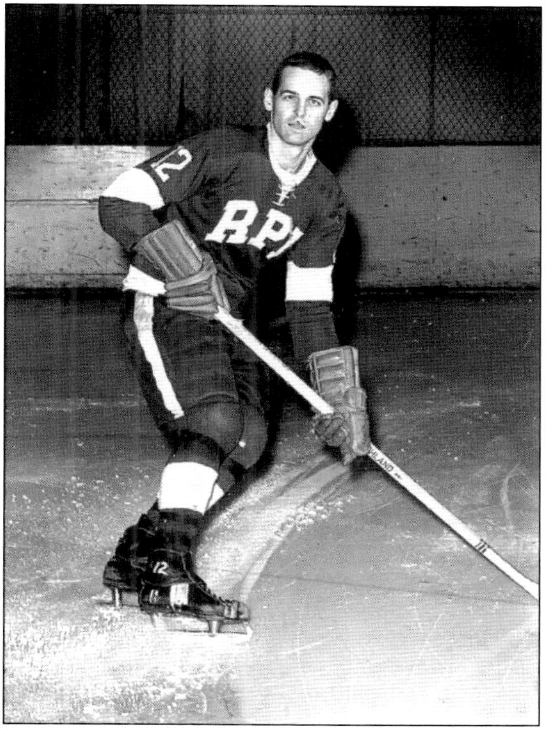

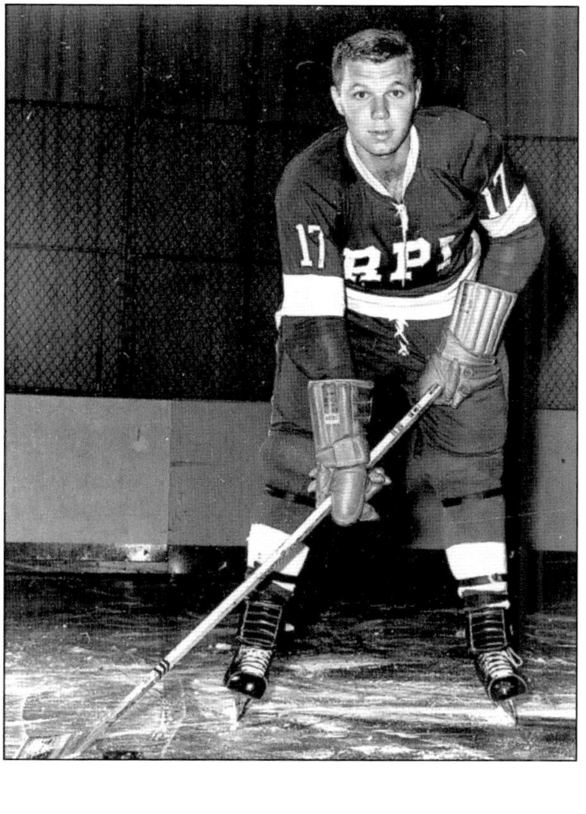

Ken Astill '63. Astill was the other co-captain during the 1962–1963 season, the last for Ned Harkness as the head coach at RPI. Astill had his best season as a senior, picking up 49 points. He followed his time at RPI by playing Senior A hockey in the Ontario Hockey Association.

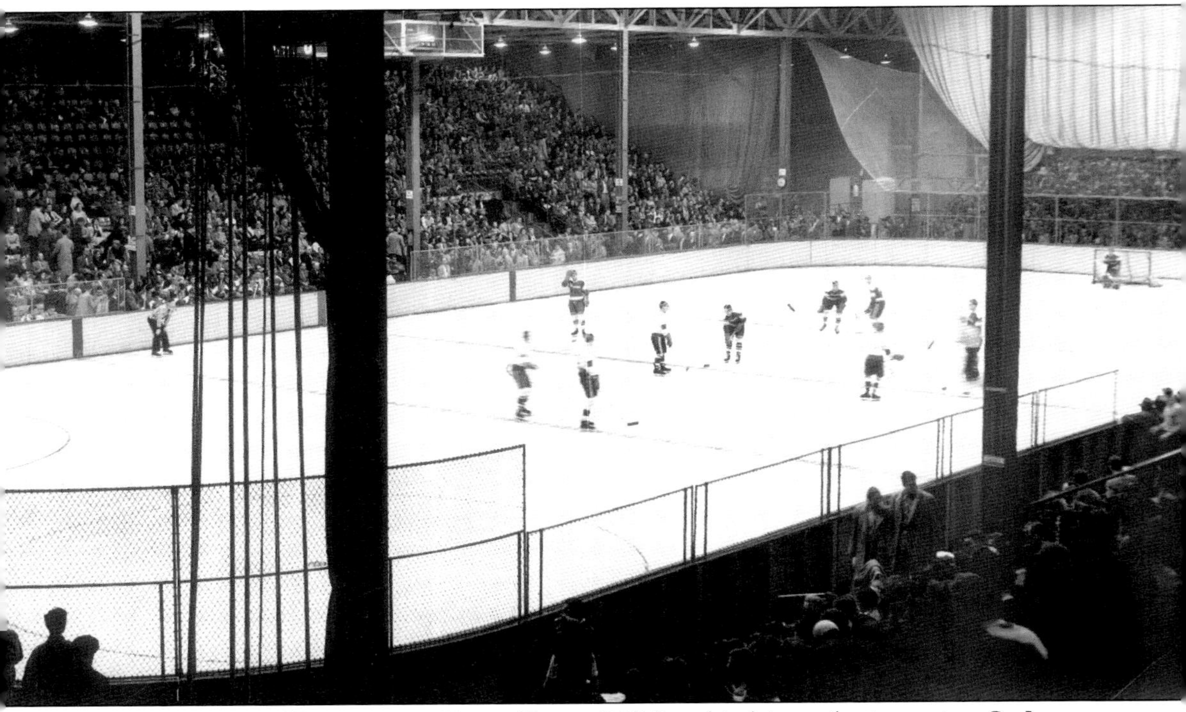

THE RPI FIELD HOUSE IN THE EARLY YEARS. RPI (in white) is on the ice against St. Lawrence University (in red) in the early years of the program. This interior view shows just how annoying the posts were in the original building. The chain-link fence is still present as the only protection for the crowd and is much lower than the Plexiglas is in the current building. This view looks toward section two (southwest), so the front of the building is in the upper right-hand corner. There is little separating the players from the crowd. Spectators stood in the nearside corners, which was possible then because the ice was at the same level as the floor and there were no railings guarding access. A good crowd is on hand. Crowds in excess of 5,000 were regular in the 1950s and early 1960s because the team was very successful and there was little else to do in the area.

Three

The 1960s and 1970s

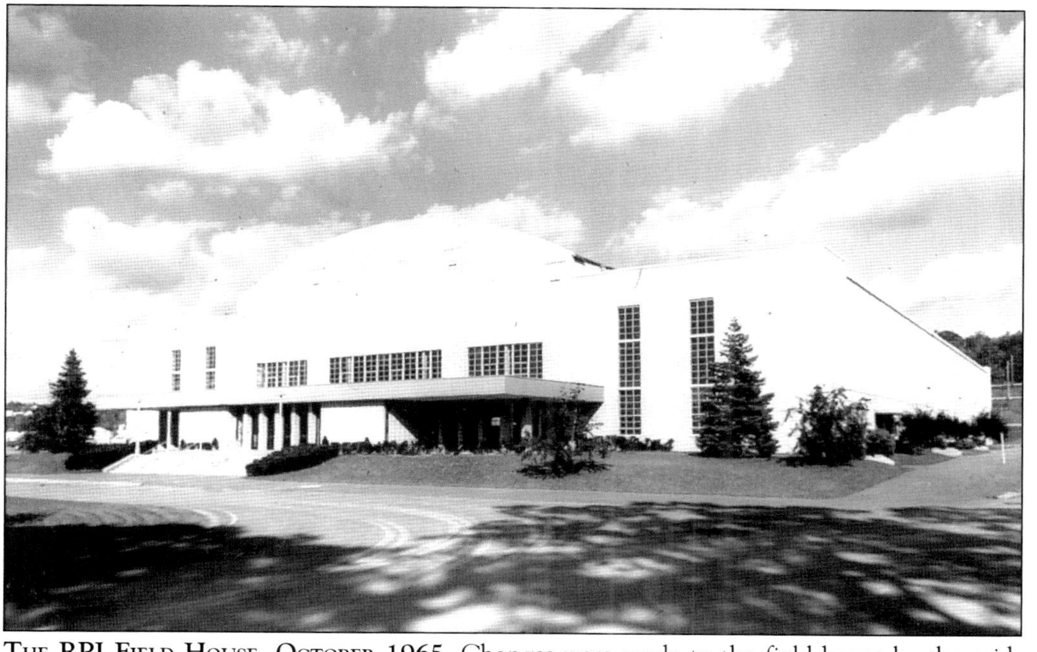

The RPI Field House, October 1965. Changes were made to the field house by the mid-1960s. A ticket booth and lobby were added to the front of the building. Since the field house was originally a navy warehouse, amenities such as these were not in the original plan. Considering the poor weather that plagues Troy much of the year, this was a logical addition to the facility.

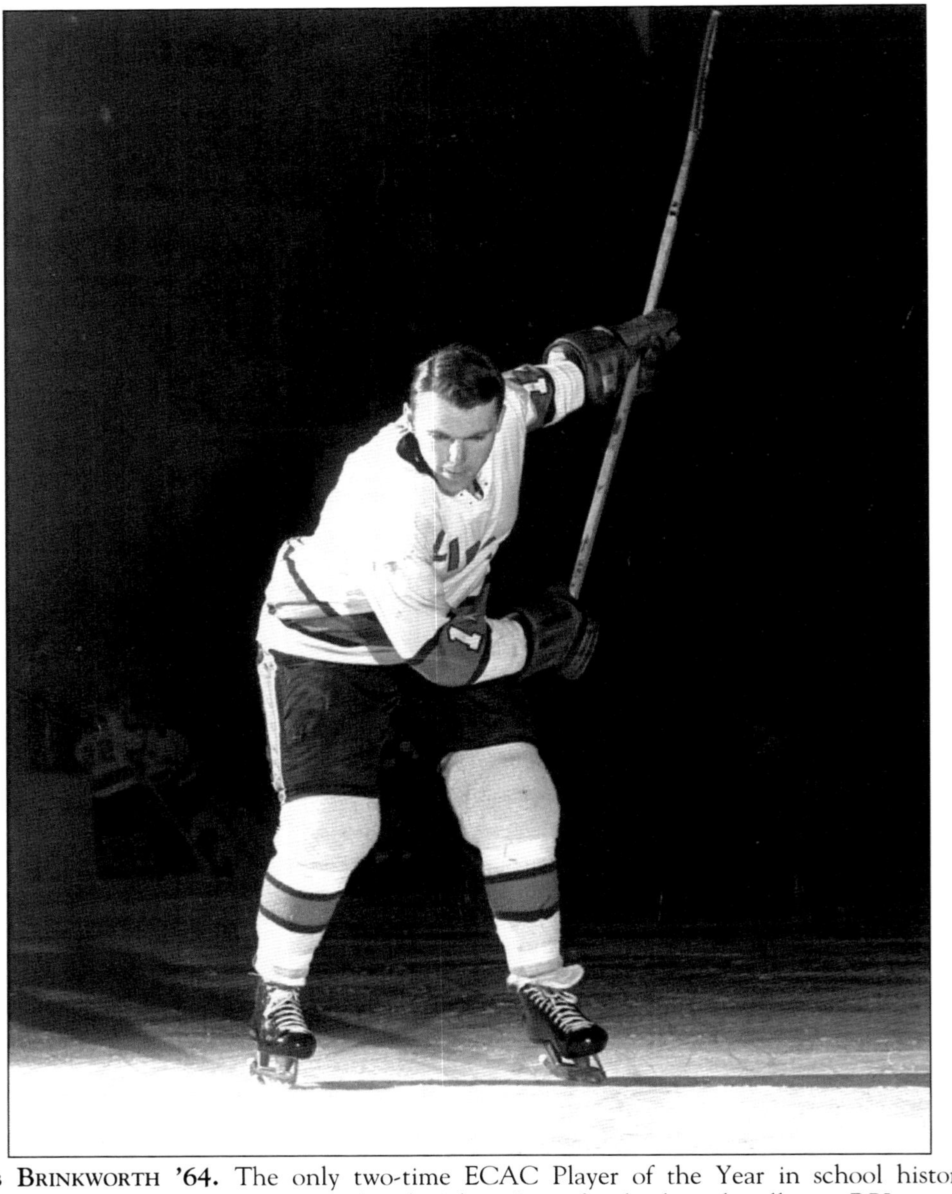

Bob Brinkworth '64. The only two-time ECAC Player of the Year in school history, Brinkworth, a Toronto native, is tied with Adam Oates for third on the all-time RPI scoring list. He was ECAC Sophomore of the Year in the 1961–1962 season and an East All-American in his junior and senior seasons. He tallied 216 points during his collegiate career, with 110 points from goals, and led the team with 71 points in the 1961–1962 season and 75 points in the 1962–1963 season. Brinkworth was third on both the school lists for career goals and points. Had freshmen been allowed to play in the 1960s, it is conceivable that another 70-point season (as all his were) in his freshman year would have placed Brinkworth at the top of both lists. He was the first player to have a sustained minor-league career, playing for the Baltimore Clippers and the Providence Reds of the American Hockey League (AHL) along with the Port Huron Wings of the International Hockey League (IHL). While playing in the minors, he also worked at Hewlett Packard.

RUBE BJORKMAN. A 1951 graduate of the University of Minnesota and a silver medalist at the 1952 Olympics, Bjorkman was hired after Harkness left in 1963. His one season was a great success as RPI. The team went 18-8 overall and advanced to the NCAA Tournament, losing to the University of Denver in the semifinals but beating Providence to win third place. He found recruiting for RPI difficult and lacked the Ontario connections both Harkness and Kearns had. After one season, he left RPI to coach at the University of New Hampshire.

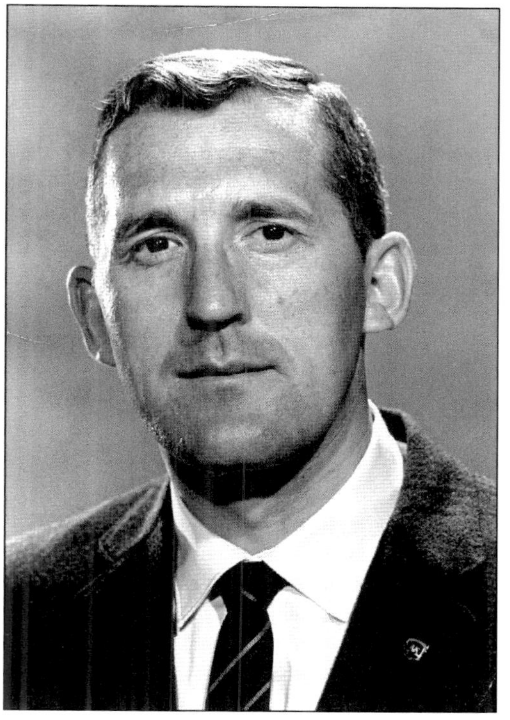

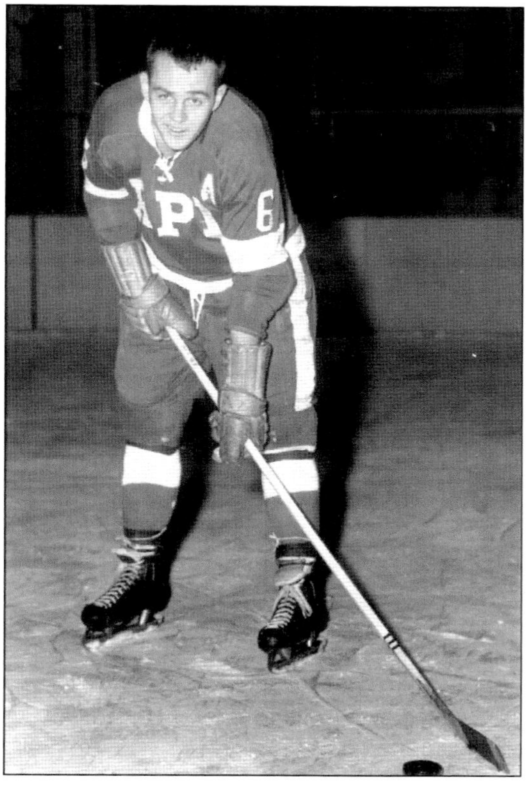

FRED KITCHEN '65. Kitchen was a biology major at RPI who later attended Albany Medical College and became a doctor. He was named an All-ECAC first-team defenseman in 1964, when RPI made a run for the NCAA title. Kitchen was also a second-team choice on the ECAC All-Tournament team that year, as RPI's first trip to Boston resulted in a 3-1 defeat in the semifinals at the hands of St. Lawrence University, a team that RPI has never defeated in the ECAC or NCAA playoffs.

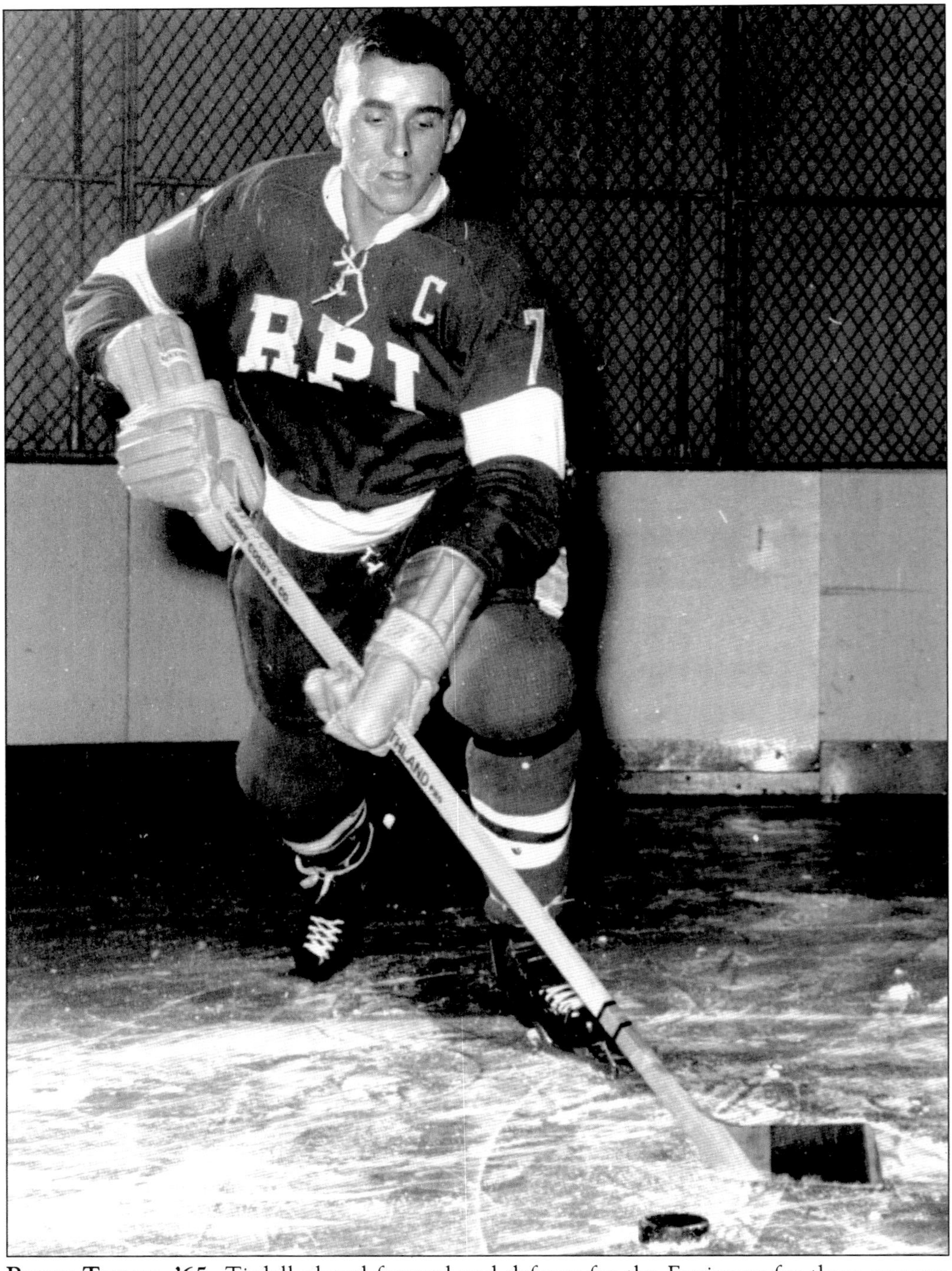

BRUCE TISDALL '65. Tisdall played forward and defense for the Engineers for three seasons. After receiving his bachelor's degree in management, he continued with graduate work at the University of Western Ontario and played hockey for their team. (Canadian schools allow for more years of eligibility.) He returned to Troy in December 1965 as part of the Mustangs team that won the RPI Invitational Tournament, defeating RPI 11-1 en route to the title.

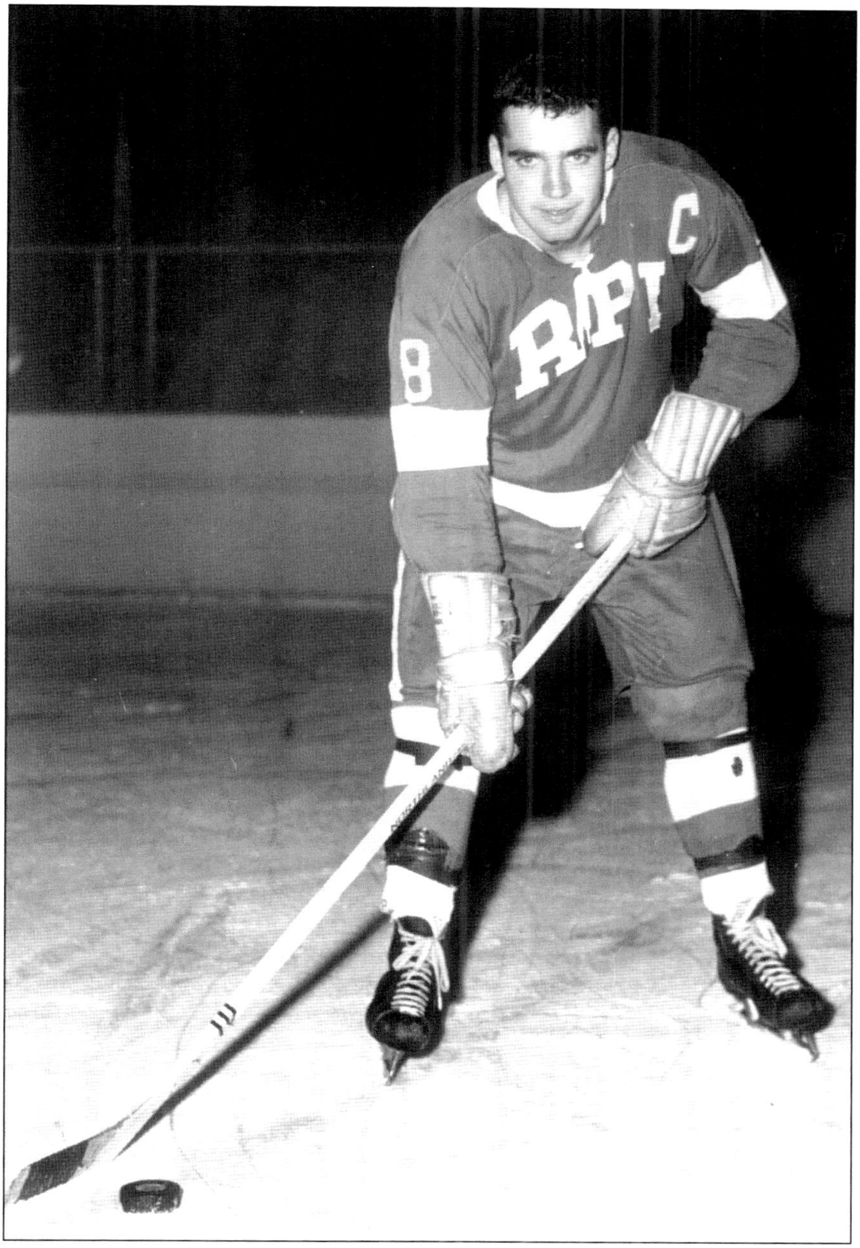

JERRY KNIGHTLEY '65. Knightley was a two-time East All-American in the 1963–1964 and 1964–1965 seasons. He captained the Engineers both those seasons (with Bob Brinkworth in 1963–1964), in which he also led the team in scoring. His production declined after the departure of Brinkworth. The team fared poorly the following season after the loss of these two speedy forwards, and RPI went 3-19. Knightley finished his career with 90 goals and 97 assists during his three seasons on the varsity team, playing at a time when freshmen could not compete at the varsity level. At the 1964 NCAA Tournament in Denver, he picked up two assists in the win over Providence College and was named to the All-Tournament second team. His 75 points in the 1963–1964 season are tied for fifth best in school history.

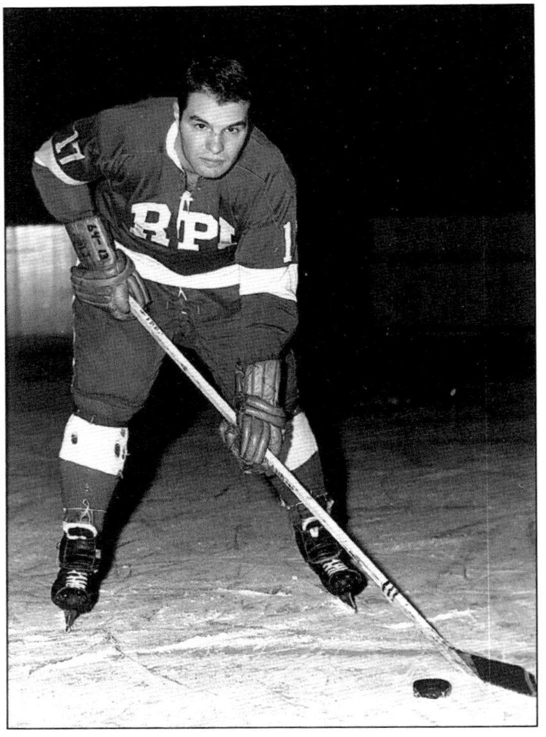

Tony Mancini '65. Mancini received degrees in both architecture and building science. He began his hockey career as a goaltender, earning a 5-2 record in the 1961–1962 and 1962–1963 seasons. In the 1962–1963 season, he also played forward for two games. After not playing in the 1963–1964 season, he returned as a forward in 1964 and picked up four points in 18 games. A switch like this is seldom seen today.

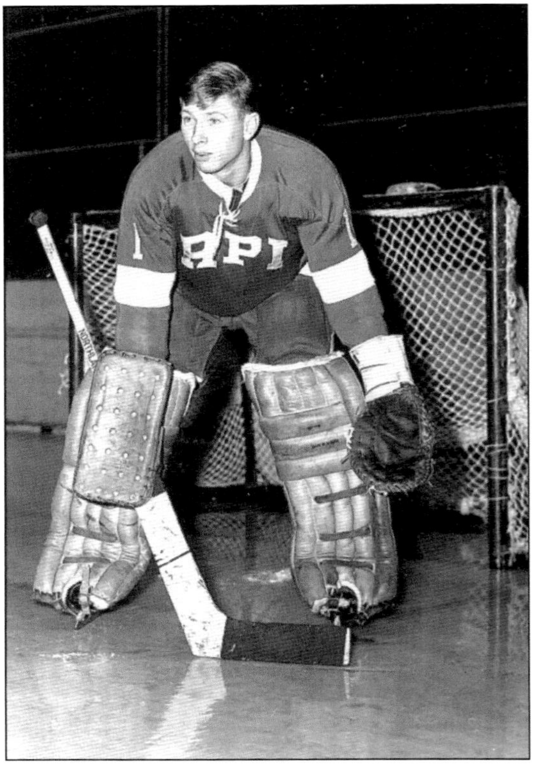

Bill Sack '65. Sack took over as the primary goaltender succeeding Tony Mancini during the RPI Invitational Tournament in the 1962–1963 season. He compiled a 35-29-3 record in three seasons with five shutouts. He is remembered by many for the abrupt manner in which his career ended. Against Boston University on February 20, 1965, at 4:41 of the second period, Sack's right skate became stuck while he was making a save, and he broke his right fibula, finishing his season and career.

PETE RUSSEL '66. Russel was a forward and co-captain of the 1965–1966 squad when things hit bottom for the program. RPI finished 3-19 and was outscored 163 to 46 in the season. Russel picked up 15 points, the lowest of his career, after exceeding 30 each of the two previous seasons. The problem was a lack of numbers, not a lack of talent.

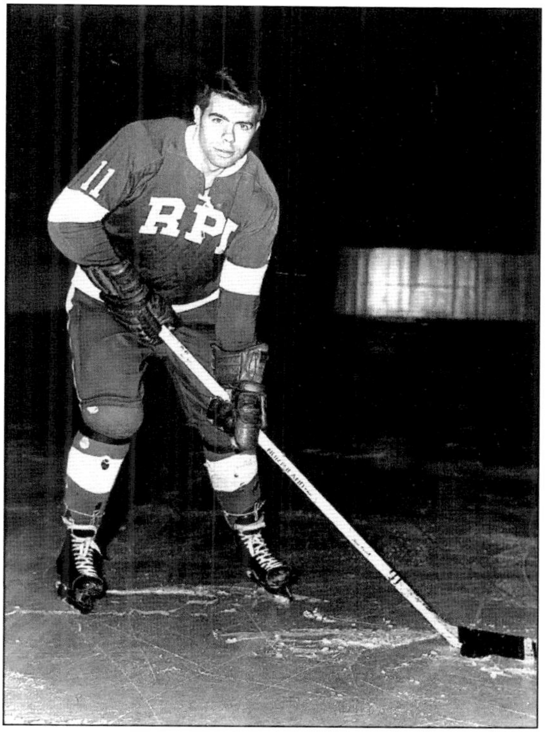

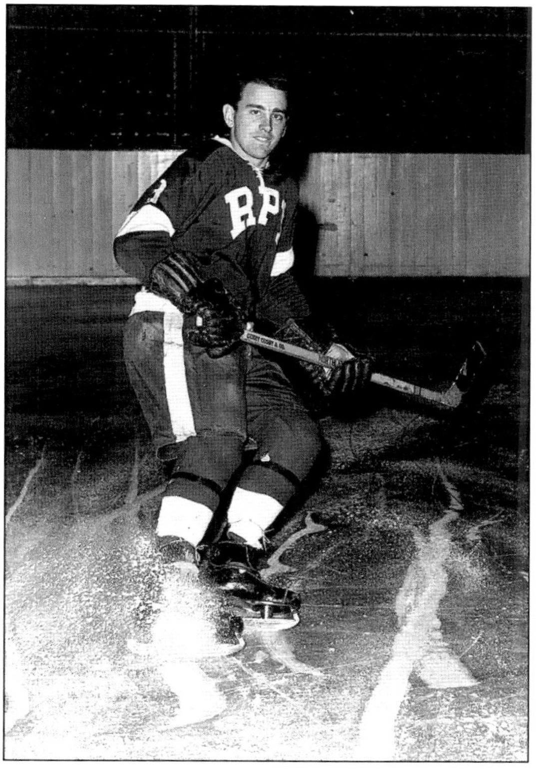

AL JONES '66. Jones, a defenseman, was a second-team All Tri-State selection in the 1964–1965 season, but he became one of the overworked blue-liners the following year. He finished his career with 38 points, earning 20 in his senior season. After graduation, Jones became a dentist.

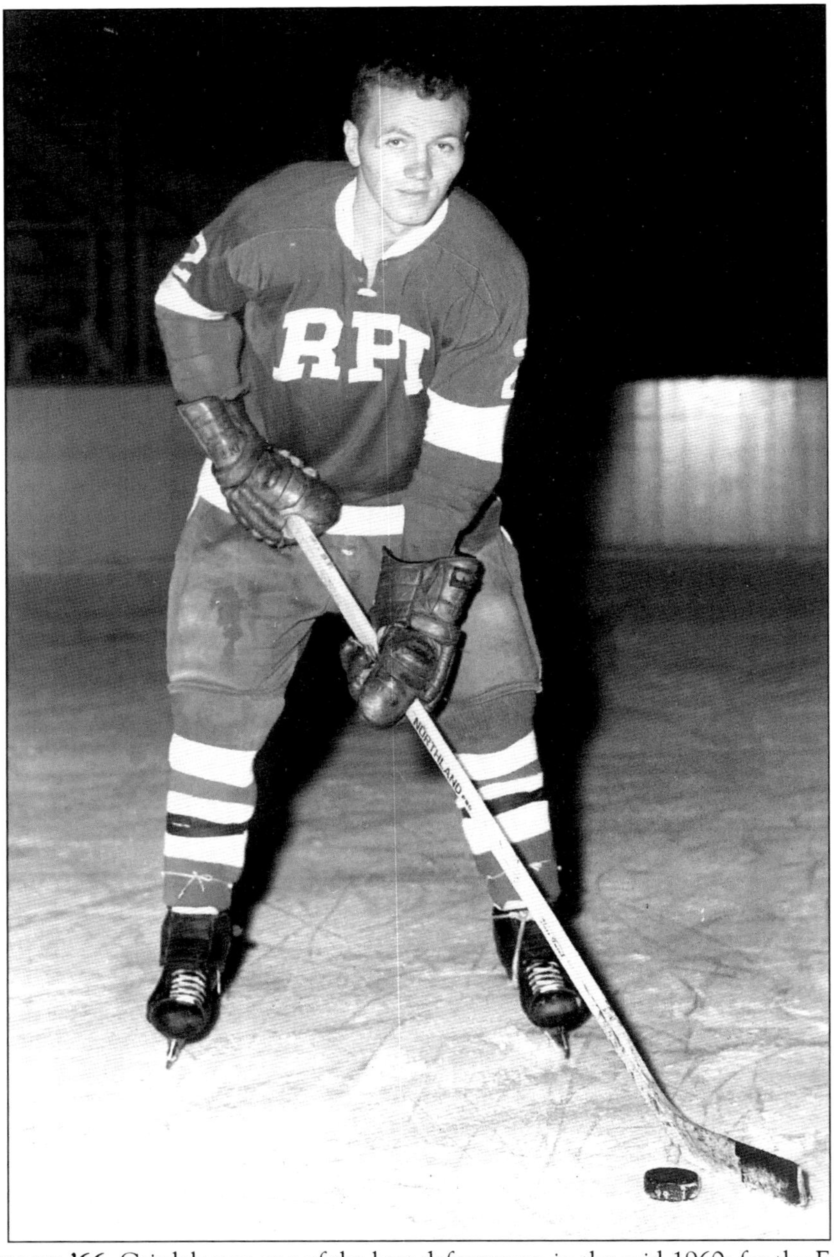

BILL GRISDALE '66. Grisdale was one of the best defensemen in the mid-1960s for the Engineers. The recruiting problems that plagued Rube Bjorkman came back to haunt Garry Kearns in the 1965–1966 season, Grisdale's last, and the team could not stay competitive. There were only three defensemen who played regularly that year—Grisdale, Jones, and Ted Bowser '68—and that is not enough to compete in most games. Grisdale picked up 18 points in his senior year and was co-captain of the squad with Russel. He also picked up a hat trick versus Hamilton College in one of the team's three wins (the others were against Middlebury College and the University of Pennsylvania). RPI won three games and lost two when the score was within two goals. In the other 17 games that season, RPI lost every time.

DALE WATSON '69. RPI began to turn things around in the 1966–1967 season when Watson became eligible to play as a sophomore. He scored 65 points in 24 games, helping RPI to finish with an 8-15-1 record. The following year, he was an All-ECAC second-team forward and also became involved in one of the most bizarre games in RPI history. Late in the second period against Colgate in January 1968, he was involved in a shoving match with Mike Babcock. Sticks started swinging, players left the benches, and referee Giles Threadgold assessed so many penalties that the game was called at 19:10 of the second period with Colgate winning 5-1.

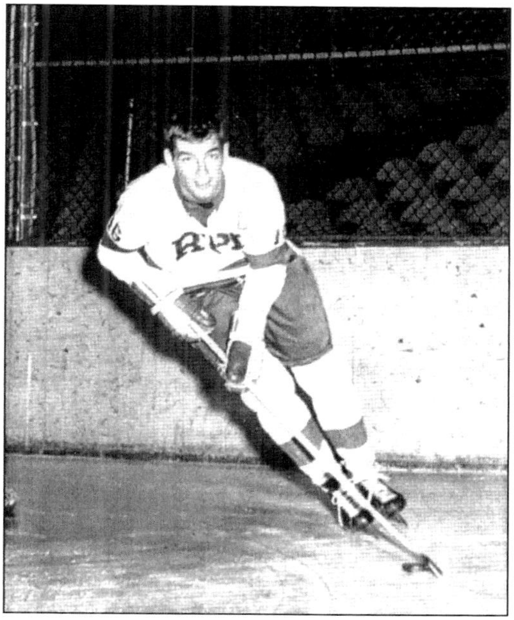

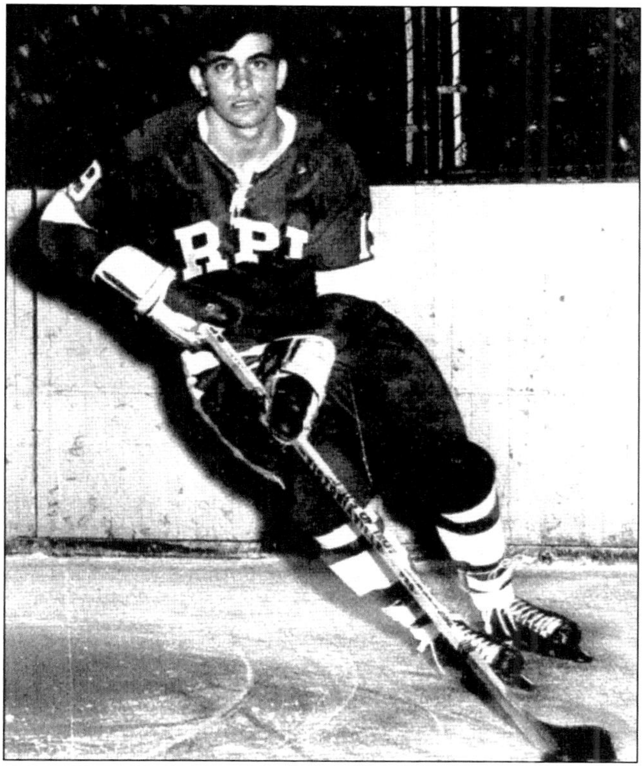

DOUG HEARNS '71. Hearns scored only four goals his sophomore year, but one was big. He beat Ken Dryden of Cornell in overtime on December 4, 1968, and scored in a game in which no one expected RPI to be close. Hearns improved steadily over his career, scoring 8, 18, and, finally, 43 points during his three seasons, but none of those points were as big as the one against Cornell. Hearns was captain during his senior year in the 1970–1971 season.

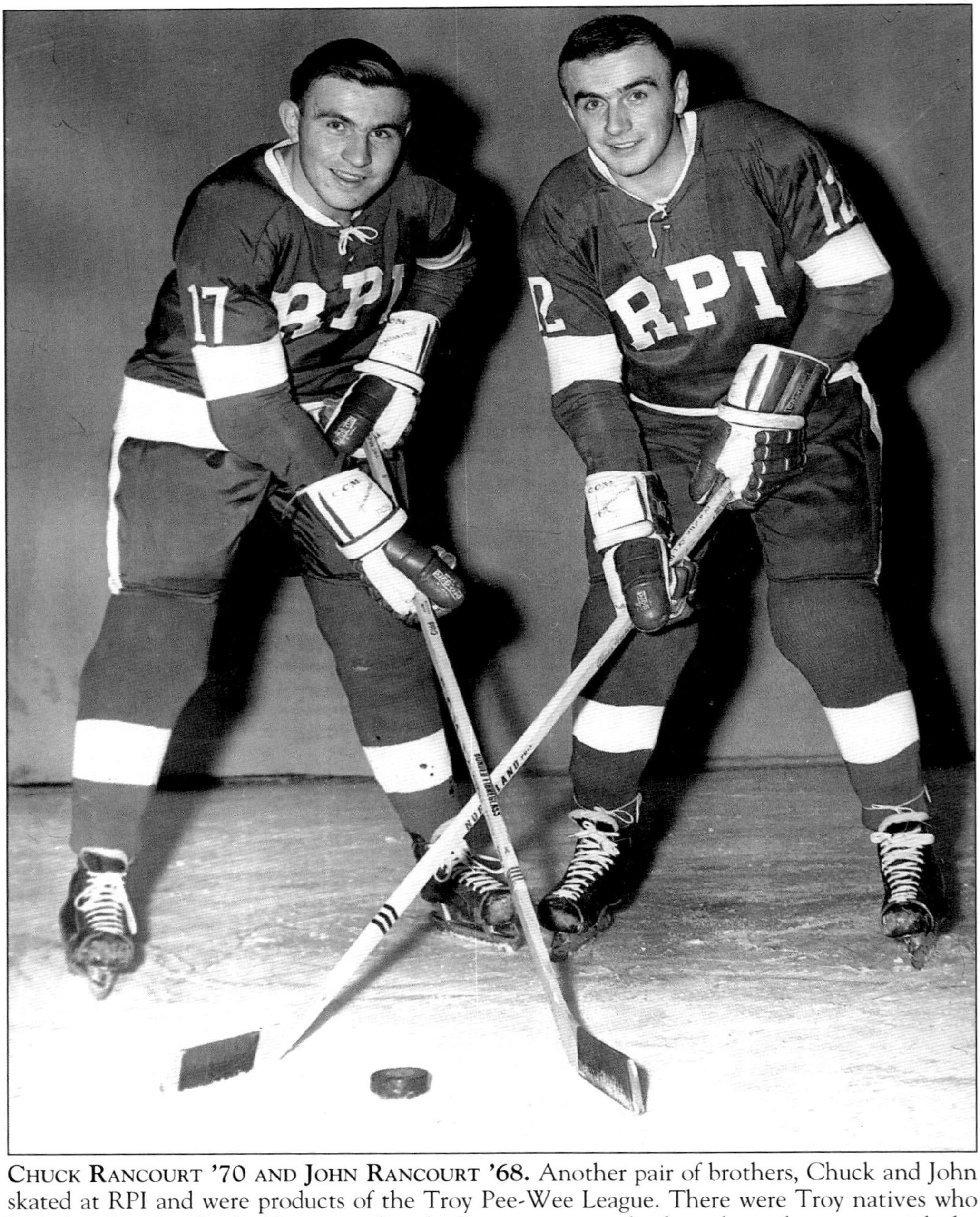

CHUCK RANCOURT '70 AND JOHN RANCOURT '68. Another pair of brothers, Chuck and John skated at RPI and were products of the Troy Pee-Wee League. There were Troy natives who had played earlier for the Engineers, but the Rancourts were the first who truly grew up with the team. John played the most, getting into 60 games over three years and scoring 41 points. Chuck scored 12 points his sophomore year but saw only limited duty in his next two seasons. A third brother, Jim Rancourt '73, played two games on the varsity team in the 1970–1971 season. All the brothers stayed at RPI for advanced degrees. John earned a bachelor's and master's degree in management and an MBA; Chuck earned a bachelor's and master's degree in management; Jim earned a bachelor's degree in management and an MBA. Chuck still works for RPI as the director of patents and licensing.

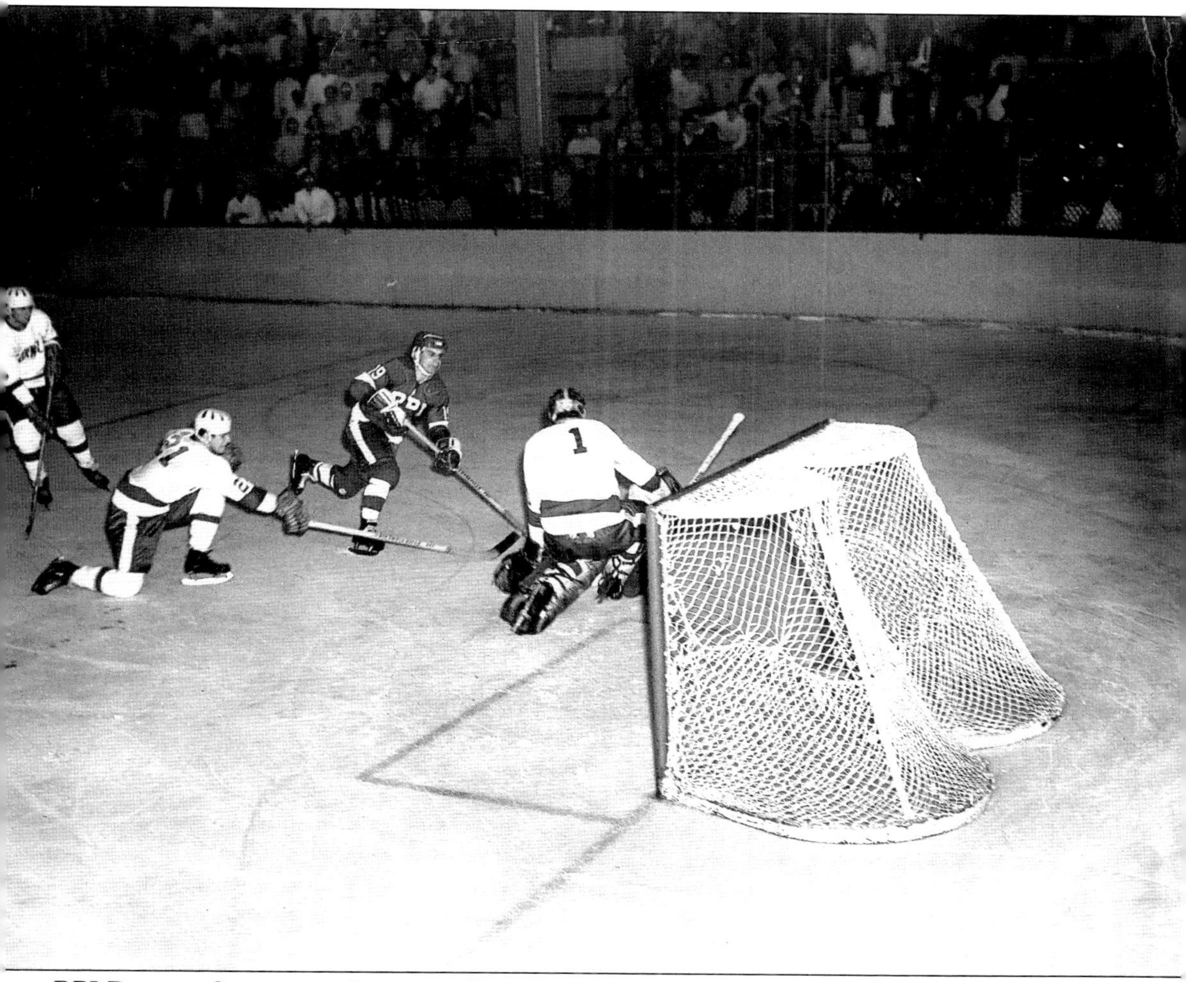

RPI Defeats Cornell in Overtime. Doug Hearns takes his shot against Ken Dryden. Hearns kept the puck low and beat Dryden at 6:09 of overtime to give RPI a 4-3 victory. Since Harkness left RPI for Cornell, things had gone well for the Big Red. Cornell won the national title in 1967, but RPI was not having the same success. In 1964, the ECAC divided its hockey programs into two divisions, and RPI, along with similar smaller schools such as Clarkson College of Technology and St. Lawrence University, opted to remain in the higher classification. As the program fell on hard times in the late 1960s, there was talk of moving the team down to the second division, on the assumption that RPI could not effectively recruit and compete. All that became academic when Hearns scored his goal, and the Engineers showed they could skate with the best team in the East.

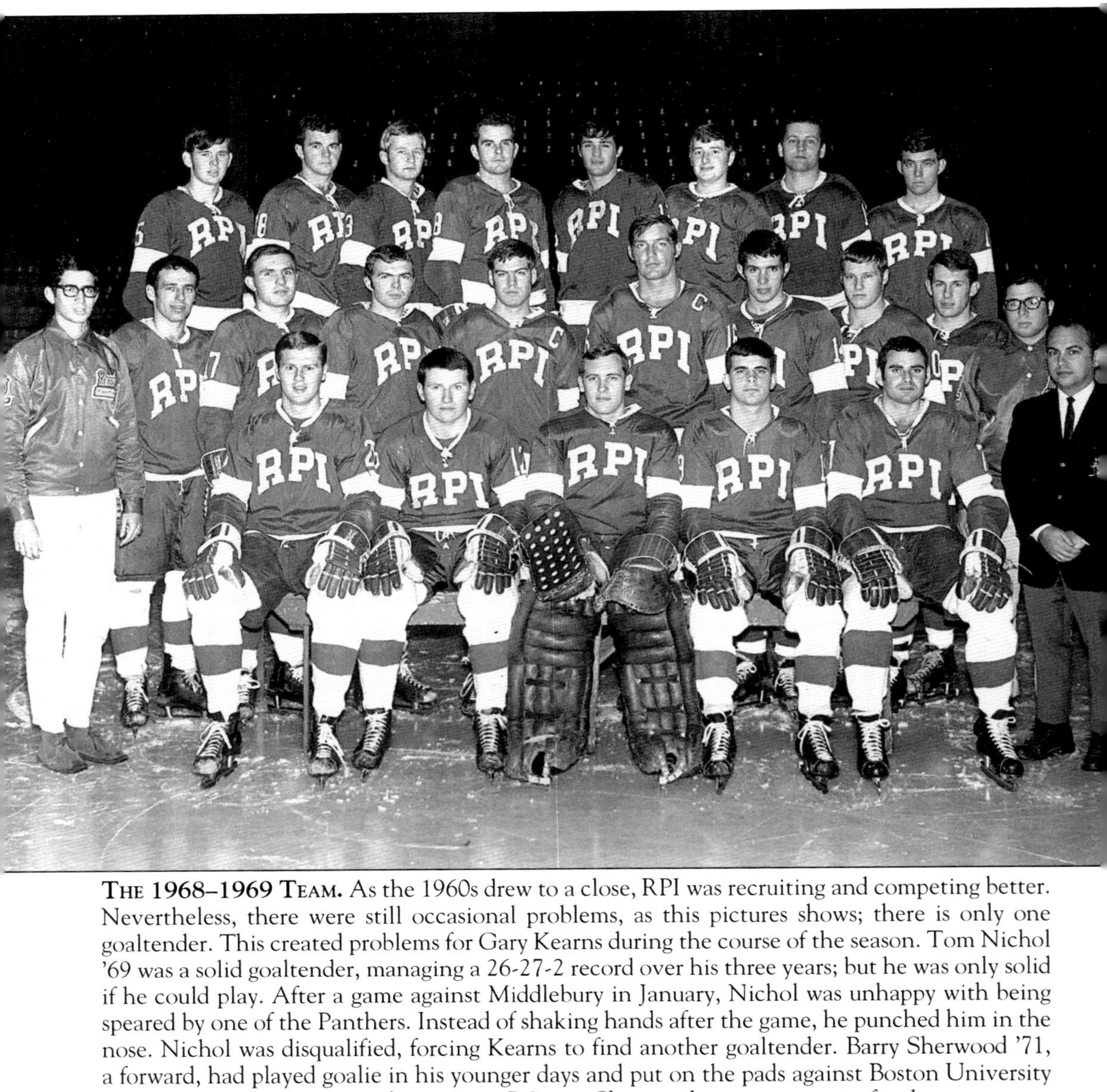

The 1968–1969 Team. As the 1960s drew to a close, RPI was recruiting and competing better. Nevertheless, there were still occasional problems, as this pictures shows; there is only one goaltender. This created problems for Gary Kearns during the course of the season. Tom Nichol '69 was a solid goaltender, managing a 26-27-2 record over his three years; but he was only solid if he could play. After a game against Middlebury in January, Nichol was unhappy with being speared by one of the Panthers. Instead of shaking hands after the game, he punched him in the nose. Nichol was disqualified, forcing Kearns to find another goaltender. Barry Sherwood '71, a forward, had played goalie in his younger days and put on the pads against Boston University the next Tuesday, getting a shutout in a 7-0 win. Sherwood was in net again for the next game, a loss to Montreal. Nichol returned, but when he was unavailable for the Merrimack game in February, defensemen Brian Dickey '69 went between the pipes and picked up the win.

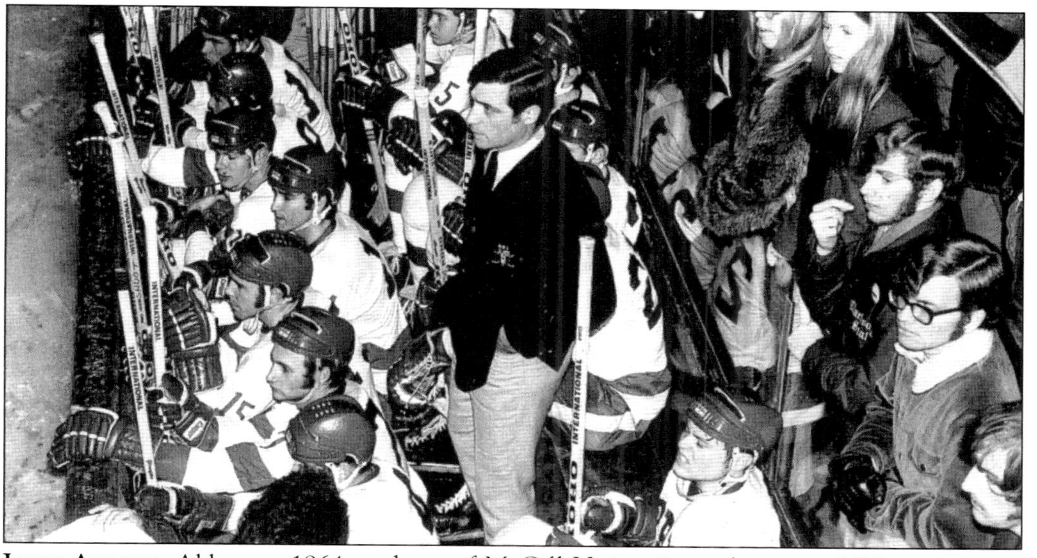

Leon Abbott. Abbott, a 1964 graduate of McGill University and native of Edmonton, was hired as the replacement for Garry Kearns when Kearns returned to architecture. Abbott's first year was poor, and the Engineers finished 15th in the conference. In the next two seasons, the Engineers returned to their winning ways, finishing with records of 16-7-2 and 17-9-1. They lost at Boston University in the ECAC playoffs both years. In 1972, Abbott left RPI to take up the head coaching job at Boston University.

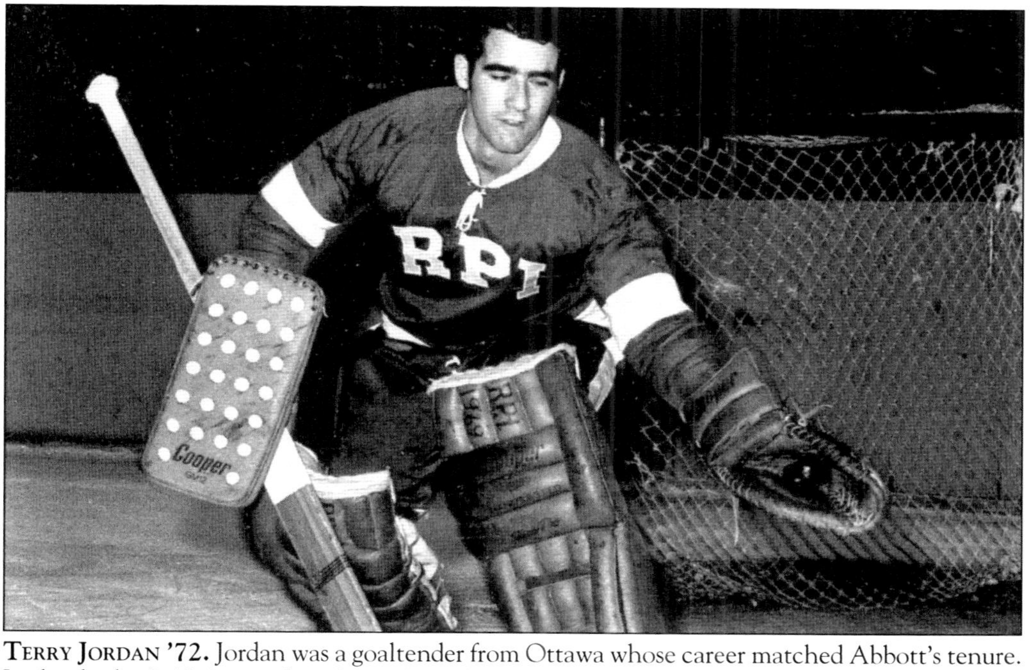

Terry Jordan '72. Jordan was a goaltender from Ottawa whose career matched Abbott's tenure. Jordan had a 7-12-1 record in the 1969–1970 season as the regular goaltender. He improved to 12-5-2 record over the next two seasons, when he shared time with Bob Mallion '73 and Don Cutts '74. He received his bachelor's degree in nuclear science, possibly the only hockey player at the institute ever to have done so.

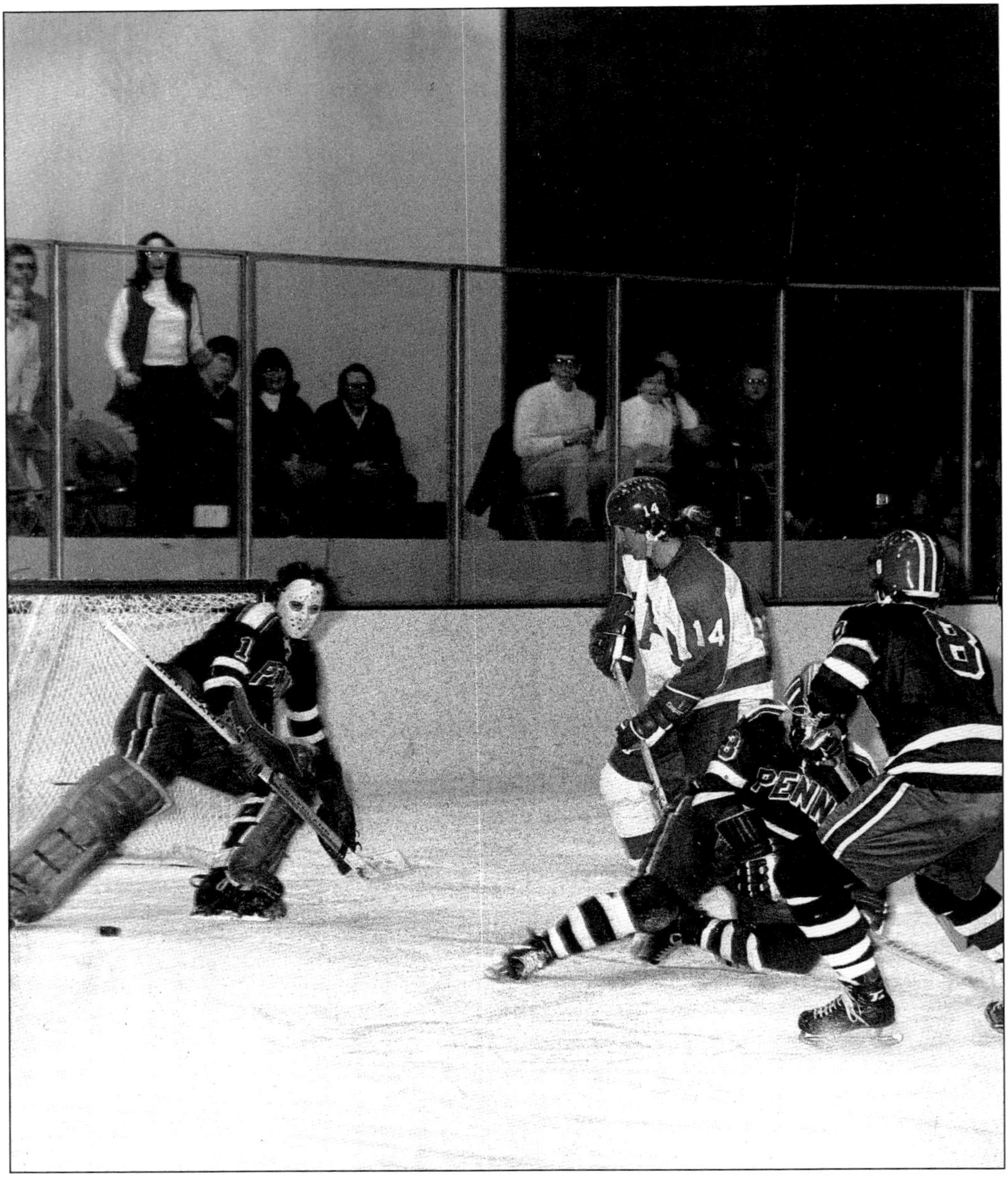

John Donahoe '73. Donahoe is shown in action against the University of Pennsylvania at the Houston Field House. Donahoe scored 42 points as a member of the junior varsity (or freshman) team and then moved up to varsity and picked up 23 points in his sophomore year. He was shifted to right wing for his last two seasons and responded with 38 and 35 points. RPI made the ECAC playoffs for three years running during his career, but they lost by at least six goals in the quarterfinals each time. This picture shows the east end of the field house with spectators on the stage. The chain-link fence is gone, and Plexiglas is now placed above the boards, though it is still lower than what is currently in the building. The University of Pennsylvania was a member of the ECAC at this time, but they dropped their hockey program after the 1977–1978 season.

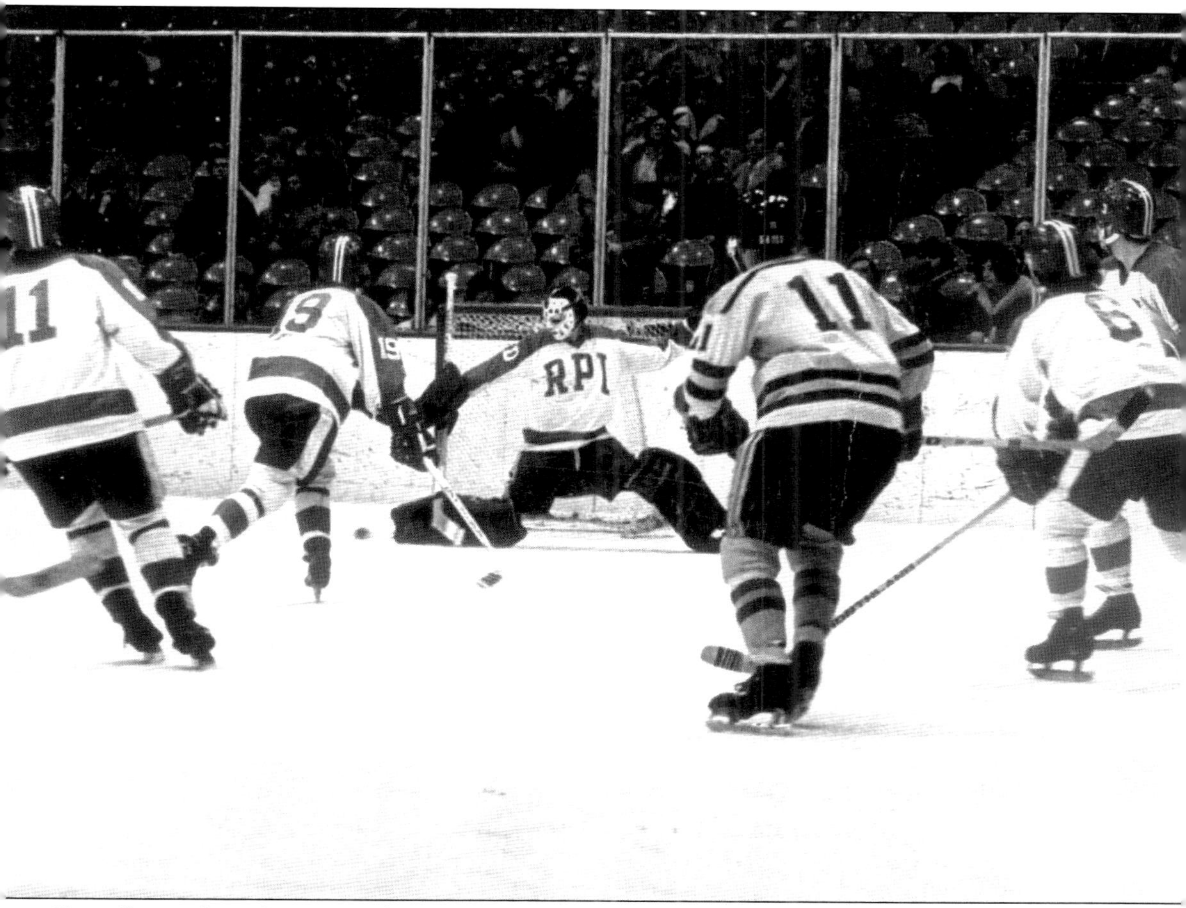

Don Cutts '74. Cutts, a Calgary native, was the first player at RPI to gain both national attention and large professional interest while still in college. His was the last class that could not play on the varsity team as freshmen. RPI began using freshmen in the 1971–1972 campaign, though a rules quirk prevented all the other ECAC schools except St. Lawrence University and Clarkson College of Technology from doing the same. Cutts took over the starting role his sophomore year, earning ECAC Sophomore of the Year honors, and started all 81 games in his career, finishing with a 40-38-2 record. He was picked 97th by the New York Islanders in the 1973 NHL draft and 48th by the Houston Aeroes in the WHA draft, the first player in school history to be drafted. After spending many years in the Central Hockey League (CHL) and the IHL with Muskegon, Forth Worth, Fort Wayne, and Houston, he finally made it to the NHL, appearing in six games for the Edmonton Oilers in the 1979–1980 season, with a 1-2-1 record.

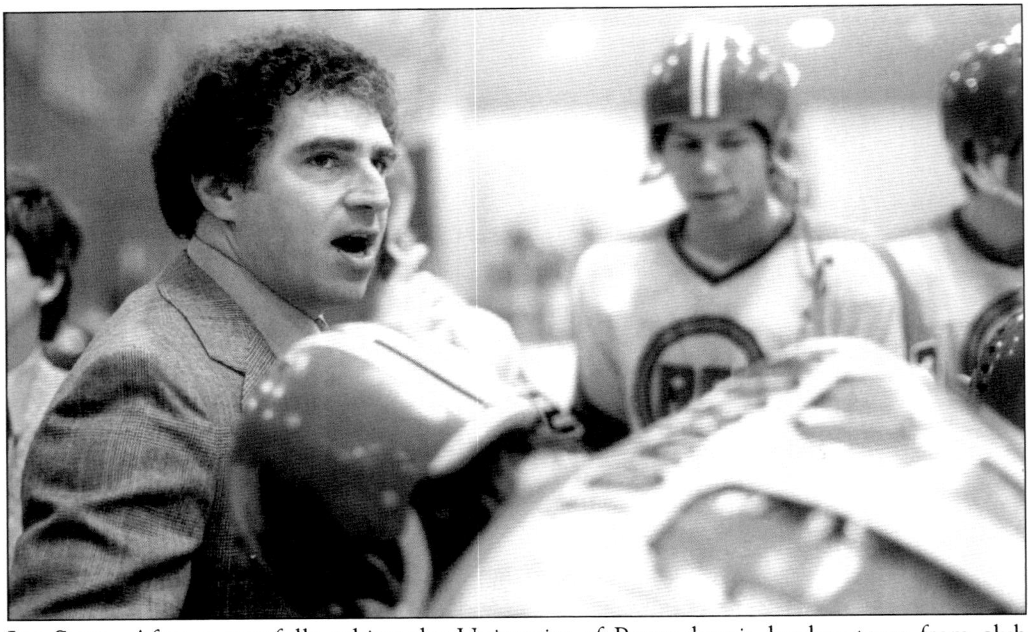

Jim Salfi. After successfully taking the University of Pennsylvania hockey team from club to varsity status, Salfi moved over to RPI once Leon Abbott departed. He graduated from St. Lawrence University in 1963 and served as the Saints' captain his senior year. The Engineers performed well under his tenure, with only two losing seasons. However, they were not able to advance in the playoffs, and recruiting players without offering full scholarships became more of a challenge. Salfi left RPI in 1979 and now coaches the Capital District Selects junior team.

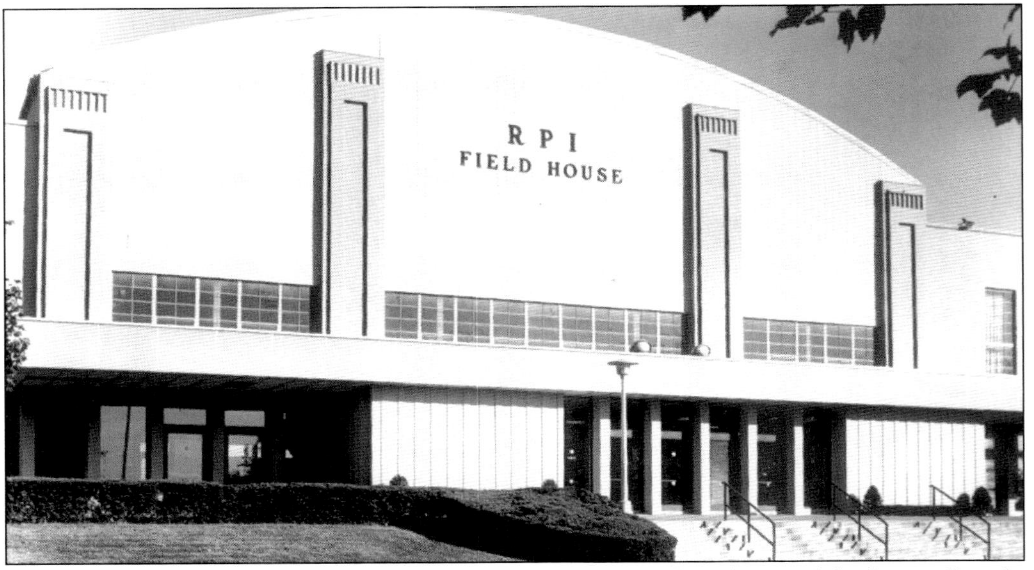

The RPI Field House in the Mid-1970s. The curved roof is still in place, and the front still reads, "RPI," so this picture is no later than 1978. There are few differences between this picture and the current field house, most notably that the windows above the lobby are now painted over. The building is approximately 30 years old and is starting to show its age, particularly the interior.

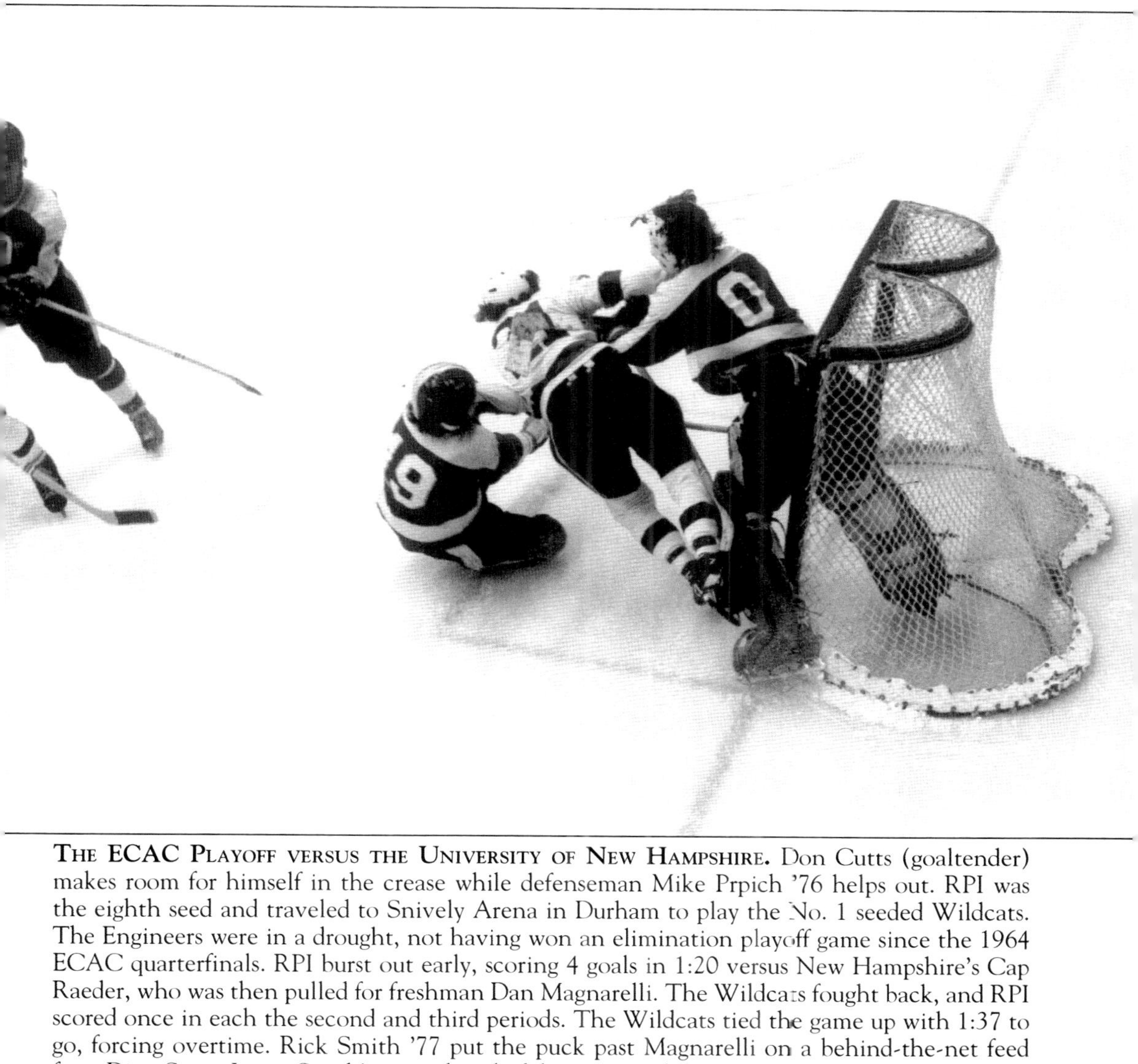

The ECAC Playoff versus the University of New Hampshire. Don Cutts (goaltender) makes room for himself in the crease while defenseman Mike Prpich '76 helps out. RPI was the eighth seed and traveled to Snively Arena in Durham to play the No. 1 seeded Wildcats. The Engineers were in a drought, not having won an elimination playoff game since the 1964 ECAC quarterfinals. RPI burst out early, scoring 4 goals in 1:20 versus New Hampshire's Cap Raeder, who was then pulled for freshman Dan Magnarelli. The Wildcats fought back, and RPI scored once in each the second and third periods. The Wildcats tied the game up with 1:37 to go, forcing overtime. Rick Smith '77 put the puck past Magnarelli on a behind-the-net feed from Dino Serra. It was Smith's second goal of the game and the season (his only two), and RPI knocked off the top-ranked Wildcats.

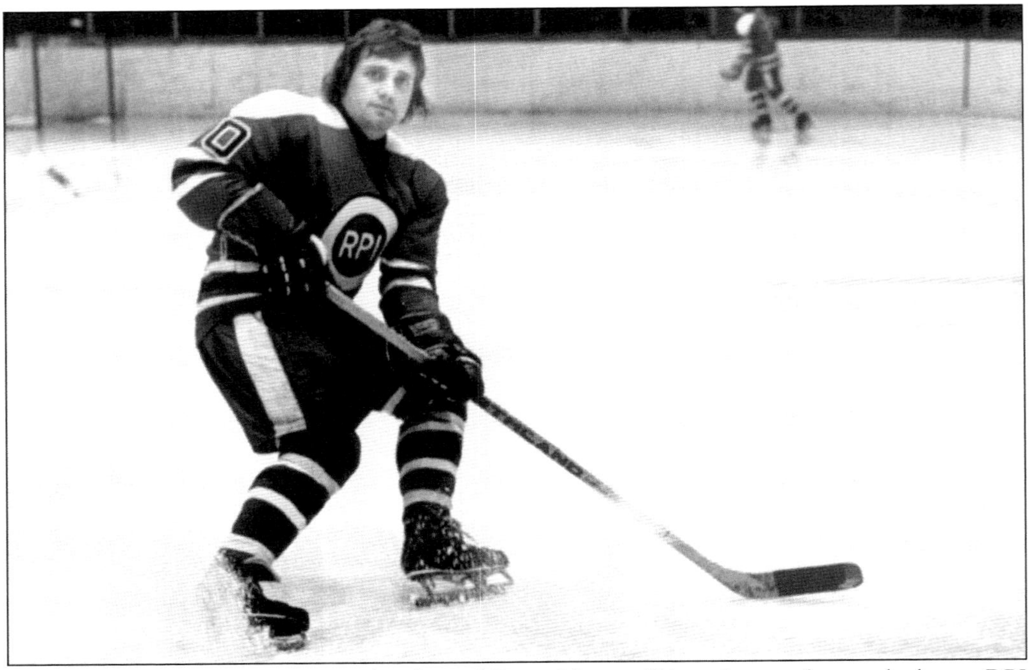

DON HEARNS '75. The younger brother of Doug Hearns '71 and one of several players RPI recruited from Milton, Ontario, Don picked up three assists in the RPI playoff victory against the University of New Hampshire. He led the team in scoring his sophomore year with 40 points and ended his career with a total of 134. Hearns was one of the fastest skaters for his day.

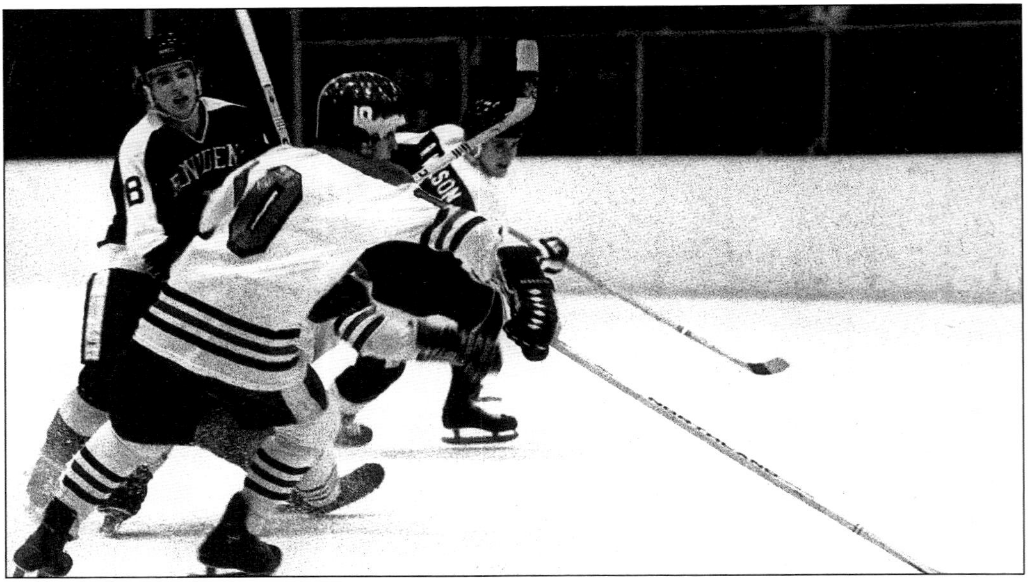

RON INCH '77. A center from Sault Ste. Marie, Ontario, Inch played only three seasons for the Engineers. He scored 17 goals and had 38 assists during his time on the team. He then left to play in the U.S. Hockey League (USHL) with Traverse City and the Southern Hockey League (SHL) with Winston-Salem the following season. This is not the last time a player with eligibility left to pursue a professional career.

BARRY MARTINELLI '76. Martinelli led or tied for the team lead in scoring in each of the three complete seasons he played, finishing with 155 points (55 from goals). He was able to play only one game during the 1972–1973 season before being forced to sit out for a year. Problems arose because Martinelli transferred from a Canadian junior college. Transfers from junior colleges in the United States are not required to wait a year, but the NCAA had different rules for transfers from Canada. Martinelli was forced to play on the junior varsity team for a season before returning to varsity. He is tied with John Carter and Steve Stoyanovich for the most overtime goals scored in a career with three. Like Carter, Martinelli got all three of his in the same season, picking up goals against McGill, Loyola, and the University of New Hampshire during the 1973–1974 season. He continued his career in hockey by coaching and was the longtime head coach at the University of Western Ontario. During his tenure, the Mustangs visited Troy in 1990 for the RPI Invitational Tournament.

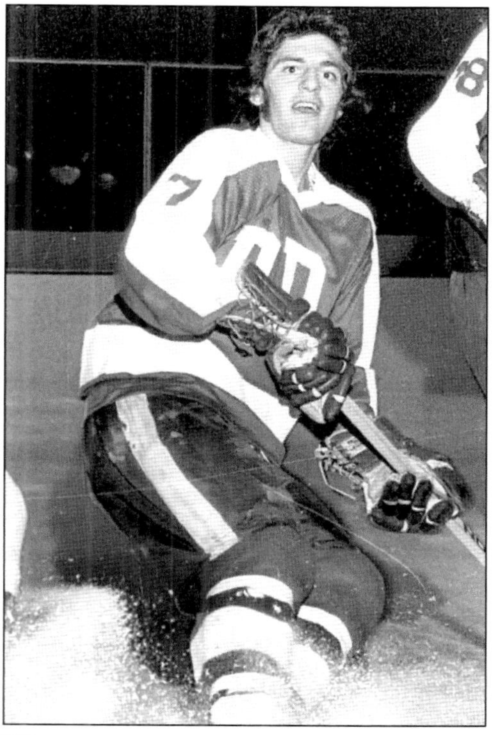

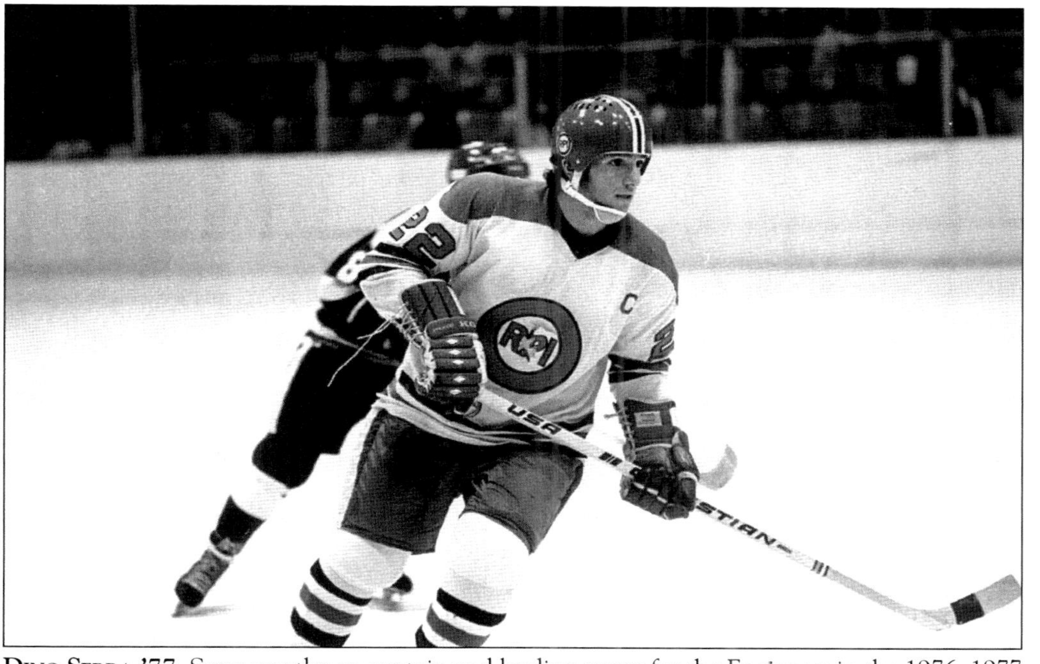

DINO SERRA '77. Serra was the co-captain and leading scorer for the Engineers in the 1976–1977 season. His 46 assists that year are fifth best in school history, and he finished with 164 points in his career. A center from Niagara Falls, Ontario, Serra is the man that set up Rick Smith for the winning goal in the ECAC playoffs versus the University of New Hampshire in 1974.

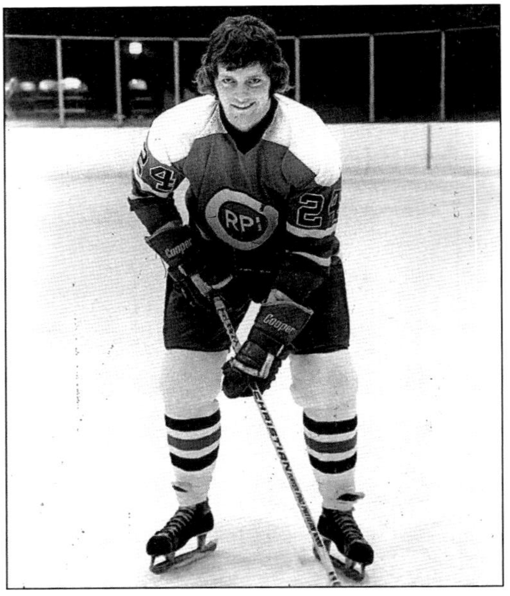

Don Armstrong '78. Armstrong was co-captain during the 1977–1978 season, which was his best scoring season with 51 points. Armstrong improved his scoring every season, going from 3 to 37 to 47 and, finally, 51 points. He received a bachelor's degree in chemistry from RPI and continued on to a career as an orthopedic surgeon in Ontario.

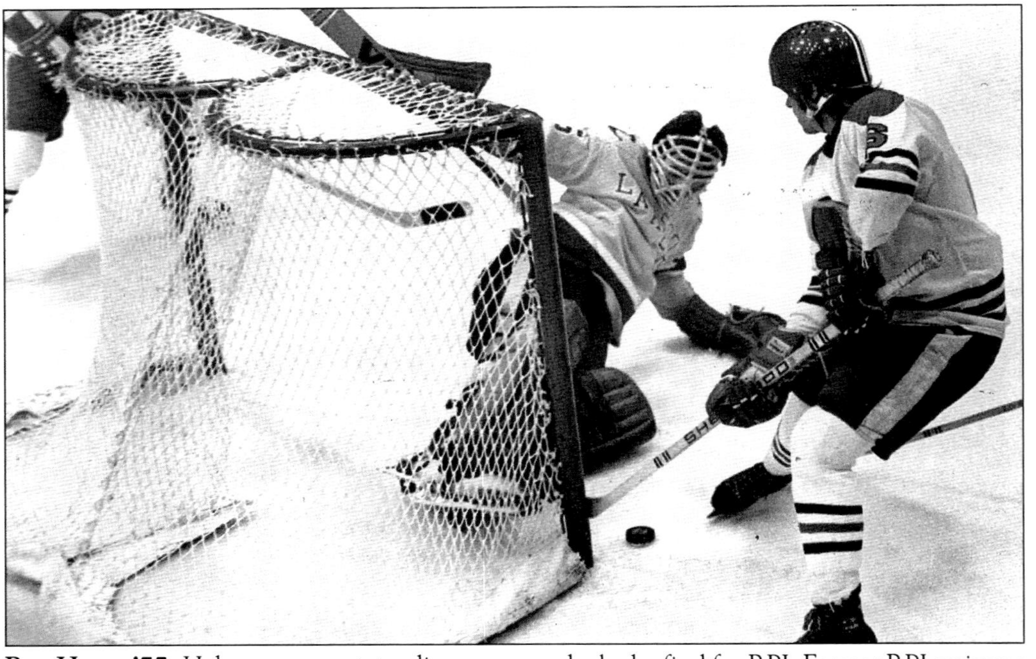

Pat Hahn '77. Hahn was an outstanding scorer and a lucky find for RPI. Former RPI assistant coach John Marks had gone to scout a teammate of Hahn's on the Pembroke Junior Lumber Kings, but he ended up recruiting Hahn instead. A prolific scorer his last two seasons, with 56 and 59 points, he average a shade under 2 points per game for the last 58 games of his career. He scored the second of the four first-period goals that knocked Cap Raeder out of the ECAC quarterfinals versus the University of New Hampshire in 1974. His only return to the playoffs was in his senior year, the 1976–1977 season, when he helped the Engineers to finish sixth in the ECAC. However, they were unable to get past Cornell in the quarterfinals, and that game was the last in Hahn's collegiate career.

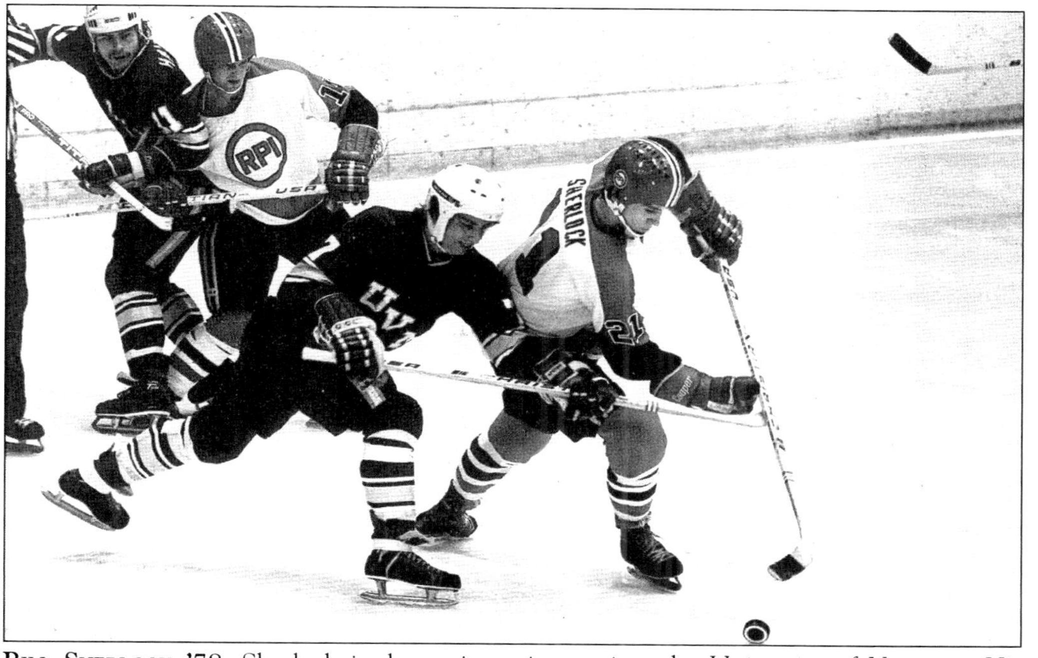

BILL SHERLOCK '78. Sherlock is shown in action against the University of Vermont. His senior year scoring (41 points) equaled his previous three years combined. Sherlock scored the Engineers' fourth goal in the wild ECAC quarterfinals game against Boston College in 1978, the first playoff game ever played by RPI in the field house, which the Engineers lost in overtime 7-6. His uncle Dave Creighton was an NHL player with Boston, Toronto, Chicago, and New York.

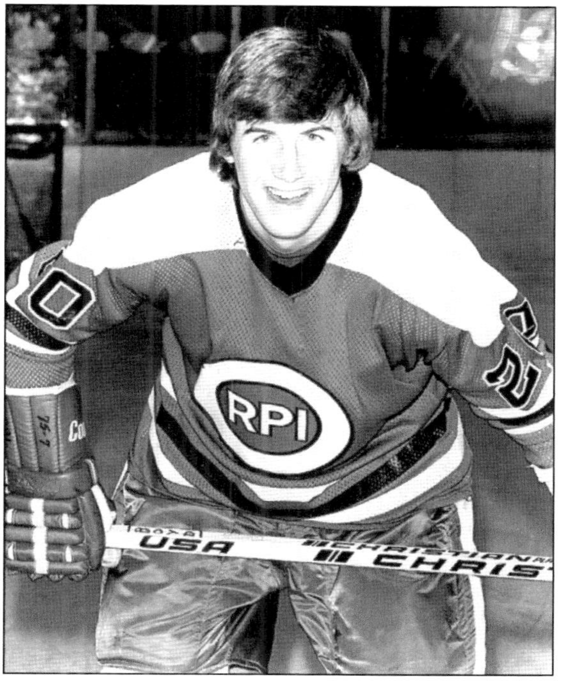

DON BOYD '79. Boyd was co-captain of the 1978–1979 team, the last under Jim Salfi, which finished 13th in the ECAC. He was drafted by the St. Louis Blues in the 12th round, the 191st pick overall. After RPI, he moved around the minor leagues and played for Port Huron of the IHL, Salt Lake of the CHL, the Baltimore Skipjacks of the AHL, and a stint with the short-lived Schenectady Chiefs of the ACHL.

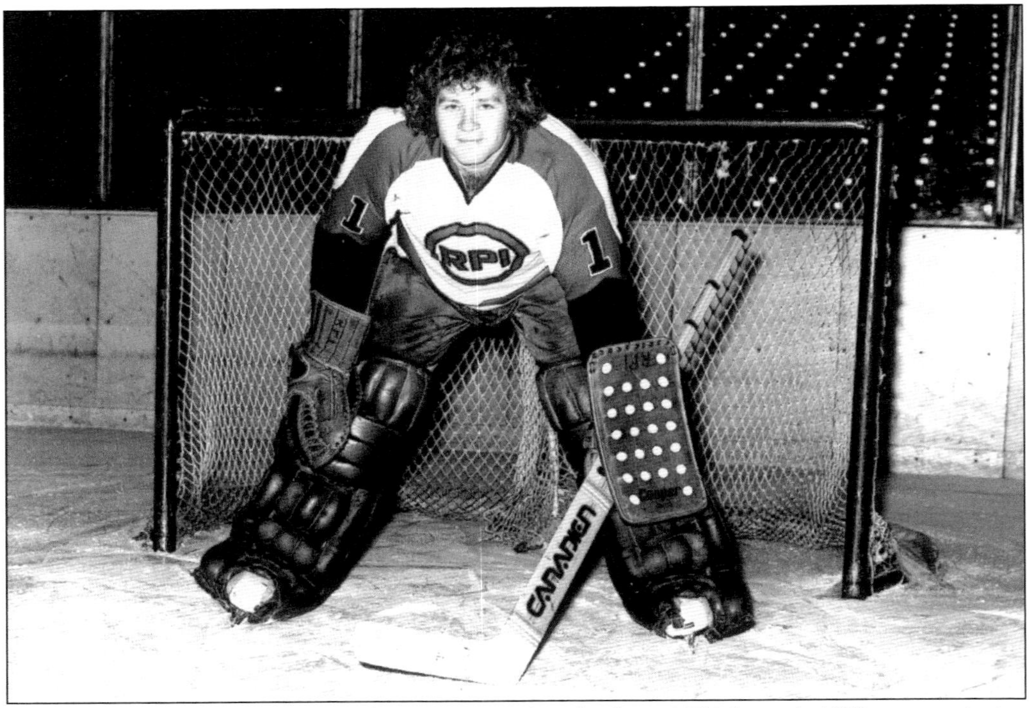

IAN HARRISON '79. Harrison was the primary goaltender from 1976 through 1979, accumulating a 37-24-2 mark over that stretch. He was in net for the 1978 ECAC quarterfinals versus Boston College, making 31 saves in the losing overtime effort. RPI only led in that game for 1:18 in the third before Boston College tied it up again. After college, Harrison played briefly for the Flint Generals in the IHL.

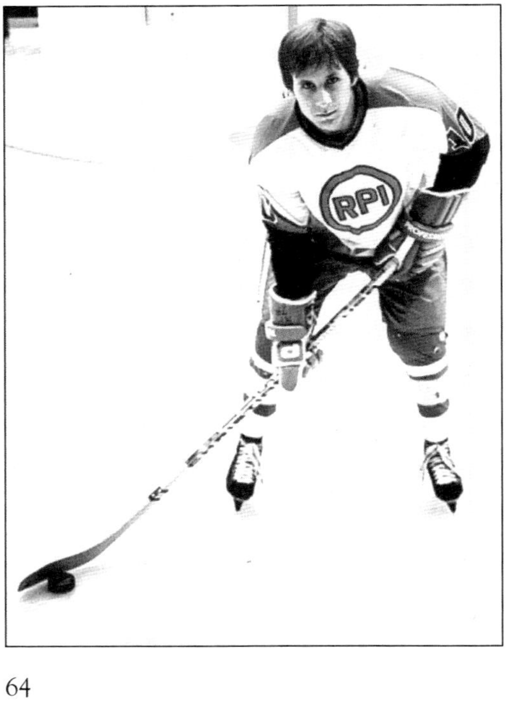

RONN TOMASSONI '80. A steady right wing from Minnesota, Tomassoni scored 48 points in 91 games at RPI. He was one of the few alums to go into coaching after college instead of a professional career. Tomassoni is known to most in the college hockey world as the man who succeeded Bill Cleary as the coach of the Harvard Crimson.

Four

The Addesa Years

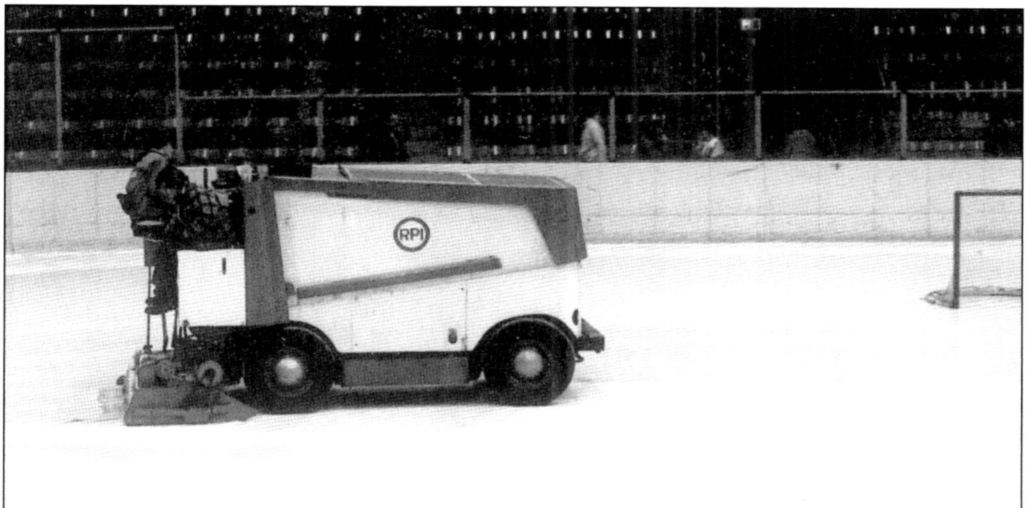

The Zamboni. The bullet logo is prominently displayed on the Zamboni ice machine. This is the field house in the late 1970s. It was soon renamed the Houston Field House, following the death of former RPI president Livingston W. Houston in 1977. The rework of the building was a few short years away.

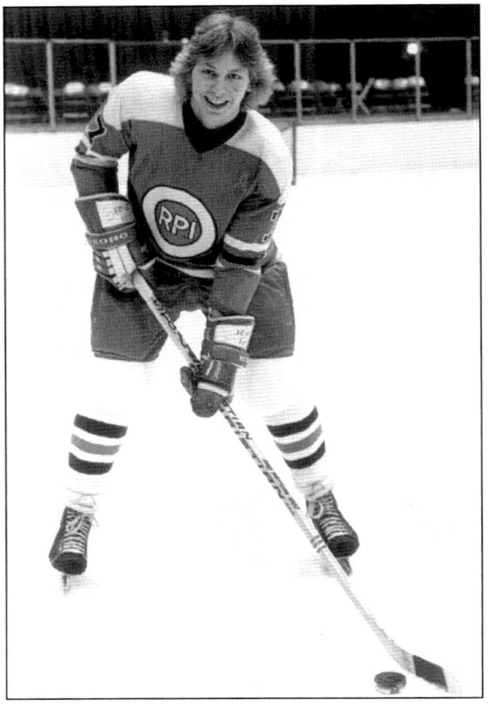

Steve Stoyanovich '80. Stoyanovich, co-captain from 1978 to 1980, led the team in scoring his sophomore and junior seasons with 52 and 47 points. The second RPI player to be drafted, he was taken by the New York Islanders as the 69th pick in 1977. He made it to the NHL after two-plus seasons in the minors, playing 23 games with the Hartford Whalers in the 1983–1984 season and scoring 8 points.

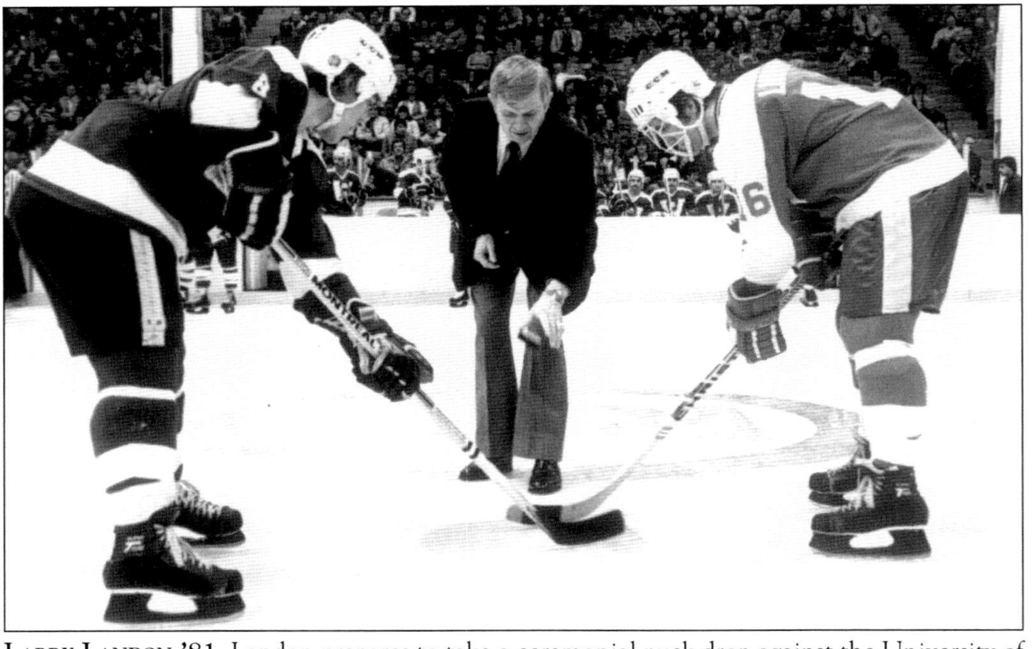

Larry Landon '81. Landon prepares to take a ceremonial puck drop against the University of Vermont. Two-time co-captain for both the 1979–1980 and 1980–1981 teams, he scored 157 points in his career. Landon was drafted by the Montreal Canadiens as the 137th pick in 1978, and he played in the NHL for Montreal in the 1983–1984 season (two games) and Toronto in the 1984–1985 season (seven games).

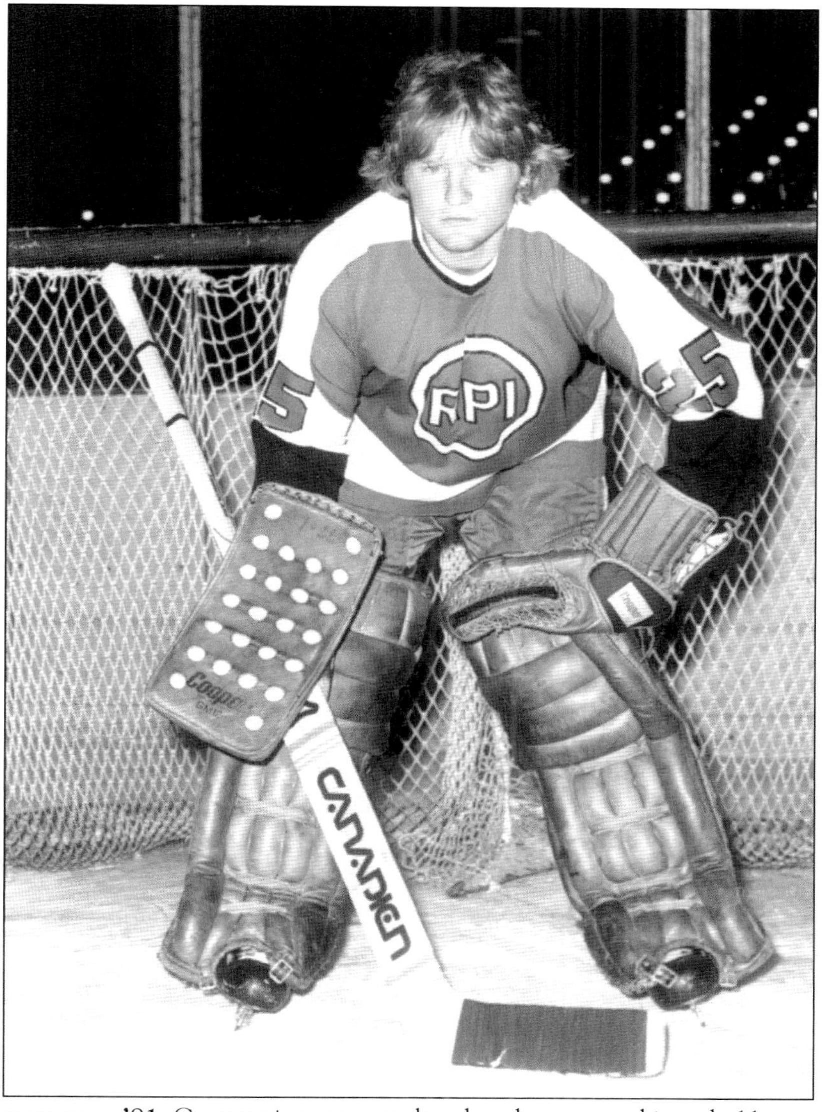

KEVIN CONSTANTINE '81. Constantine was a goaltender who appeared in only 11 games during his freshman and sophomore years, earning a 5-4 record. He became the starting goaltender in the 1979–1980 season and finished with a 13-9 record, including one shutout. He left school after that season and ultimately began a career in coaching. His path started in the USHL, after which he went to the IHL as an assistant coach for the Kalamazoo Wings. The Kansas City Blades hired Constantine in 1991 as a head coach. During the first season, he won the IHL championship. After another season with Kansas City, he was hired by the NHL's San Jose Sharks as their head coach. He was dismissed during his third season with San Jose, became an assistant with Calgary, and moved to the Pittsburgh Penguins as a head coach in 1997. Sent packing by Pittsburgh in 1999, he became a mid-season replacement for the New Jersey Devils in 2002 but was dismissed after a first-round loss in the playoffs. He had the distinction of coaching two first-round upsets of top-seeded teams, when San Jose defeated Detroit in 1994 and Pittsburgh beat New Jersey in 1999. He is currently coaching in the Western Hockey League (WHL).

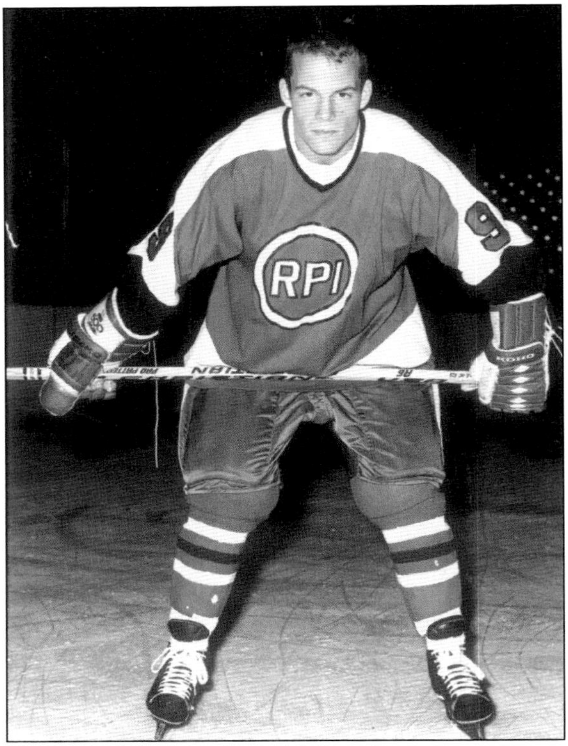

Jacques de St. Phalle '82. A small right wing, de St. Phalle was a native of Philadelphia who attended Deerfield Academy. A point-a-game forward (81 points in 81 games), he left RPI after his junior season and transferred to the University of Wisconsin. After sitting out for a year, he finished his collegiate career with the Badgers, playing seven games in the 1982–1983 season.

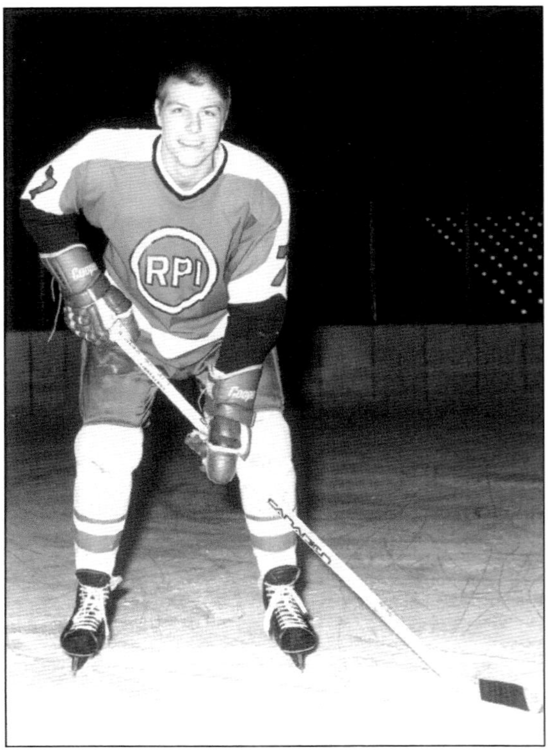

Dave Stoyanovich '82. Dave Stoyanovich, the younger brother of Steve Stoyanovich '80, played both left wing and center during his career at RPI. Co-captain of the 1981–1982 squad, he never scored more than 15 points in a season. After graduation, he played in the IHL for Flint and Kalamazoo. He then moved on to the AHL and played for Binghamton and Nova Scotia. In the late 1980s, he ended up playing in Great Britain.

MIKE MCPHEE '82. After scoring 115 points in his first three seasons, McPhee's hopes for a stellar senior season were dashed when he was injured after playing only six games. However, the Montreal Canadiens drafted him in the sixth round of the 1980 draft, and after playing in the AHL, he was brought up to the parent team. In 1986, he reached hockey's ultimate goal when the Montreal Canadiens won the Stanley Cup. He is the only RPI alum to have his name on the cup.

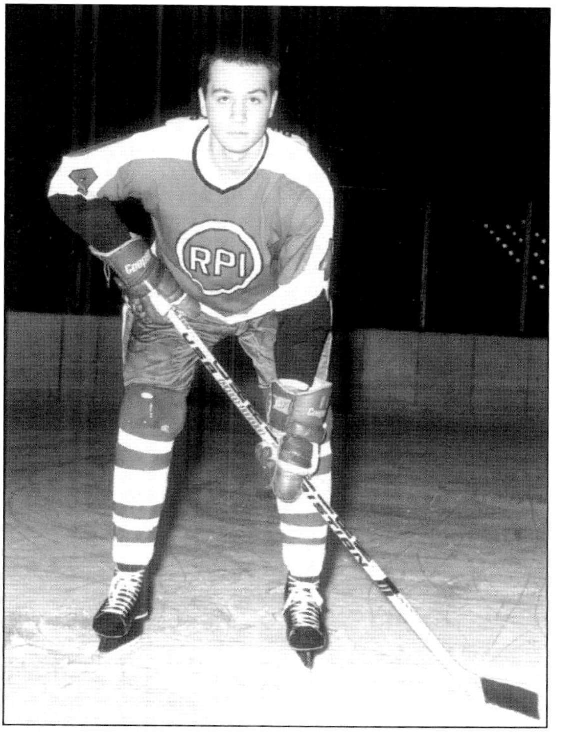

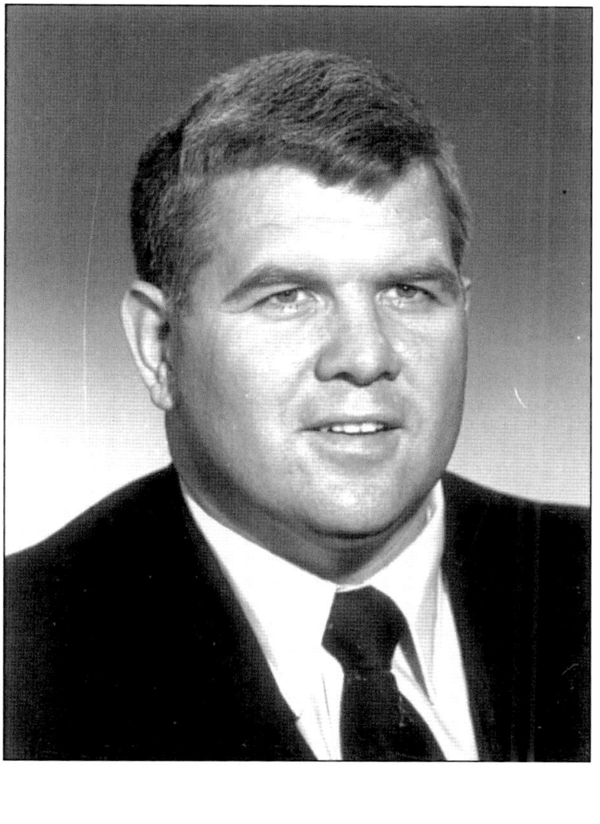

MIKE ADDESA. A graduate of Holy Cross in 1966, Addesa coached at his alma mater for three seasons before switching over to RPI after Jim Salfi left in 1979. RPI returned to the playoffs in 1980 and 1983 but could not get past the first round. Recruiting became somewhat easier once the institute began granting full athletic scholarships, and the talent coming in paid off. RPI returned to the top of the east in 1984 and 1985.

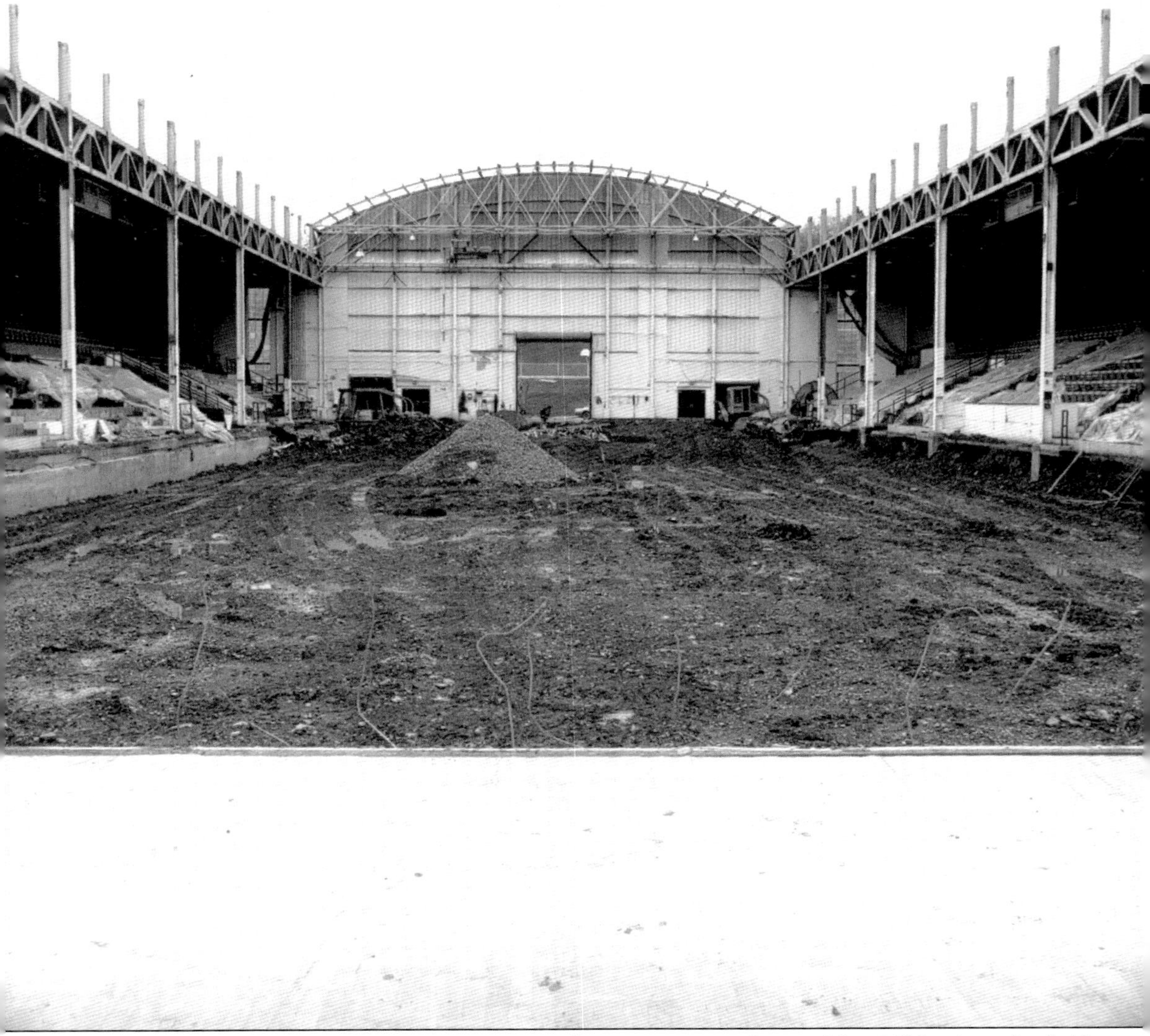

Houston Field House Reconstruction. This picture was taken in May 1983, when the field house was extensively modified. In addition to the obvious new roof, other upgrades included the removal of all but four of the columns that obstructed fans' views; also, the center scoreboard was removed, and two new scoreboards were installed, one at each end of the building. The ice surface was lengthened, making it a standard 200- by 85-foot size. The ice was sunk down two and a half feet and was placed atop a new concrete surface that housed more efficient tubing. The locker rooms were modified, and a new training facility and weight room were added. All of these renovations were necessary to bring the arena up to modern standards, without which it would be difficult to recruit. Additional changes have been made in subsequent years, most notably the return of a center-ice scoreboard.

MARTY DALLMAN '84. Second-team All-ECAC in his senior season, Dallman scored the game-winning goal against Colgate in the second game of the ECAC quarterfinals in 1984. That series sent RPI to the ECAC semifinals for the third time overall and the first time in 10 years. He finished his RPI career with 163 points and later played six games in the NHL with the Toronto Maple Leafs.

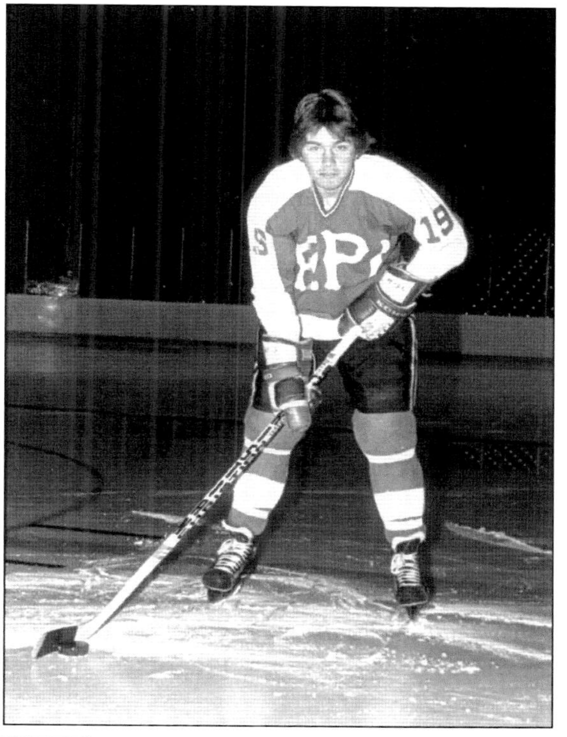

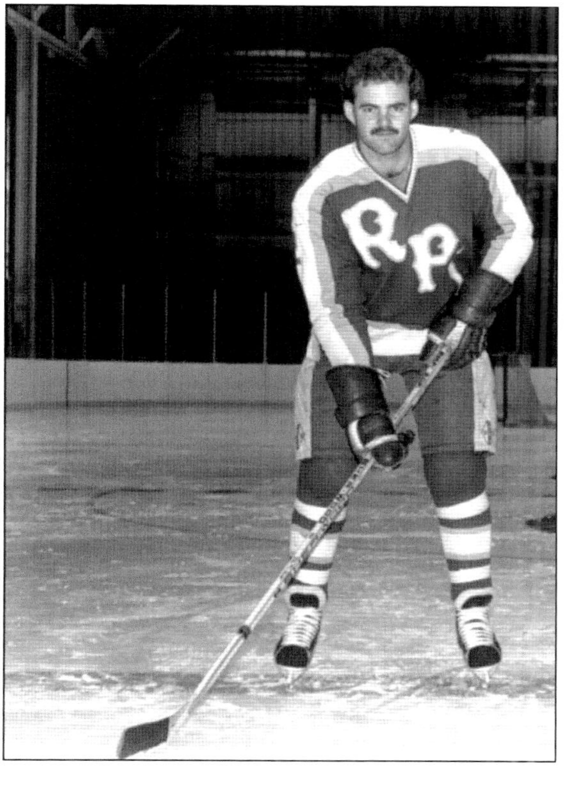

TIM FRIDAY '85. Friday scored the game-winning goal in the first game against Colgate during the 1984 ECAC quarterfinals, RPI's first postseason win in 10 years. He picked up 34 points (29 were assists) on the phenomenal scoring 1984–1985 team. Friday was named to the NCAA All-Tournament team in 1985, and he went on to play 23 games with the Detroit Red Wings in the 1985–1986 season.

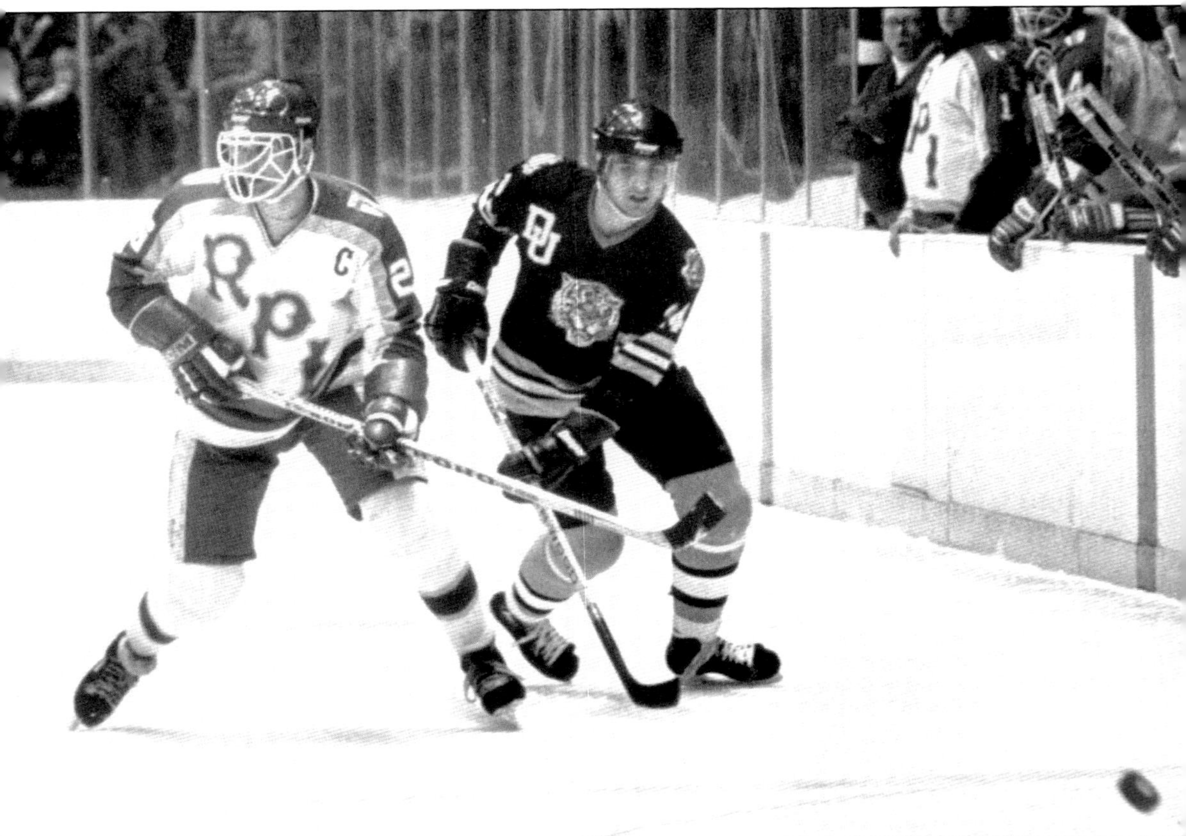

KEN HAMMOND '85. Hammond, a blue-liner, was named an East All-American in the 1984–1985 season, earned a place on the All-ECAC first team, and was a member of the 1985 NCAA All-Tournament team. He is pictured here in 1984, when he was co-captain of the team along with Mike Dark. The opposition is Dalhousie University. Hammond was part of an outstanding defensive corps that succeeded by limiting the number of shots the opponents could take. In the 1984 NCAA semifinals versus the University of North Dakota, RPI outshot the Fighting Sioux 93-52. It was the outstanding performance by North Dakota's goaltender Jon Casey that let the Sioux advance and finished RPI's season. Hammond finished his RPI career with 77 points and signed with the Los Angeles Kings, playing three games for them in the spring of 1985. He played for eight different NHL teams—the last was Ottawa in the 1992–1993 season—for a total of 193 games.

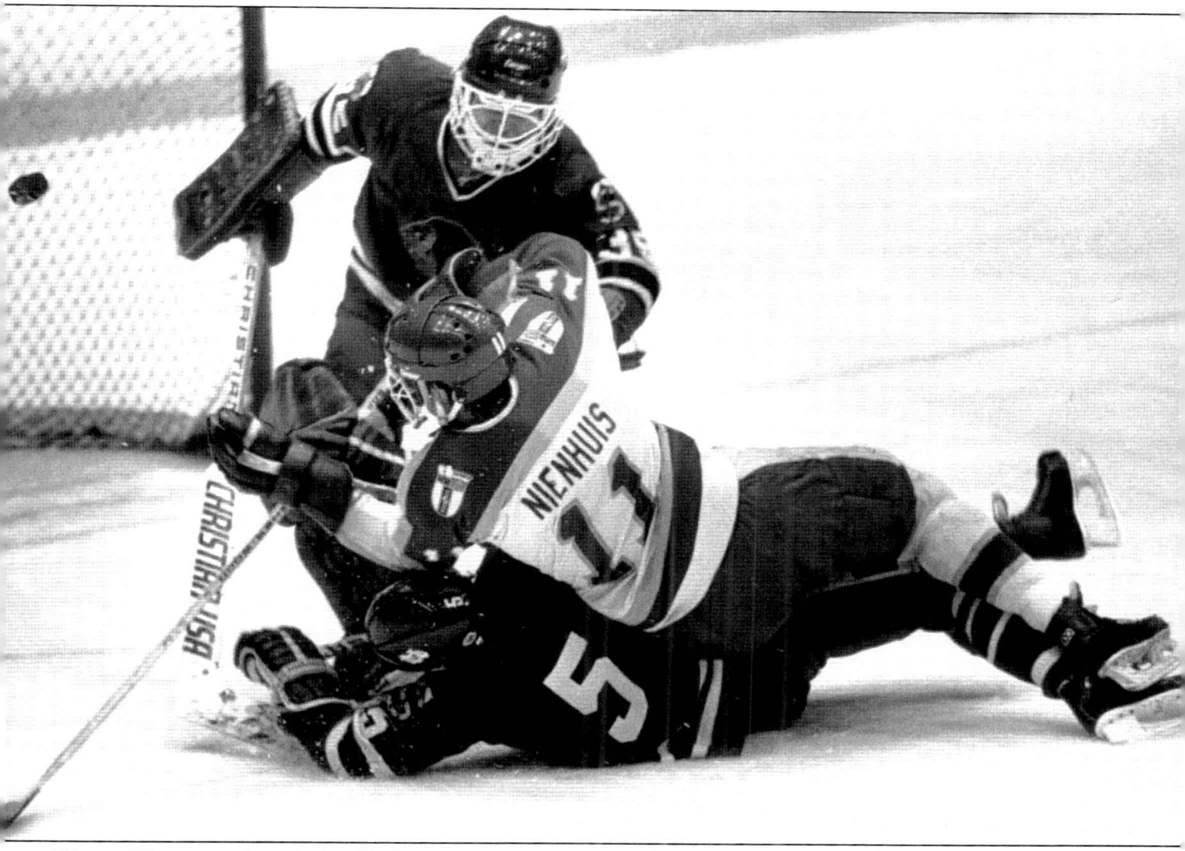

Kraig Nienhuis '86. It finally happened on March 10, 1984. After 11 previous appearances in the ECAC Tournament, RPI made it to the final and came away with a trophy. At 10:31 of the third period, Nienhuis scored the game-winning goal against Boston University. Adam Oates followed up with two insurance goals, and the Engineers skated out of Boston Garden with a 5-2 victory. Nienhuis is shown here trying to reach the airborne puck in front of North Dakota's net, as both teams participate in the 1984 NCAA quarterfinals at the Houston Field House. Jon Casey is the goaltender and Scott Sandelin is the defenseman underneath Nienhuis. Mike Addesa and some players were critical of the officiating in the series, as they felt the western officials called a game that was more to the favor of the University of North Dakota. Nienhuis left RPI after the championship in 1985 and signed with the Boston Bruins, playing 87 games over parts of three seasons. He then continued in the minors, including three games for the Albany Choppers.

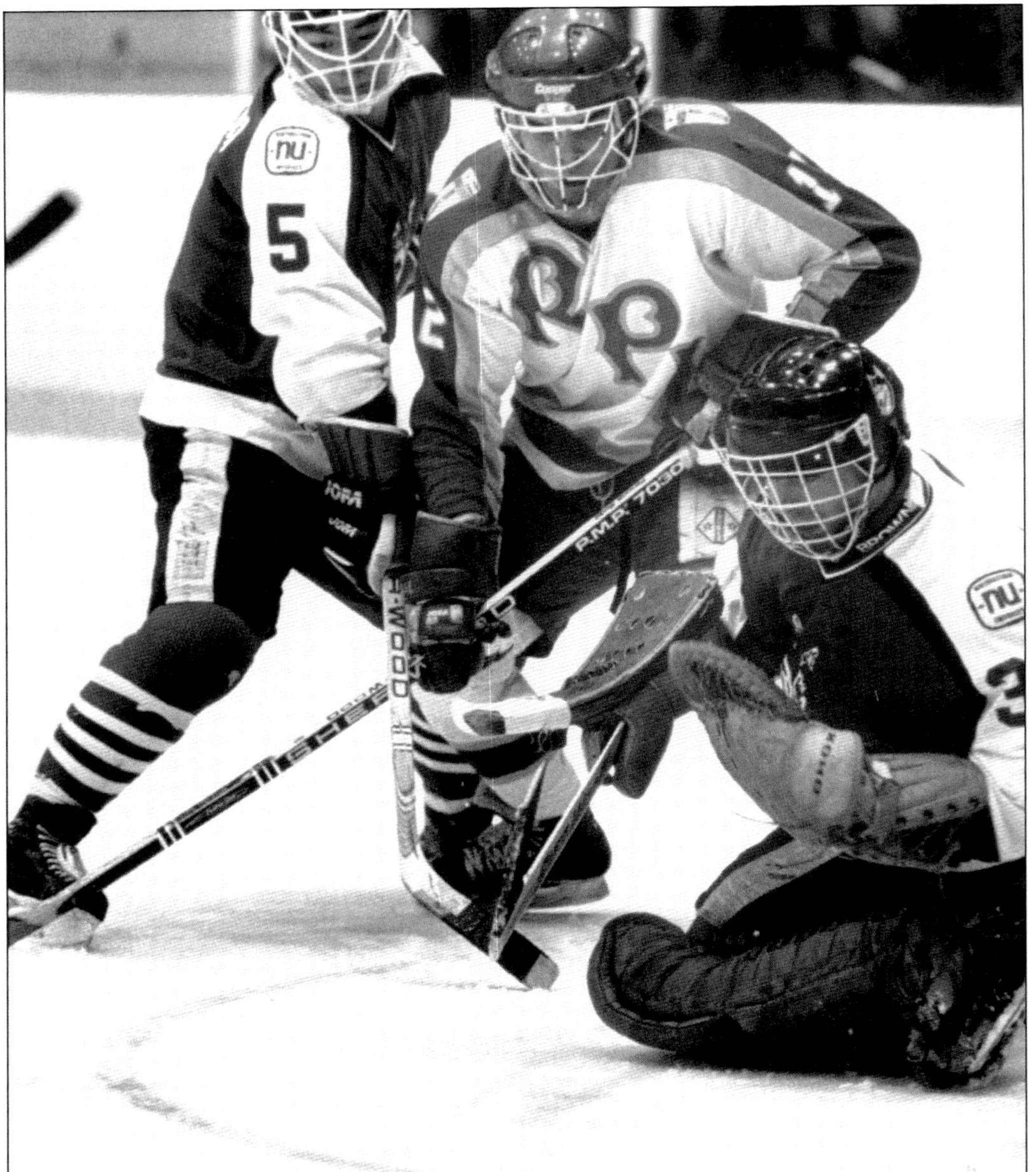

ADAM OATES '86. Oates tries to reach the puck in front of Northeastern's goaltender at the field house in 1984. One of the greatest passers in the history of hockey, Oates holds the career and season records for assists at RPI, with 150 and 60 in the 1984–1985 season, respectively. His 216 points have him tied for third on the school's list, while the point totals in his last two seasons (83 and 91) are school records as well. He could score and had 66 goals in three seasons, including the game-winning goal against Harvard to win the ECAC Championship game in 1985. Oates was a first-team East All-American in the 1983–1984 and 1984–1985 seasons as well as the ECAC Tournament's Most Outstanding Player in 1984. He is easily the most famous RPI alum in the hockey world, having played in the NHL until 2004 and amassing 1,420 points (1,079 assists) in 1,337 games for Detroit, St. Louis, Boston, Washington, Philadelphia, Anaheim, and Edmonton, in an almost certain hall-of-fame career.

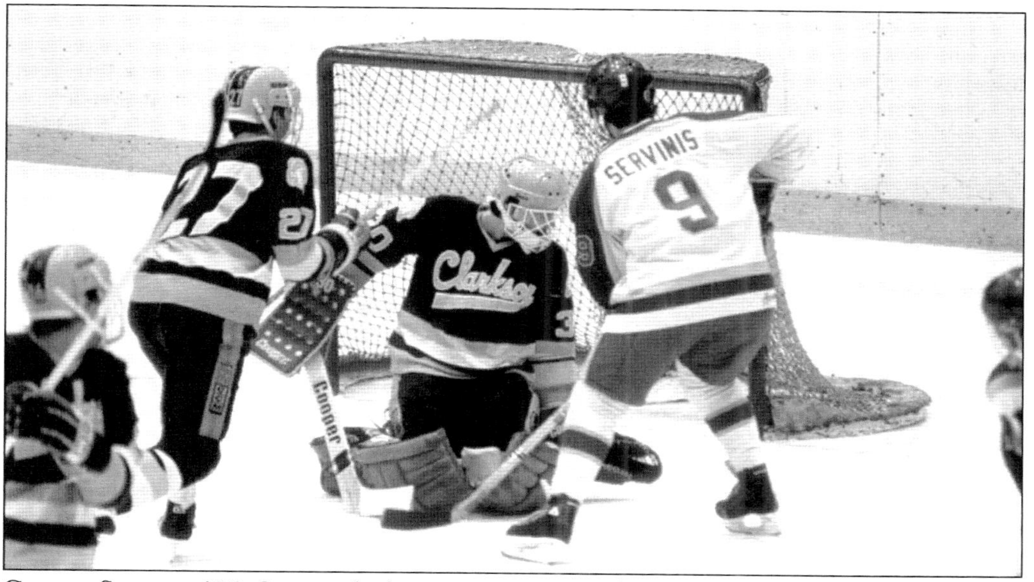

George Servinis '86. Servinis looks to score against Clarkson University. Had Servinis not spent a significant portion of the 1983–1984 season with the Canadian National Team, his statistics would stand out much more. As it is, his freshman point total of 64 and junior total of 59 are excellent numbers, and Servinis scored more goals than assists. He was the man others passed to. He was the ECAC Rookie of the Year for the 1982–1983 season.

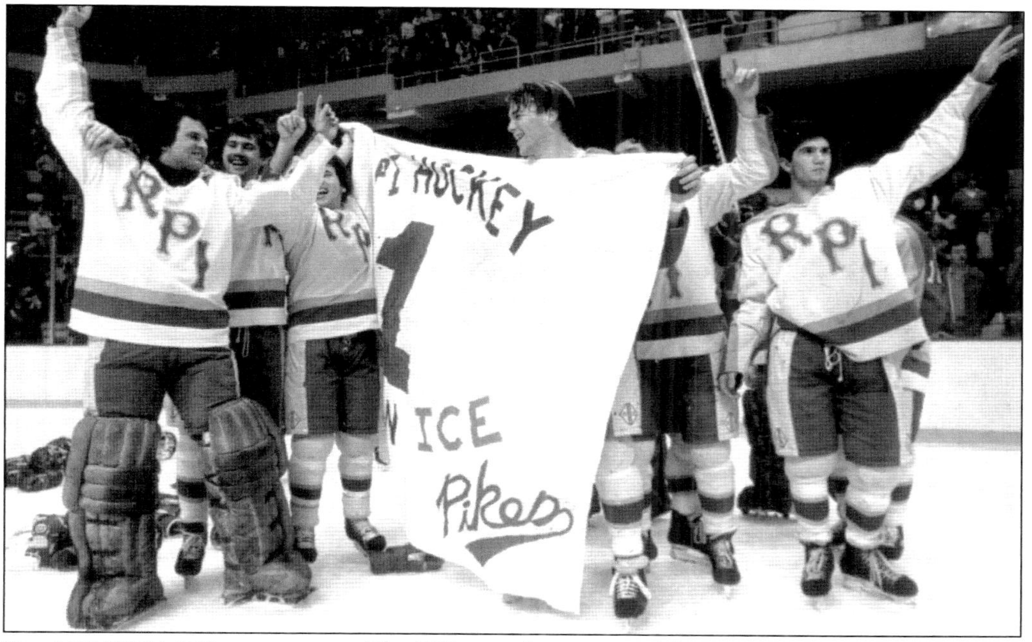

The 1984 ECAC Championship. The RPI team skates around the Boston Garden after defeating Boston University 5-2 to claim the school's first ECAC title. RPI entered the tournament with the best record in the league, knocked out Colgate 8-5 and 5-3, eliminated Clarkson College of Technology 5-4, and then beat Boston University to claim the crown. The win secured an automatic berth to the NCAA Tournament the following weekend.

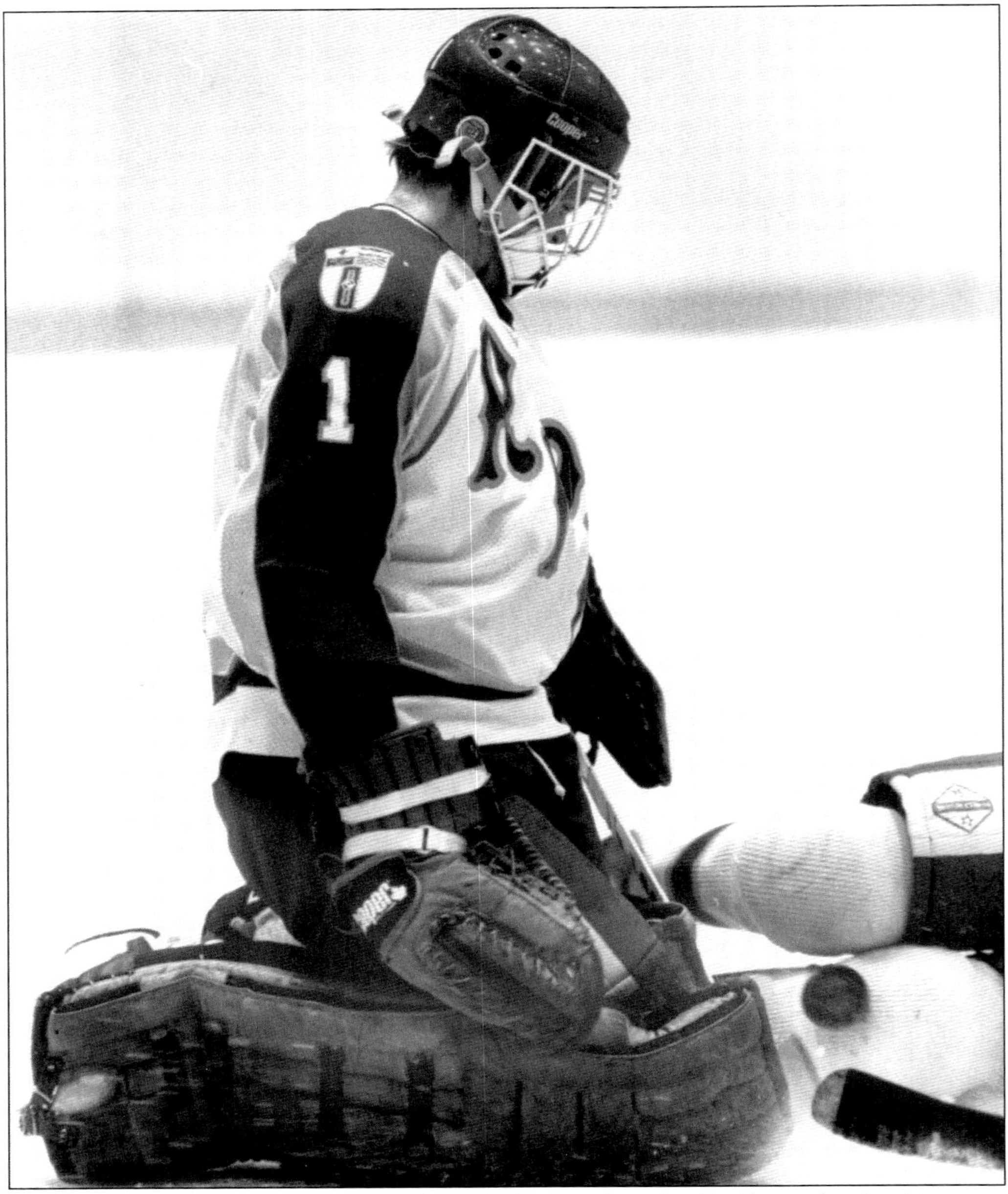

Daren Puppa '87. His career win total is only third on the school's all-time list, but his career winning percentage of .879 is a mark likely to remain untouched. He finished 54-7-1 during his two seasons at RPI, including an amazing 30-1-1 record during the 1984–1985 championship season. His only loss that year came in relief in November against the University of North Dakota. During the season, he won 29 straight starts before RPI tied Lake Superior in Game 2 of the NCAA quarterfinals. Amazingly, Puppa was never selected a first-team All-American, but he was named to the second team in the 1983–1984 season and was named the ECAC Tournament Most Outstanding Player in 1985. Puppa left RPI in 1985 and joined the Buffalo Sabres, which drafted Puppa 74th overall in 1983. With Buffalo, Toronto, and Tampa Bay, he compiled a 179-161-54 record before leaving the NHL in 2000.

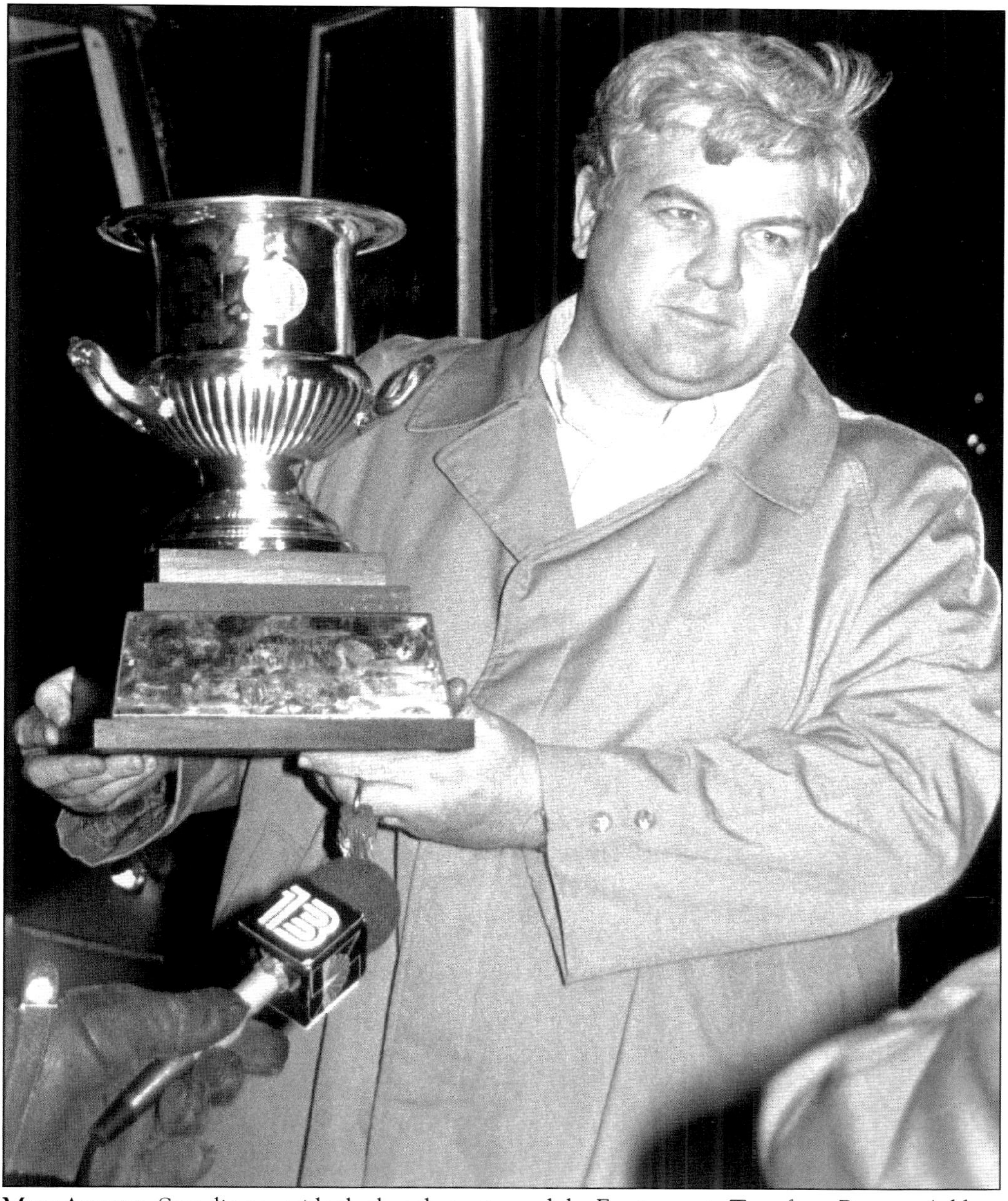

Mike Addesa. Standing outside the bus that returned the Engineers to Troy from Boston, Addesa holds the ECAC Championship trophy presented to RPI for winning the 1984 tournament. The championship was not a certainty, as RPI had a tough match against Clarkson College of Technology in the semifinal. It ended as a 5-4 victory for the Engineers, but Trini Iturralde '87 did not score the game winner until 8:08 of the third period and, in a rarity for these RPI teams, Clarkson outshot RPI 33-26. This was the third trophy for the Engineers this year; in November they had won the Empire Cup in an in-season tournament held in Glens Falls, New York, and they won the RPI Invitational Tournament in December. The hopes for a fourth trophy, the biggest prize, were derailed the following weekend when RPI lost two games to the University of North Dakota in the NCAA quarterfinals.

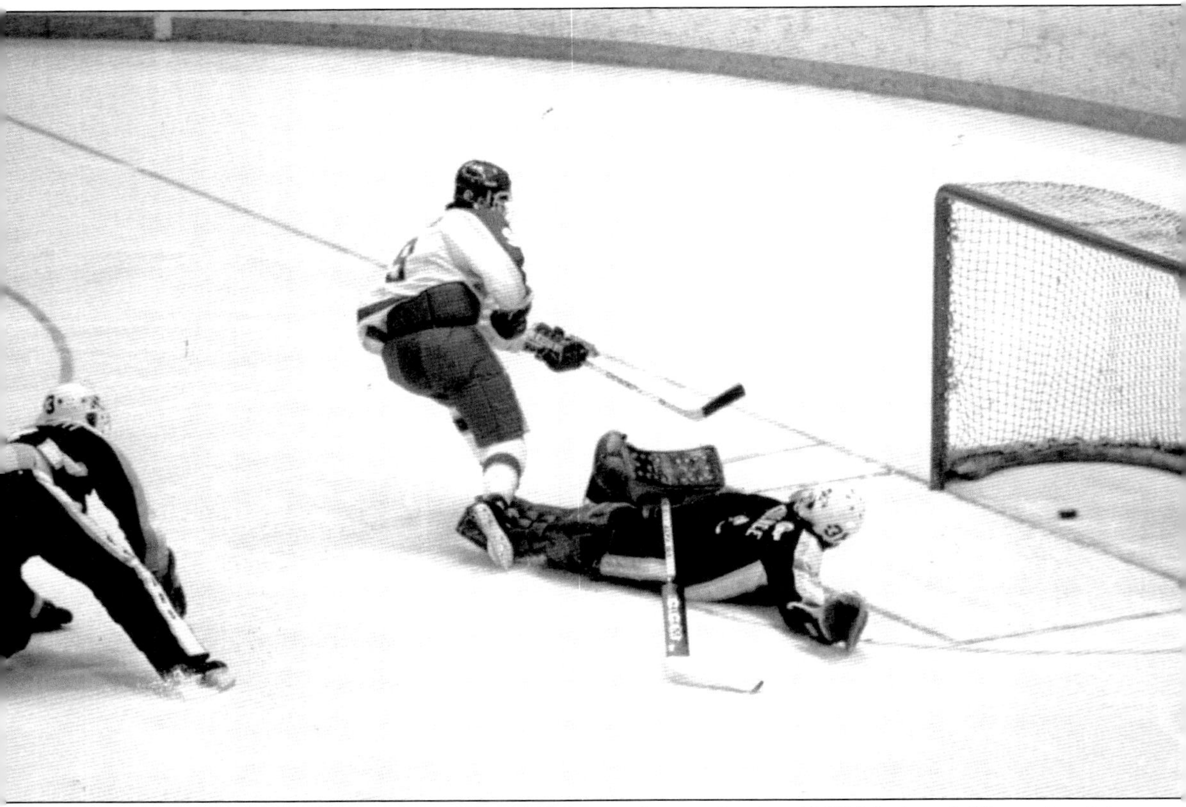

GEORGE SERVINIS SCORES THE GAME-WINNING GOAL. In the 1985 National Championship game, RPI scored first against Providence College, getting a goal from Neil Hernberg '87 4:29 into the first period during a power play. The score was 1-0 after one period. Then, RPI took two quick penalties near the beginning of the second period, giving Providence a brief five-on-three power play. While RPI was killing the second penalty, Servinis gained possession of the puck after Peter Taglianetti made an errant pass. Servinis broke free and took the shot, beating Chris Terreri of Providence for RPI's second goal. Providence struck back, scoring at the 10:00 mark of the third period, a power-play goal by Paul Cavallini. RPI held firm and won the game 2-1, with Puppa making 21 saves versus Terreri's 40. Terreri was voted Most Outstanding Player of the tournament, the last time that award went to a member of the losing team.

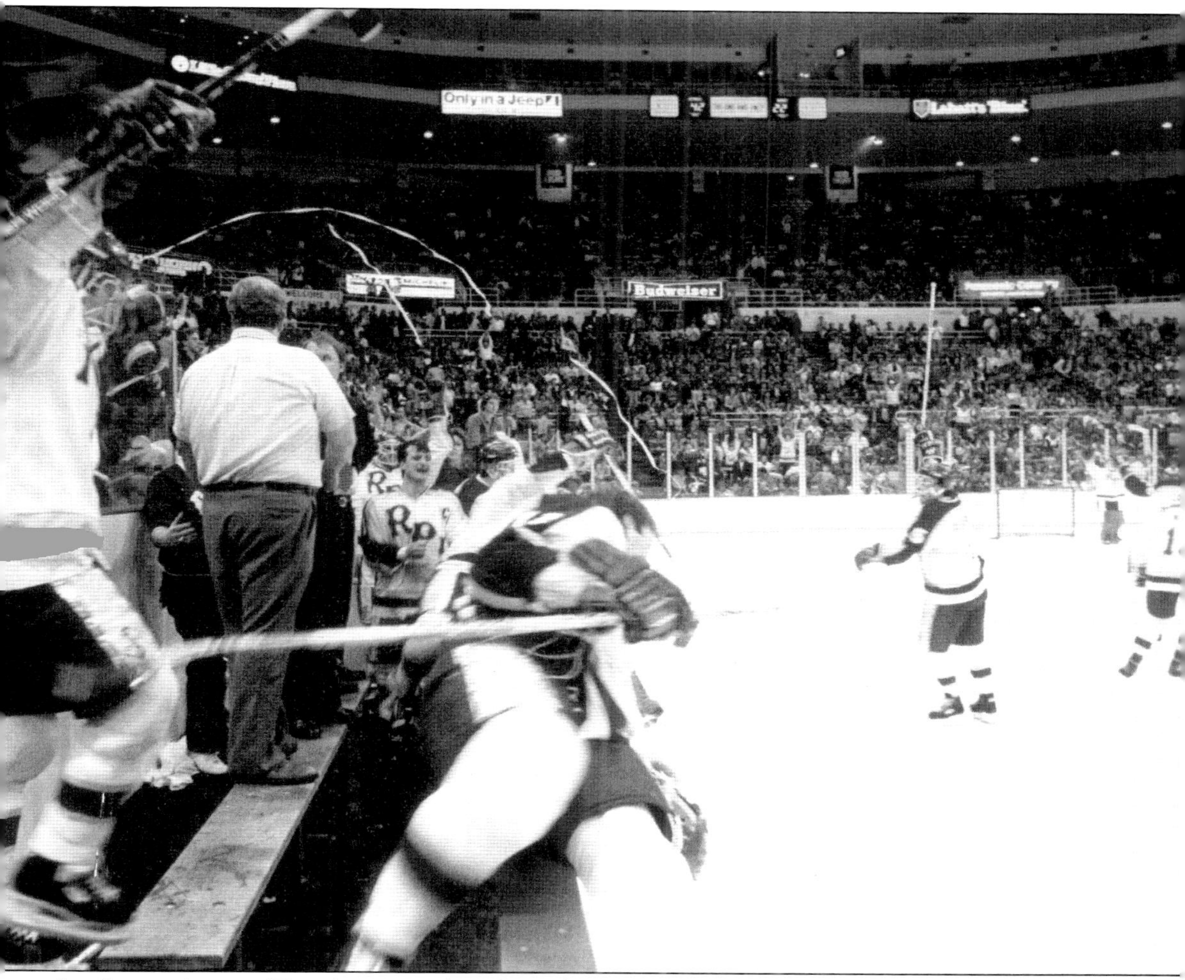

JOE LOUIS ARENA. This shot was taken from the RPI bench inside Joe Louis Arena moments after RPI beat Providence to win the NCAA title. It was the culmination of one of the most dominant seasons in college hockey. RPI never lost after November 23 and went to overtime only three times after that, all victories. The championship game was the 33rd straight game without a defeat, and the Engineers outscored their opponents by almost two and a half goals to one during the course of the season. Their .952 winning percentage in the ECAC is still the best for any team since the ECAC and Hockey East divorced in 1984. The recent parity in college hockey makes it unlikely any RPI team can ever match this performance.

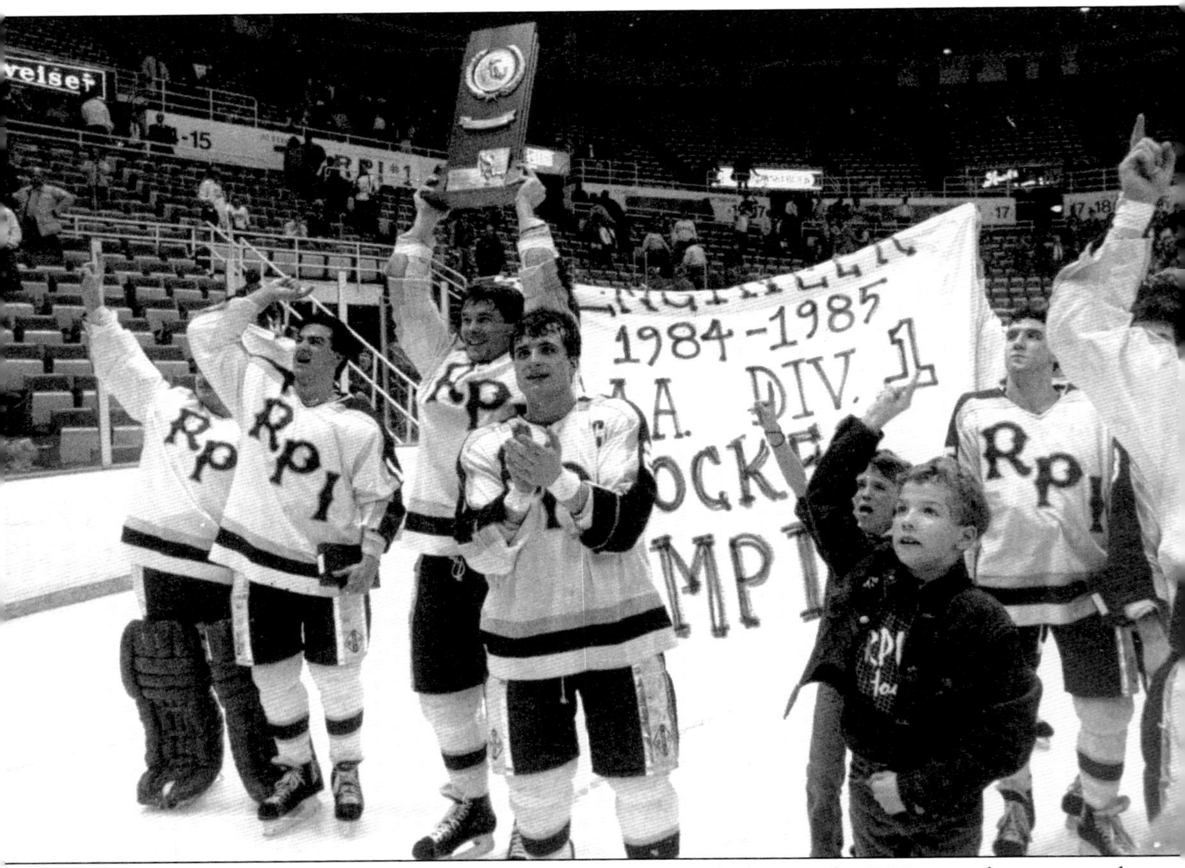

The 1985 Victory Lap. Led by team captain Mike Sadeghpour, the RPI team skates around Joe Louis Arena with the NCAA Championship trophy with a look of relief on their faces. The night before, RPI played their semifinal matchup against the University of Minnesota–Duluth. The game went into triple overtime before John Carter scored the game-winning goal, his third overtime goal of the season, to advance to the title game after 85 minutes and 45 seconds of hockey. Although Providence College also needed triple overtime to beat Boston College, their game was played a day earlier, giving the Friars added rest before facing the Engineers. This apparent inequity in the tournament format was not rectified by the NCAA until 1990.

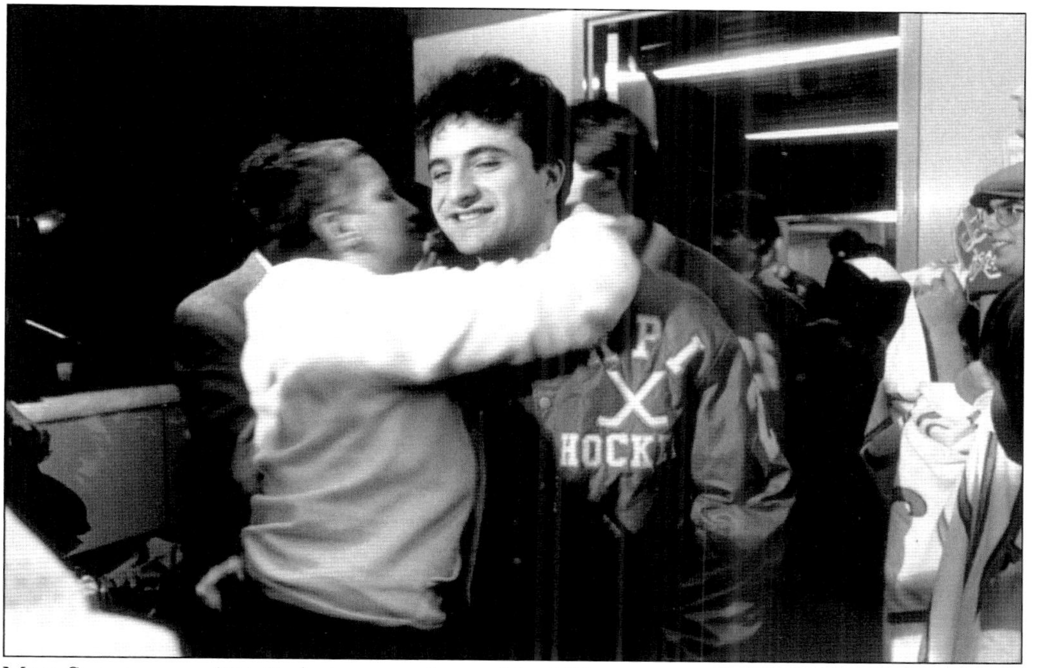

Mike Sadeghpour '85. Sadeghpour, a forward for RPI, is congratulated at the Albany County Airport as the Engineers return home. His statistics were overshadowed by others, but his leadership was key to the Engineers' victory. In 1990, he returned to RPI as an assistant coach, where he remained for three years while he earned his master's degree.

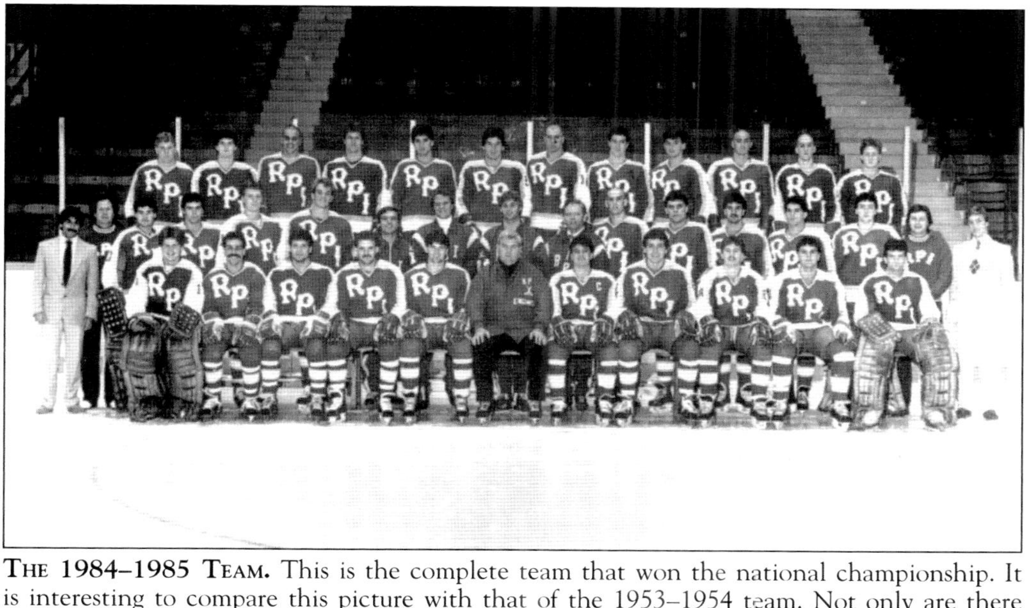

The 1984–1985 Team. This is the complete team that won the national championship. It is interesting to compare this picture with that of the 1953–1954 team. Not only are there significantly more players, but they are also physically larger, as the game of hockey had changed a great deal in the 30 years between championships.

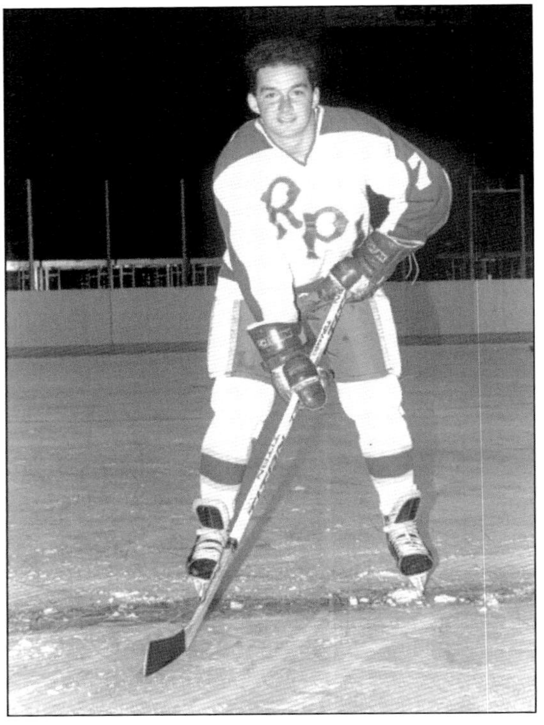

Mark Jooris '86. The No. 3 scorer on the championship team, Jooris became the leading scorer the following year, garnering 60 points in both seasons. He loved to play the University of Michigan. In three games against the Wolverines during the 1985–1986 season, Jooris scored 11 of his 34 goals, getting hat tricks in all three games. He later played for the Canadian National Team, briefly in the AHL, and for a number of years in Germany.

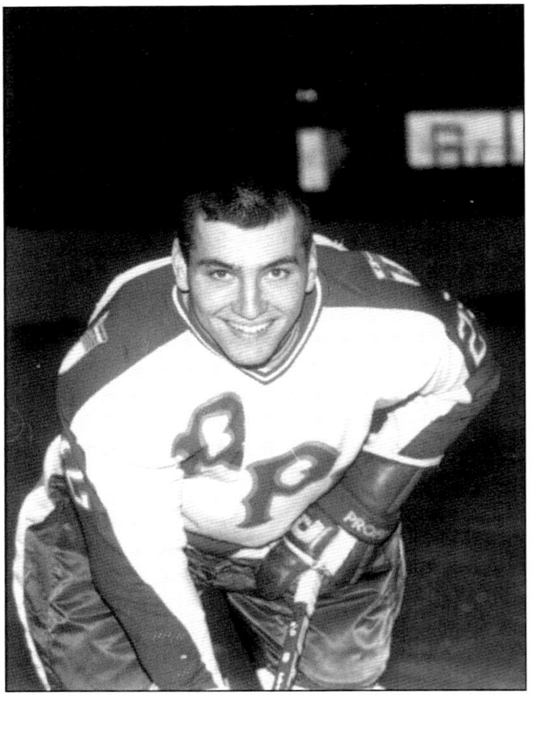

Mike Dark '86. A blue-liner who could set up the forwards, Dark picked up 83 assists in his four seasons. He could also score, picking up the first two goals against Colgate in the 1984 ECAC quarterfinals and the insurance goal against Harvard in the 1985 ECAC Championship game. Dark was a first-team East All-American in the 1985–1986 season. He turned professional after RPI and played 43 games for the St. Louis Blues, along with time in the IHL and AHL.

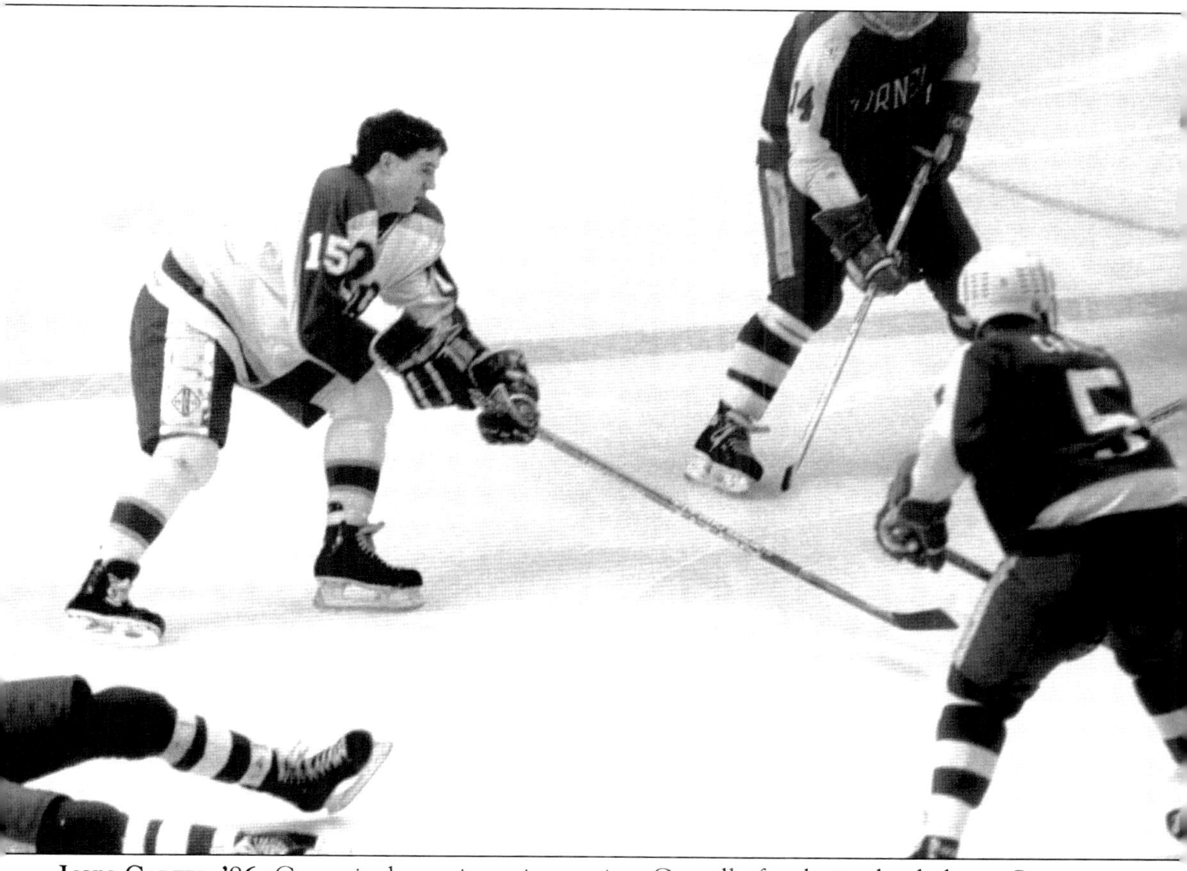

John Carter '86. Carter is shown in action against Cornell after losing his helmet. Carter was the biggest name to remain after 1985, having scored 74 and 72 points the previous two seasons. He was limited to 27 games in the 1985–1986 season, and his point total slipped to 41. In his career, he had 225 points, second only to Frank Chiarelli, and 117 goals, also second to Chiarelli. Certainly, his biggest score was the overtime game-winning goal against the University of Minnesota–Duluth in the 1985 NCAA semifinals. His 13 career hat tricks place him third on the all-time list. He was on two All-America teams, making the East's first team in the 1983–1984 season and the second team in the 1984–1985 season. Carter served as co-captain with Mike Dark for the 1985–1986 squad. After he finished his career at RPI in 1986, Carter played three games for the Boston Bruins. He jumped up and down between Boston and the farm system for a number of years. He ended up with the San Jose Sharks for part of two seasons before finishing in Worcester in the AHL in 1995.

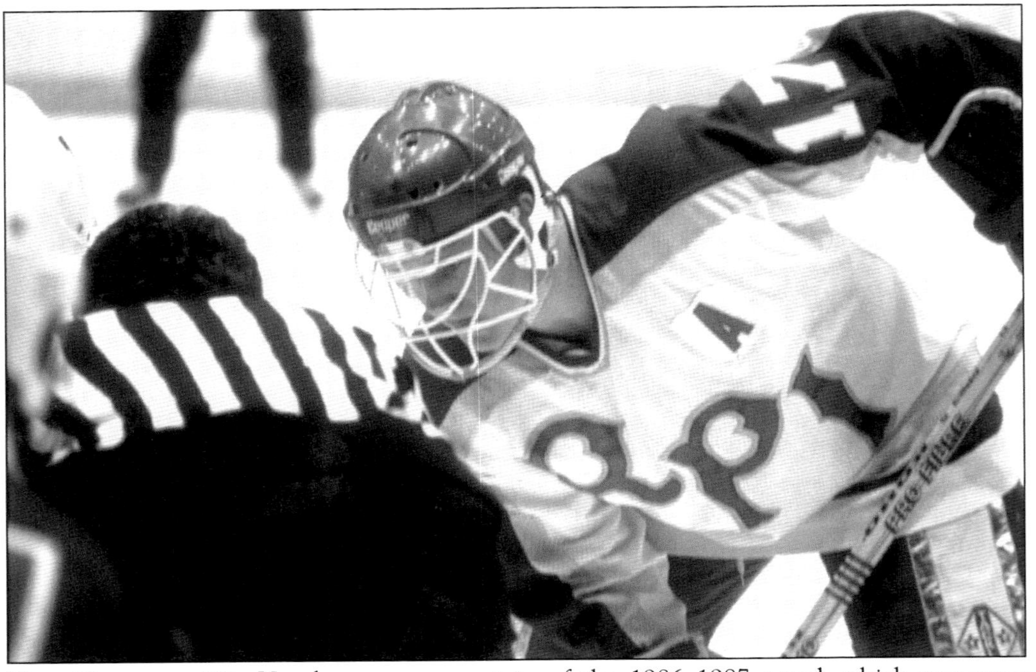

Neil Hernberg '87. Hernberg was co-captain of the 1986–1987 squad, which saw some unorthodox strategy in the playoffs. After losing Game 2 of the ECAC quarterfinals to Colgate, Addesa replaced Gavin Armstrong '90 with Steve Duncan to prepare Duncan for the mini-game. Then, on every power play, he pulled the goaltender to get an extra skater to tire Colgate's goaltender. RPI lost Game 2 but won the mini-game with Duncan and advanced.

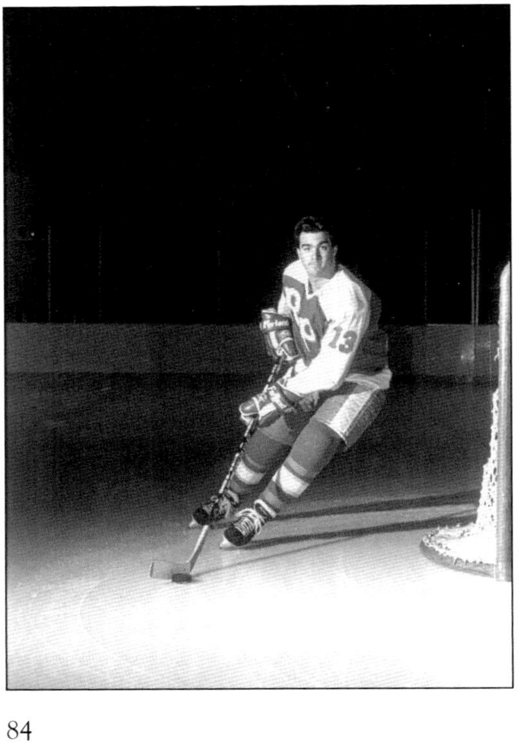

Maurice "Mo" Mansi '88. A native of Montreal, Quebec, Mansi has had some interesting hockey travels. He was bothered by injuries his junior year at RPI but came back his senior year with a solid 35-point performance. After RPI and a stint with the Canadian National Team, Mansi headed to Europe, where he played in German, Italian, and British leagues, most recently with Varese HC in Italy.

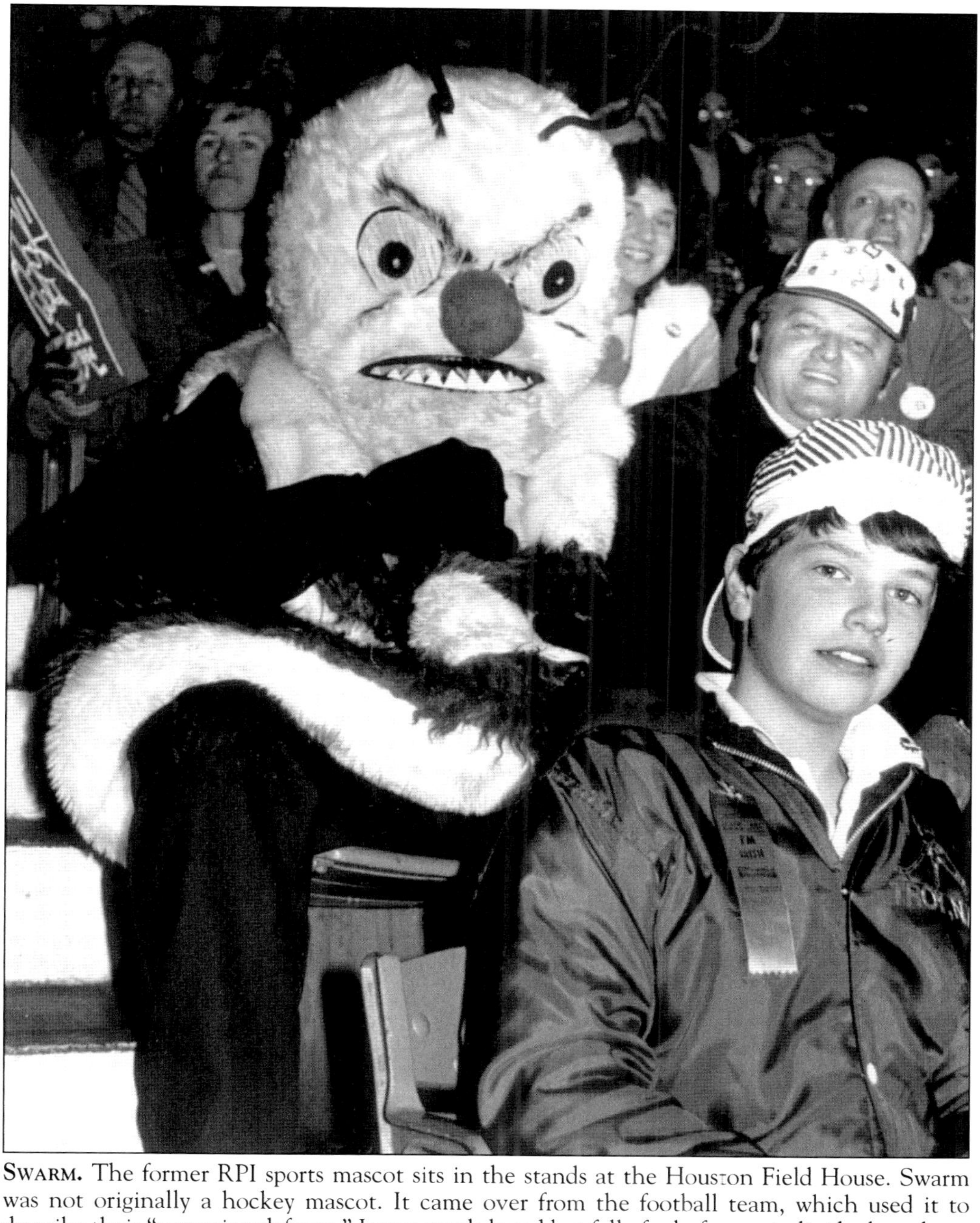

SWARM. The former RPI sports mascot sits in the stands at the Houston Field House. Swarm was not originally a hockey mascot. It came over from the football team, which used it to describe their "swarming defense." It was much loved but fell afoul of some individuals and was banished, along with Mrs. Swarm and Baby Swarm, in the early 1990s. The Engineers operated without a mascot for some time until the school went in two directions at once. The Red Hawk, which looks something like the San Diego Chicken, was introduced as the mascot for all sports except hockey. The hockey teams adopted Puckman, which is the RPI bullet logo on their pucks. Puckman existed, in art form, since the 1970s, but there was never a costume made for it. Puckman now has all the jobs that Swarm had, including leading the team onto the ice at the start of each period.

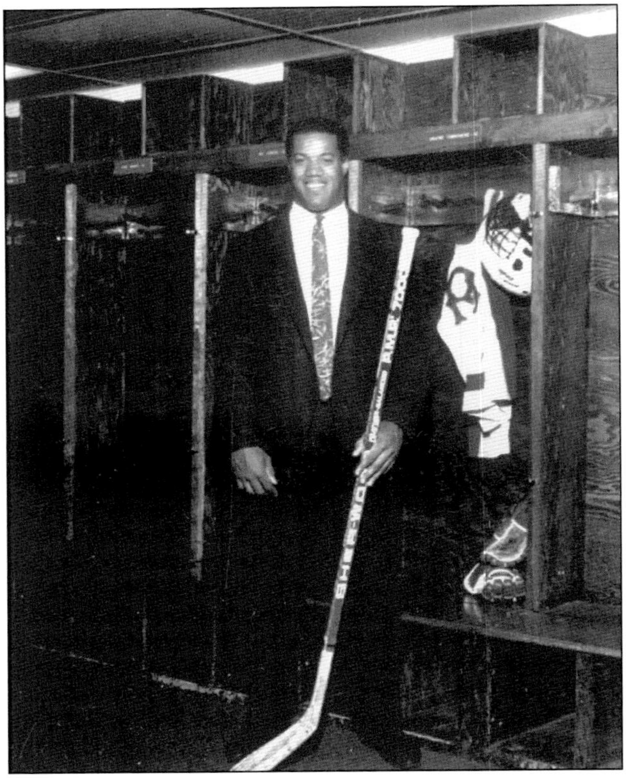

Graeme Townshend '89. Townshend is the big, powerful forward pictured here in the RPI locker room. After scoring only eight points each of his freshman and sophomore seasons, he picked up his production with 20 and 22 his junior and senior years. He returned to play in the field house as a member of the Capital District Islanders as part of his professional career, which included stints in the NHL with Boston, the New York Islanders, and Ottawa.

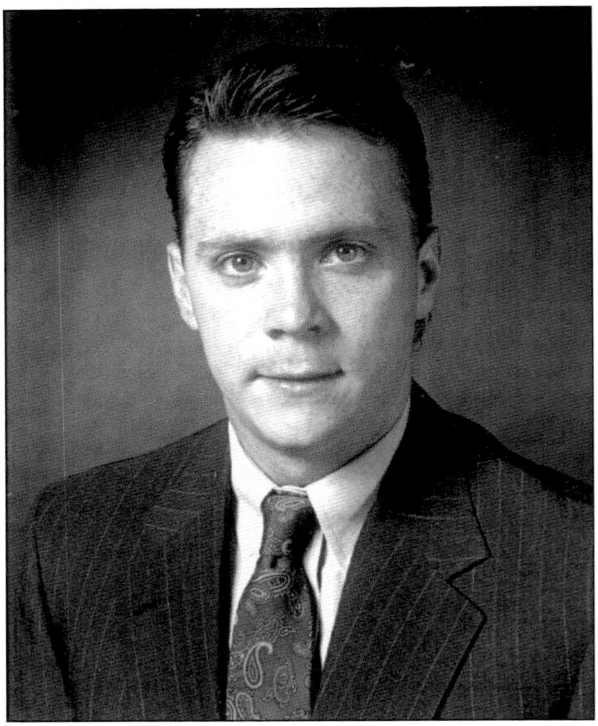

Steve Duncan '89. Duncan was a goaltender who shared duties with numerous other goalies during his four years. He won the mini-game against Colgate in 1987 to advance RPI to the ECAC semifinals. His best game was a 4-0 win over Harvard on February 20, 1988. After leaving RPI in 1990, he played in Sweden for a year. He then returned and, in 1993, became an assistant coach, a position he held for two years.

Five

The 1990s and Beyond

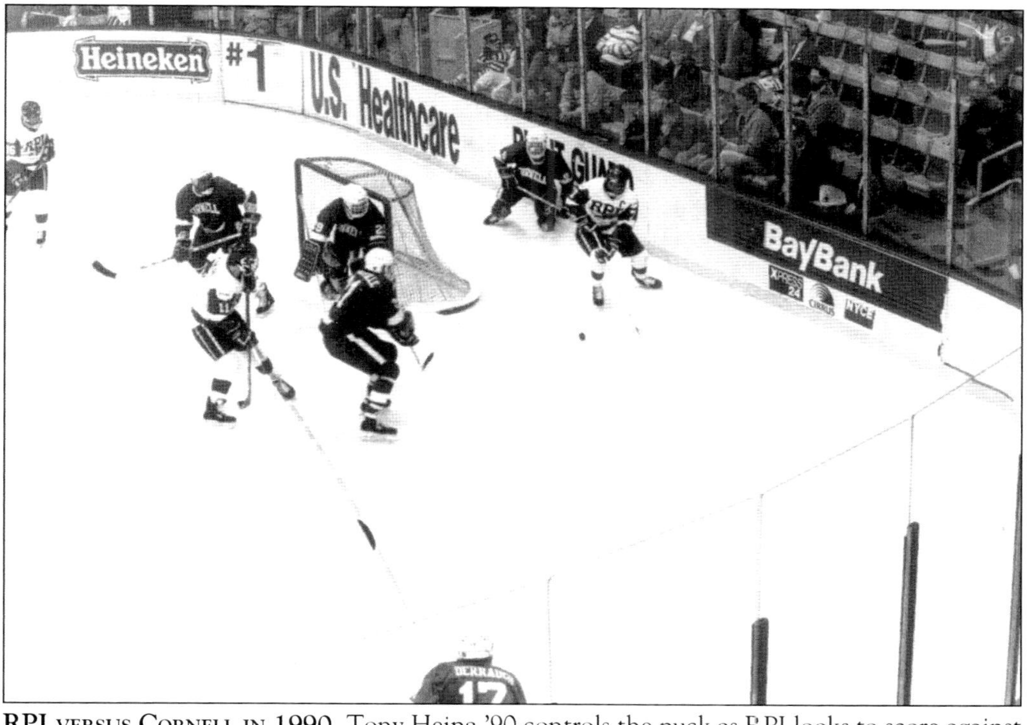

RPI versus Cornell in 1990. Tony Hejna '90 controls the puck as RPI looks to score against Cornell in the 1990 ECAC semifinals. Hejna scored the second goal of the game, and Joe Juneau put in the game winner at 12:40 of the third to advance RPI to the championship game. It was RPI's first appearance in the ECAC title game since 1985 and the first time they would lose a championship game, when Colgate defeated them 5-4.

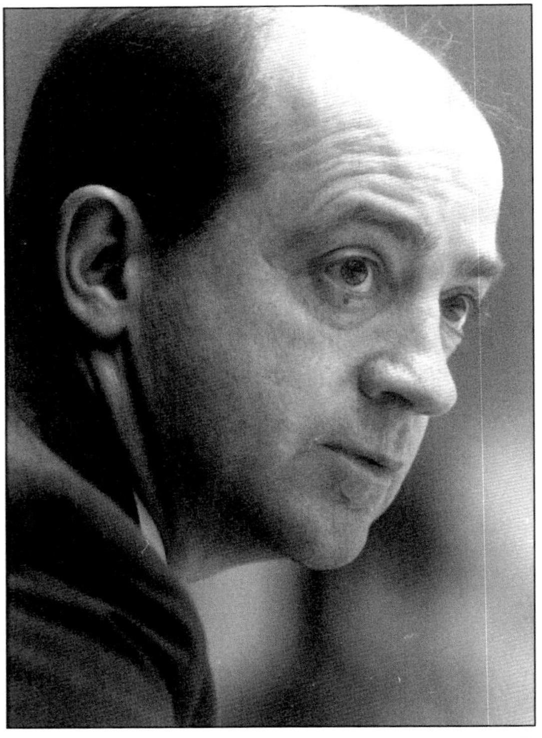

Buddy Powers. Following Addesa's resignation in 1989, Buddy Powers, then head coach at the Rochester Institute of Technology (RIT), was selected as the new RPI coach. Playing a more wide-open style, Powers's teams advanced to the ECAC semifinals in four of his five seasons at the school. Powers left in 1994 to take the head coaching position at Bowling Green, leaving with a record of 94-63-13.

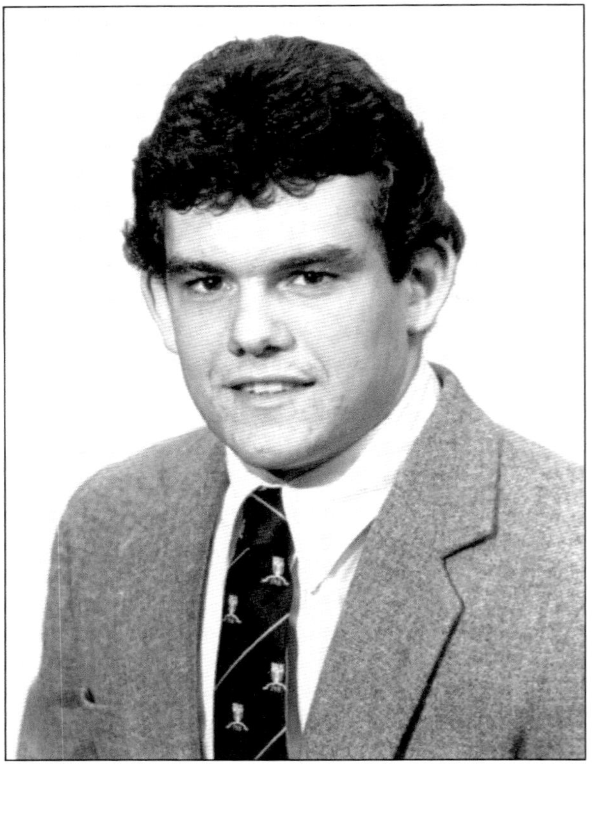

Brian Ferreira '90. One of the tri-captains of the 1989–1990 squad, Ferreira had his best season under Powers's new style, picking up 45 points. In the 1987 Colgate mini-game, it was Ferreira who got the game winner to advance the Engineers to the finals in Boston. He played in the AHL with the Maine Mariners after finishing at RPI.

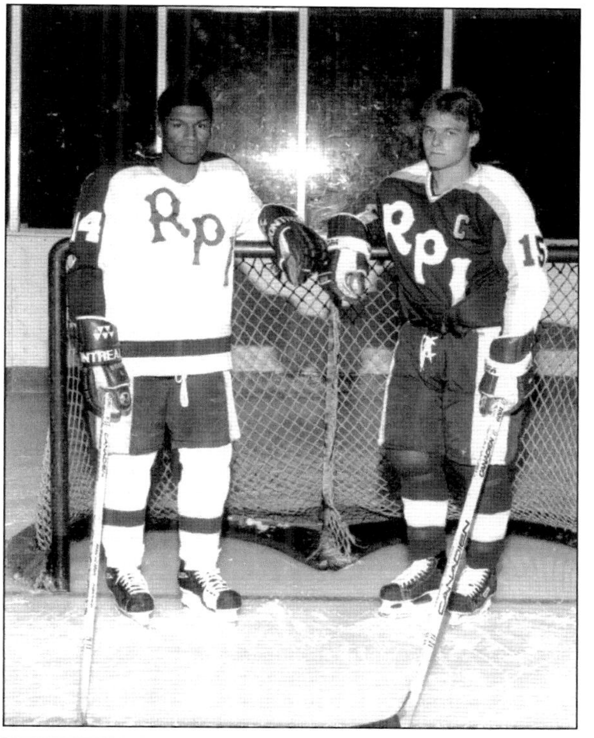

Bruce Coles '91 and Denis Poissant '90. Poissant served as a captain in his last three years at RPI, the only player ever to do that. He scored 86 points in his career. Coles followed Poissant as a co-captain for the 1990–1991 season and was a member of the 1987–1988 ECAC All-Rookie team. He picked up 165 points in his career and holds the school record for most career penalty minutes (407). Coles saw a lot of action in the minor leagues after RPI.

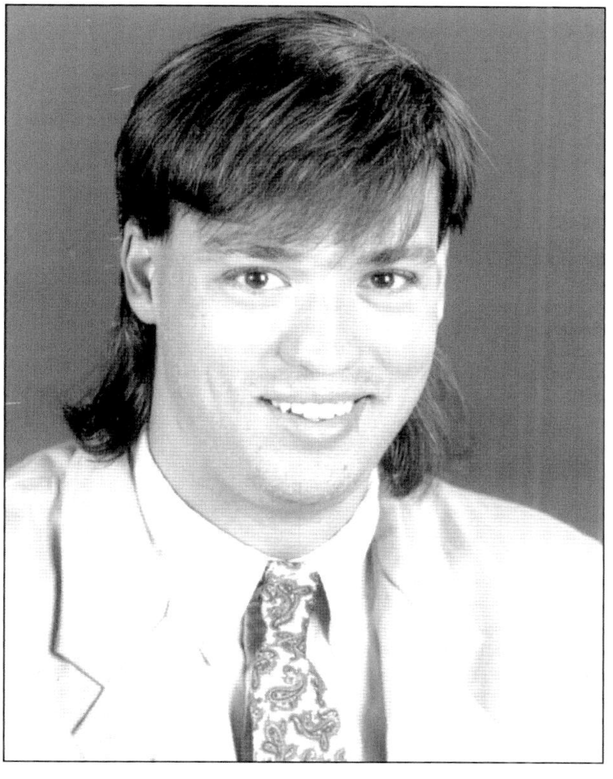

Joé Juneau '91. A talented forward, Juneau was named a first-team East All-American in the 1989–1990 season and second team in the 1990–1991 season. His career assists total of 144 are only six behind Oates's record, and his 213 points are fifth on the all-time school list. He joined the Canadian National Team after graduating from RPI with an aeronautical engineering degree, and three years later, he joined the Boston Bruins. He also played for Washington, Buffalo, Ottawa, Phoenix, and Montreal before retiring from the NHL in 2004.

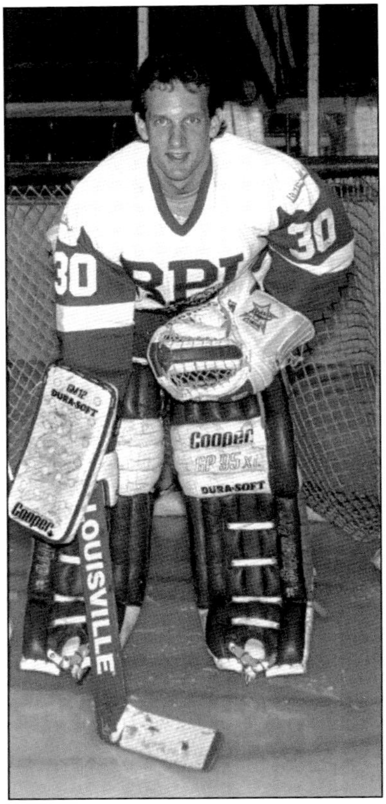

Sean Kennedy '92. Kennedy was a goaltender who shared time with Steve Duncan and Neil Little, until Little claimed the starting job. Has a 30-20-3 lifetime record with two shutouts. His most important save came against Cornell in the 1990 ECAC semifinals. With less than six minutes remaining, Cornell was given a penalty shot. Kennedy stopped Ross Lemon and preserved RPI's lead and the win.

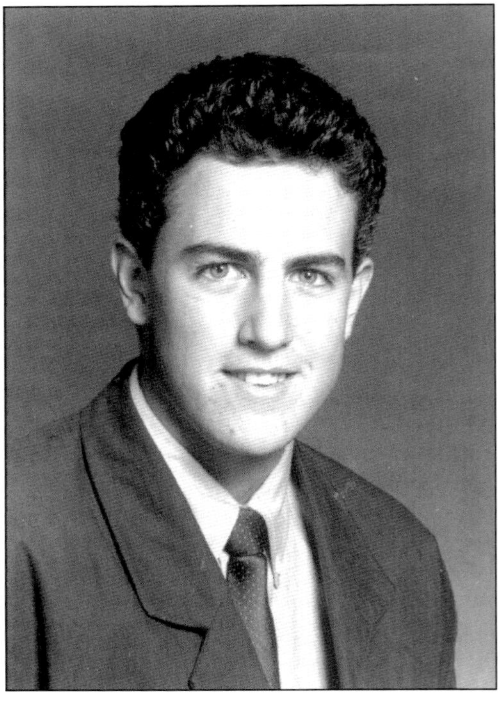

Stephane Robitaille '92. A disciplined, talented defenseman who rarely took penalties, Robitaille was a good assist man who totaled 73 over four years. His transition from college player to professional can be measured in hours. RPI lost the 1992 ECAC semifinal game to St. Lawrence University after midnight. The team returned to Troy the next day, and Robitaille was almost immediately signed to a professional contract. He traveled to Glens Falls that night to play for the Capital District Islanders against the Adirondack Red Wings.

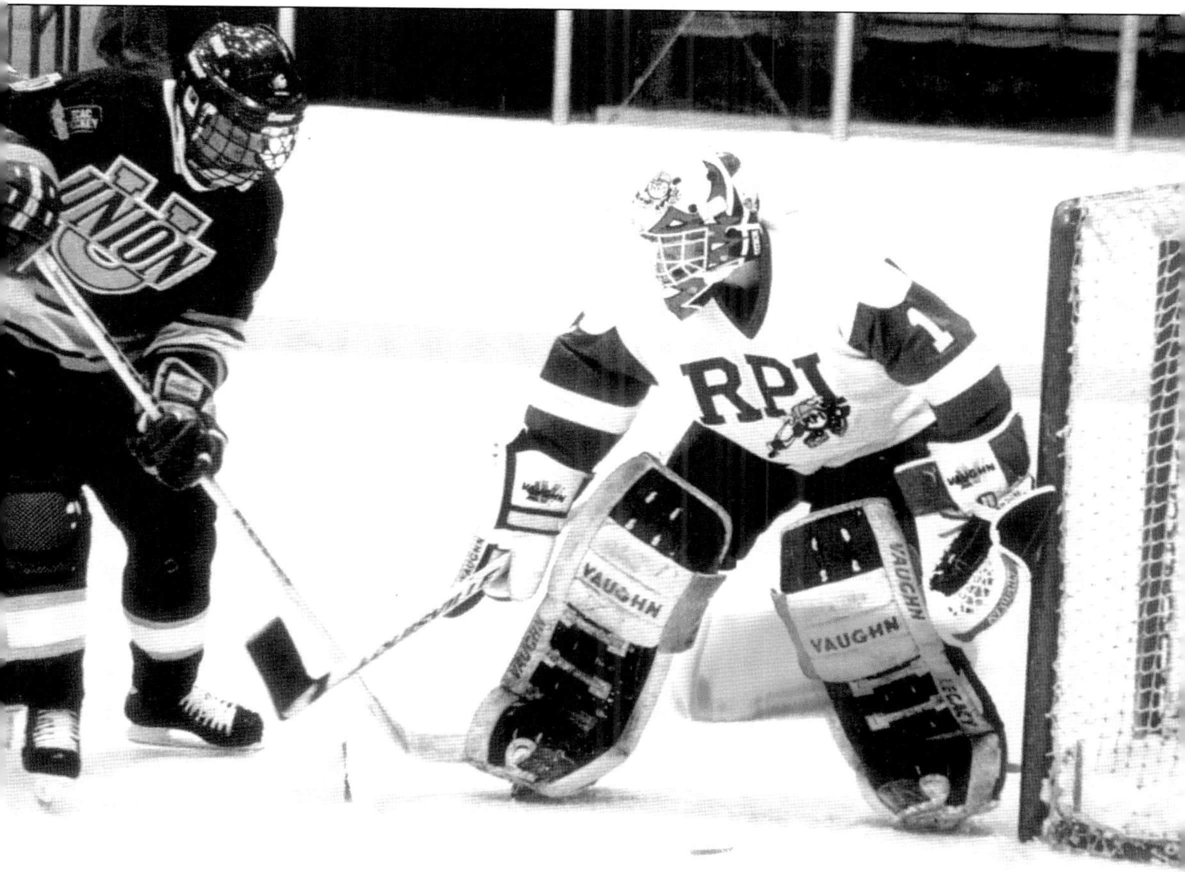

NEIL LITTLE '94. Little was the first goaltender since Daren Puppa who got a large amount of national attention. He took over the starting goaltender's job in December 1991 and held it for the rest of his college career. He was a stand-up goaltender whose 58 career victories (58-39-10) are a school record, and a number of his other career numbers are second only to Nathan Marsters. He was a second-team East All-American in the 1992–1993 season and a first-team All-ECAC pick the same season. He also made the ECAC All-Rookie team in 1990–1991. His professional career has mostly been in the minors, playing for the Hershey Bears and Philadelphia Phantoms of the AHL and one season with the Grand Rapids Griffins of the IHL. He has appeared in two NHL games, one each season in 2001–2002 and 2003–2004 for the Flyers.

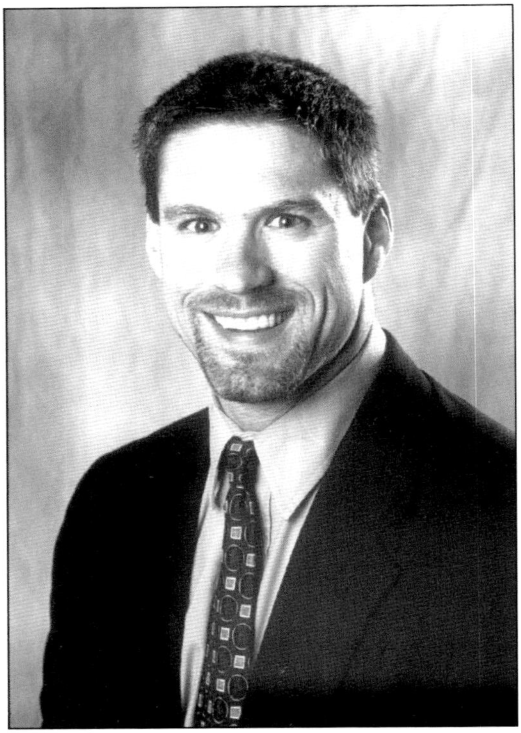

IVAN MOORE '92. Pictured as an assistant coach, Moore was the captain of the improbable 1991–1992 squad that made its way to the finals in Boston. After finishing 10th, the team defeated the University of Vermont 5-2 in Burlington with help from the Catamounts, who scored on themselves. Then, they knocked out Harvard 4-3 in overtime before falling to St. Lawrence University 6-5 in double overtime in the semifinals. Moore returned to RPI as an assistant coach in 2000 and remained for four years.

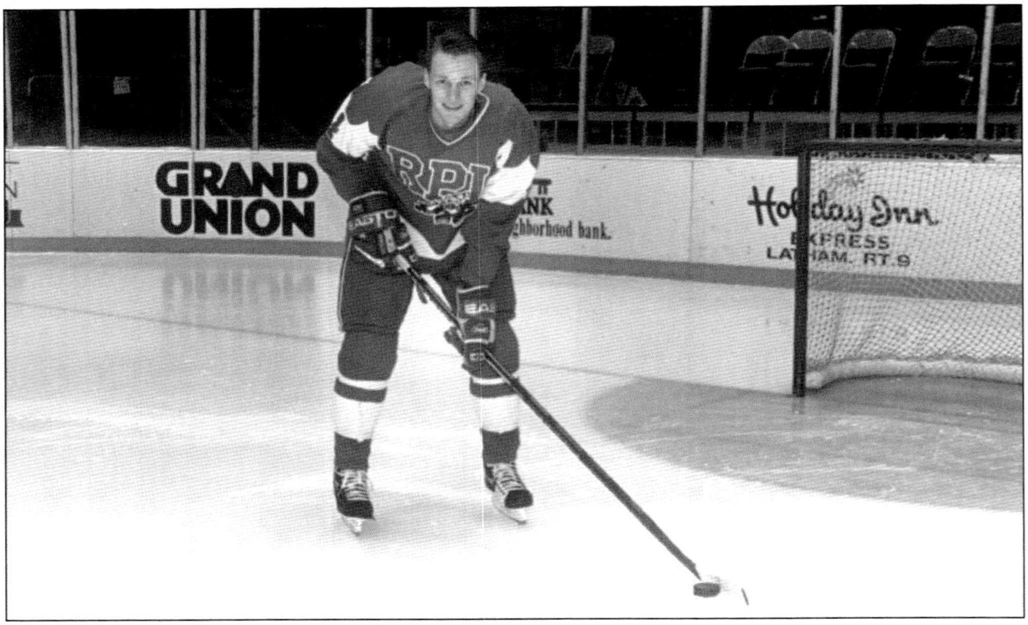

BRAD LAYZELL '94. Layzell was a solid defenseman from Beaconsfield, Quebec. Not one to enter the fray as a scorer, he developed into a good setup man, getting 44 of his 63 points from assists in his final two seasons. His blue-line work helped the Engineers increase their goal differential in his junior and senior seasons. For his efforts, he was named to the All-ECAC second team in the 1992–1993 season.

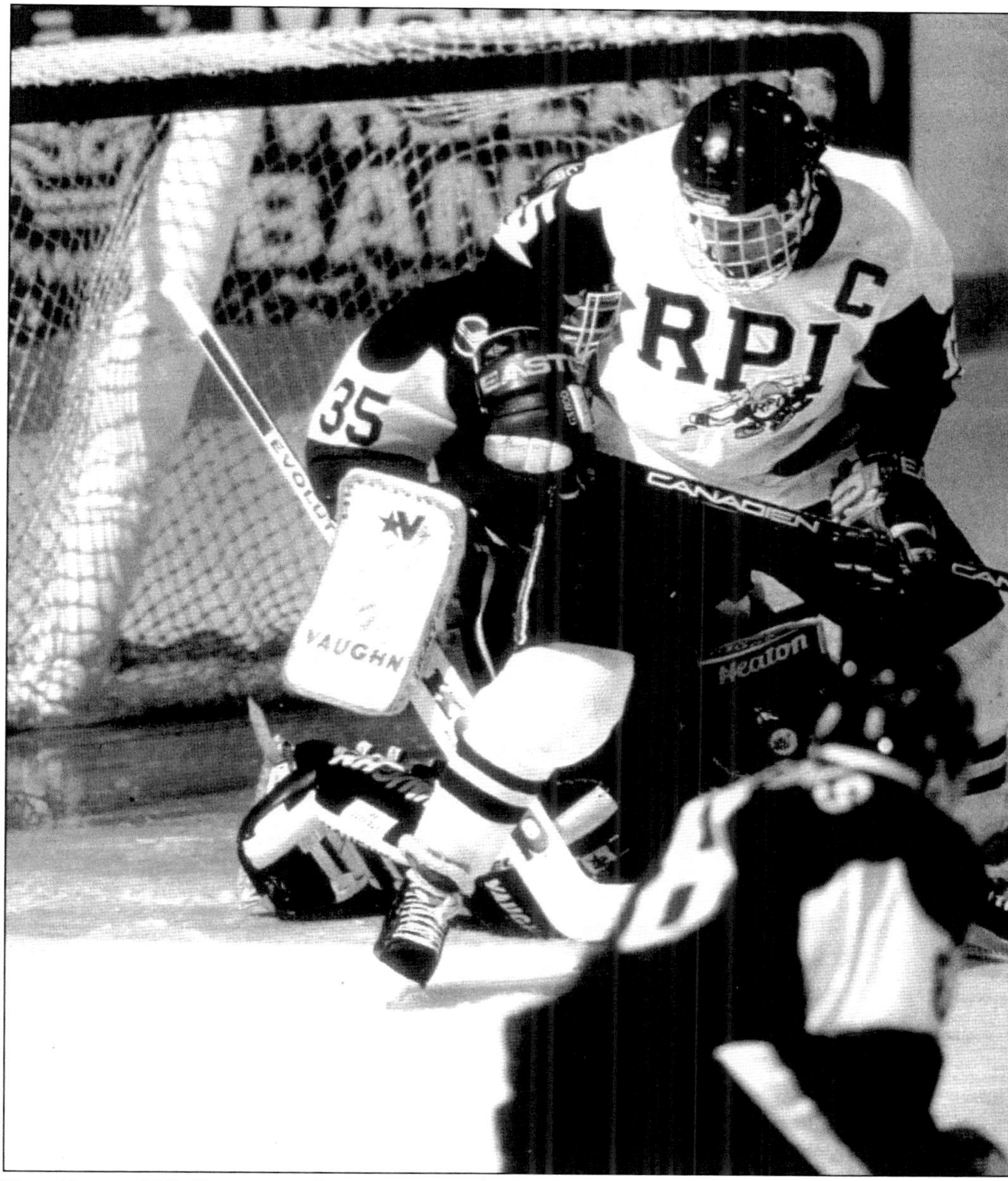

Ron Pasco '94. Pasco was the two-time solo captain of the Engineers his junior and senior seasons, the first since Ken McCutcheon '76 in the 1974–1975 and 1975–1976 seasons. His best offensive season was his senior year in which he earned 17 goals and 40 assists, when the Engineers averaged more than 4 goals per game. In the 2004 ECAC quarterfinals, after Union College took Game 1, Pasco assisted on all three goals in the second period of Game 2 to put RPI ahead for the win that forced a third game, which RPI won handily. Pasco had two more assists in the semifinals, when RPI downed Clarkson University. Although the Engineers lost to Harvard in the final, they received a bid to the NCAA Tournament, their first appearance since 1985. They were ousted by the University of New Hampshire in Albany. After graduating, Pasco continued to play hockey in the Eastern Collegiate Hockey League (ECHL), the IHL, for the Canadian National Team, and for Mannheim, Kessel, and Cologne in Germany.

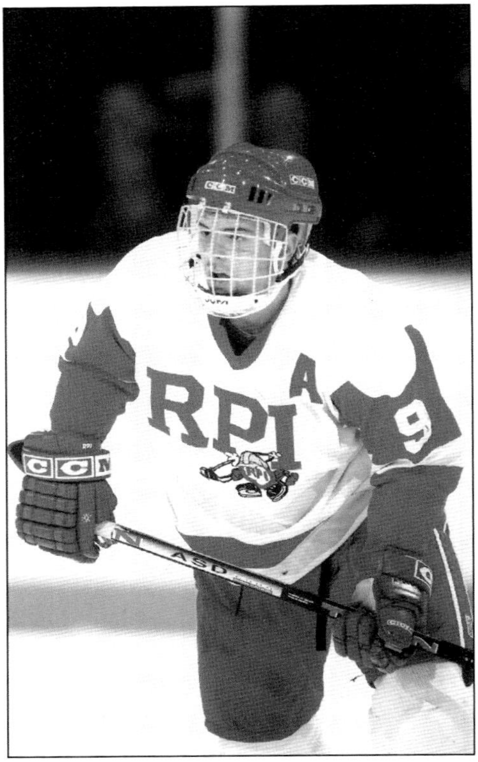

JEFF BRICK '95. Brick picked up a hat trick against the University of Massachusetts–Lowell in the championship game of the RPI Invitational Tournament in 1993. He also scored the game winner and insurance goal against Clarkson University in the 2004 ECAC semifinals. Brick was from East Lansing, Michigan, and had his best season in 1993–1994, when he scored 32 points while playing mostly on a line with Bryan Richardson and Tim Regan '96.

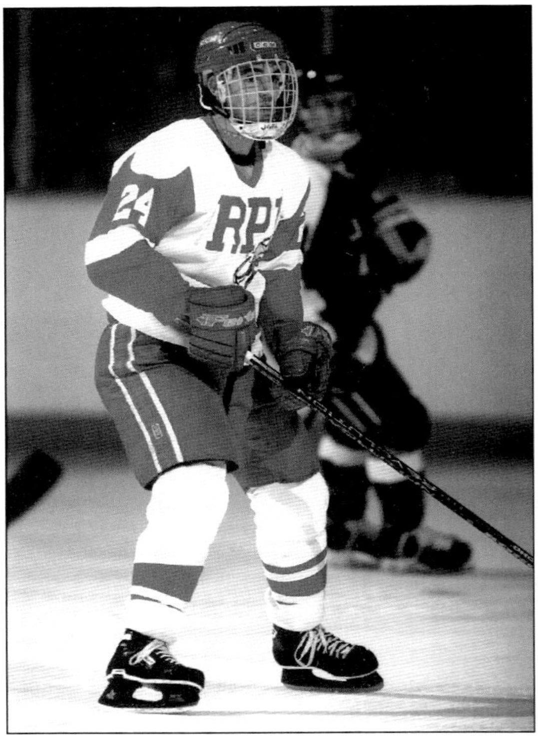

JEFF MATHEWS '95. A walk-on to Rensselaer's hockey team, Mathews improved each year and produced a 17-point performance his senior year. In the second game of the 1995 ECAC quarterfinals, Mathews assisted on both the Wayne Clarke and Kelly Askew goals in the third period that put RPI up 3-1 en route to victory. Mathews returned to RPI in 2004 as an assistant coach.

CRAIG HAMELIN '95. Hamelin, a skilled forward from Quebec, was a key ingredient in the RPI playoff run in 1995, which resulted in an ECAC Tournament championship with a 5-1 win over Princeton at Lake Placid. He scored the first goal in the second quarterfinal game against Harvard and then assisted on two goals against Princeton in the championship game. Hamelin was consistent, always scoring between 38 and 49 points during his four years at RPI. He finished his career with 171 points, 65 from goals, and played minor-league hockey through the 2000–2001 season in the ECHL, CHL, and Western Professional Hockey League (WPHL). His desire to win was extraordinary, and he was, at times, vocal about his teammates' desire or lack thereof. Hamelin was also named to the 1991–1992 ECAC All-Rookie team.

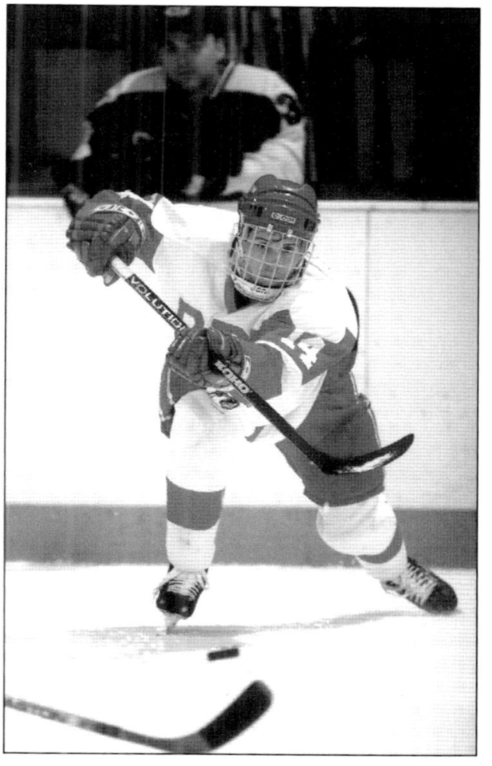

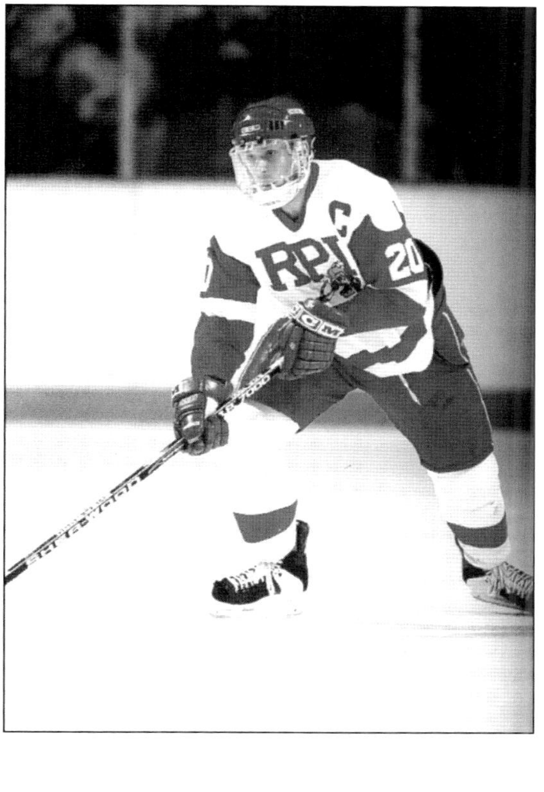

ADAM BARTELL '95. Bartell was captain of the 1994–1995 ECAC Tournament champions. A big defenseman from Buffalo, he was part of the tight defense in the 1995 playoffs. That defense allowed only five goals over four ECAC games, of which only three were at even strength. He ended his college career with a career-best 22 points his senior year and was named to the All-ECAC second team.

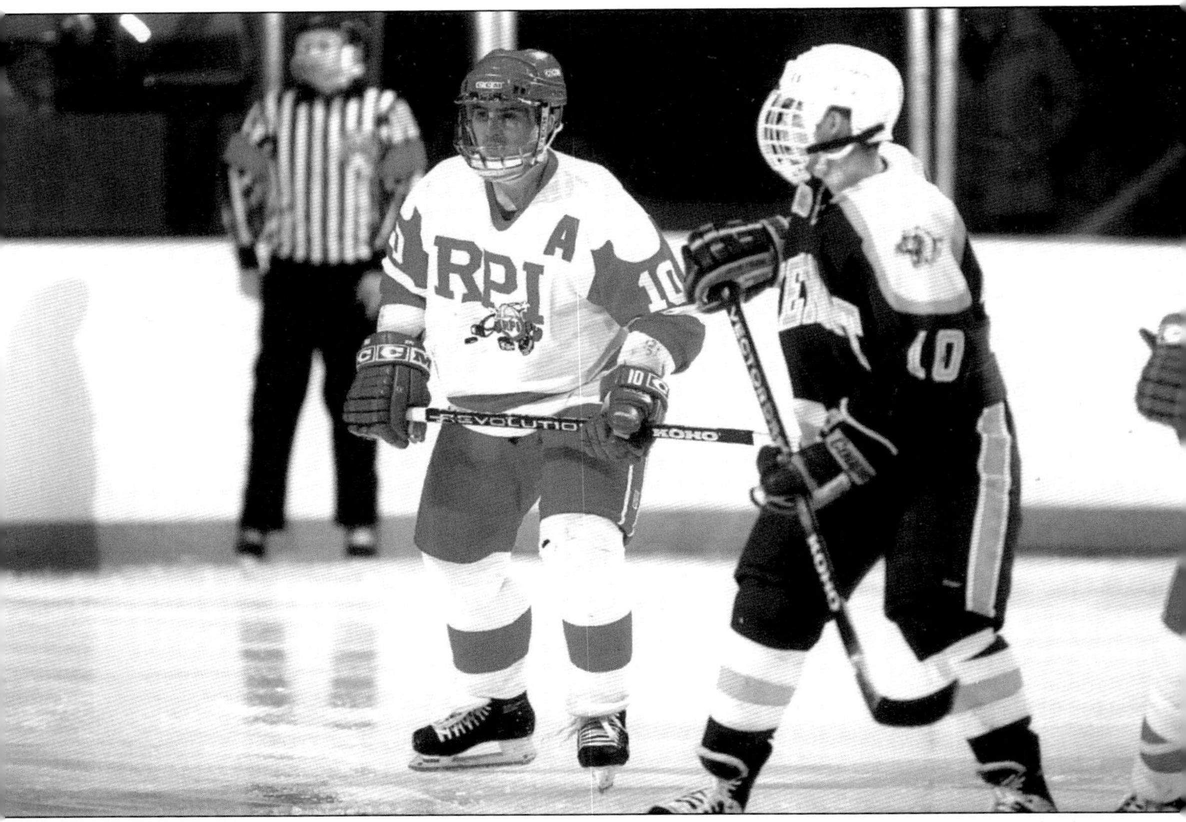

Kelly Askew '95. Askew was, quite possibly, the fastest player to don the cherry and white. When the Engineers were short defensemen in the spring of 1995, Askew was moved back to defense because he was quick. He scored the game-winning goal in the 1995 ECAC semifinals by shooting the puck straight at Colgate's Todd Brenzavich, forcing Brenzavich to back into the goal with the puck. After graduation, Askew played roller hockey with the New Jersey Rockin' Rollers. He then joined the Candian National Team for the 1995–1996 season, after which he played for a few seasons in Europe.

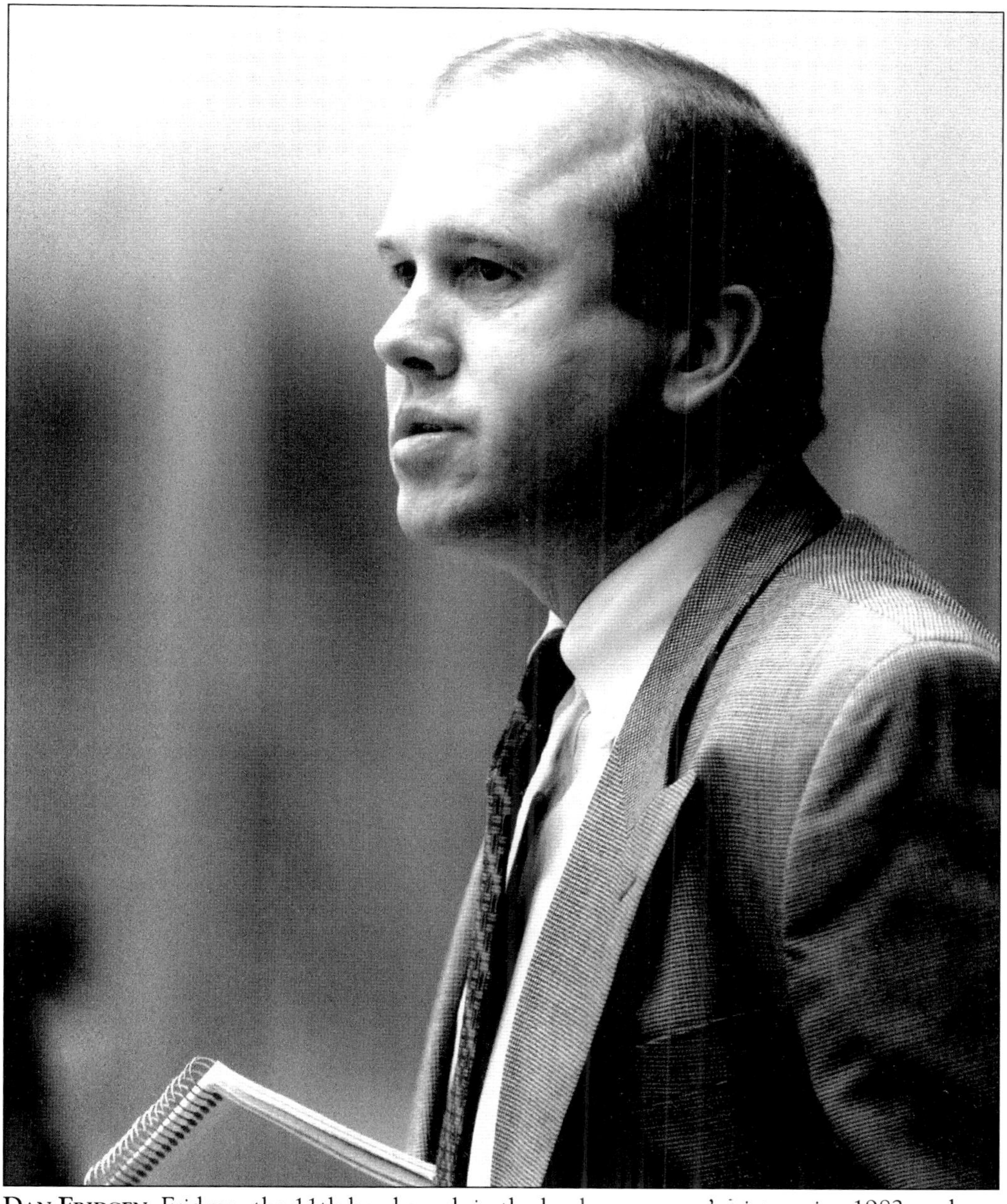

Dan Fridgen. Fridgen, the 11th head coach in the hockey program's history, is a 1982 graduate of Colgate University, where he played left wing and was known for being able to score and take penalties. He still holds the Colgate career mark for goals scored (114), goals in a season (38), and penalty minutes in a season (164). Fridgen played for the Hartford Whalers organization, including 13 games at the NHL level, where he scored two goals and had three assists. After an automobile accident cut his career short, he switched to coaching, first as an assistant at Union College and then at RPI under Buddy Powers. After Powers left for Bowling Green in 1994, Fridgen was promoted to head coach, and the team won the ECAC Championship in his first season at the helm. RPI has had eight winning seasons in his 10 years as head coach and has reached the ECAC semifinals five times.

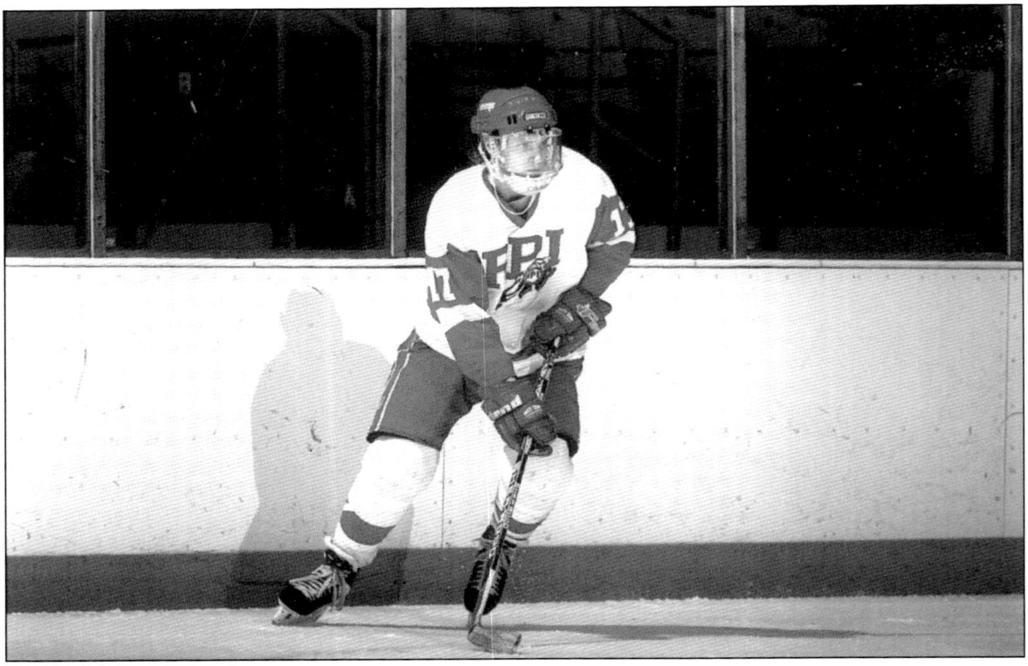

WAYNE CLARKE '95. Clarke was a right wing from Castleton, Ontario, who scored the series-winning goal against Harvard with only 6:41 left in third period of the 1995 ECAC quarterfinals. Clarke was an ECAC All-Rookie team member in the 1991–1992 season and was a steady performer, with 62 goals and 64 assists in his career. He played briefly for the St. John's Maple Leafs of the AHL.

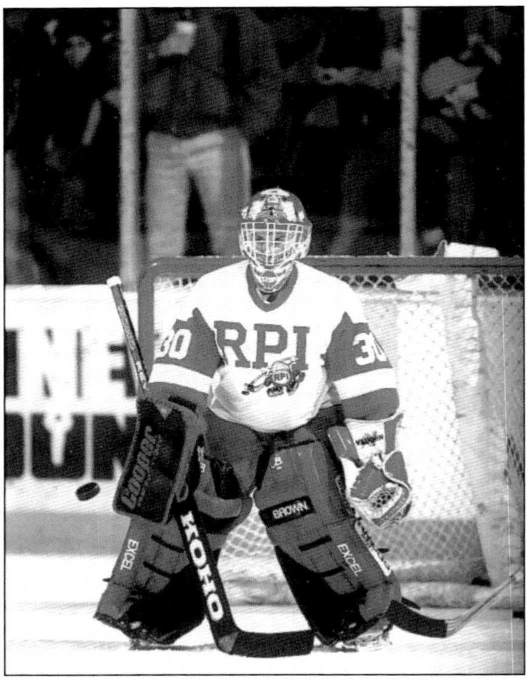

MIKE TAMBURRO '96. Tamburro was the ECAC Tournament's Most Outstanding Player in 1995, when he allowed only five goals over the course of four playoff games. It was his misfortune to be the best goaltender on a poor team the following season, as he went from a 13-8-4 record to 8-20-3, setting a school record for losses in a season. He continued his career in the minors, mostly in the ECHL, until 2002.

Jeff O'Connor '96. O'Connor was a forward who improved his scoring every year, from 5 to 8 to 25 to 28 points, while recovering from knee surgery at the start of his junior year. His best game was a hat trick versus Dartmouth in January 1995. O'Connor played in Germany after leaving RPI.

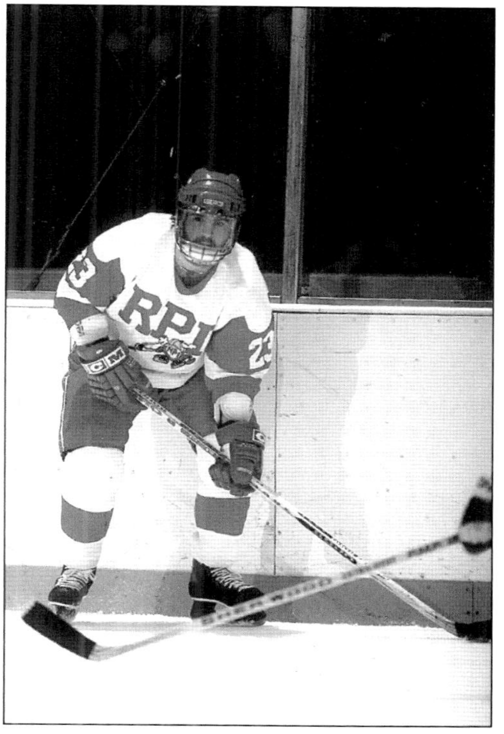

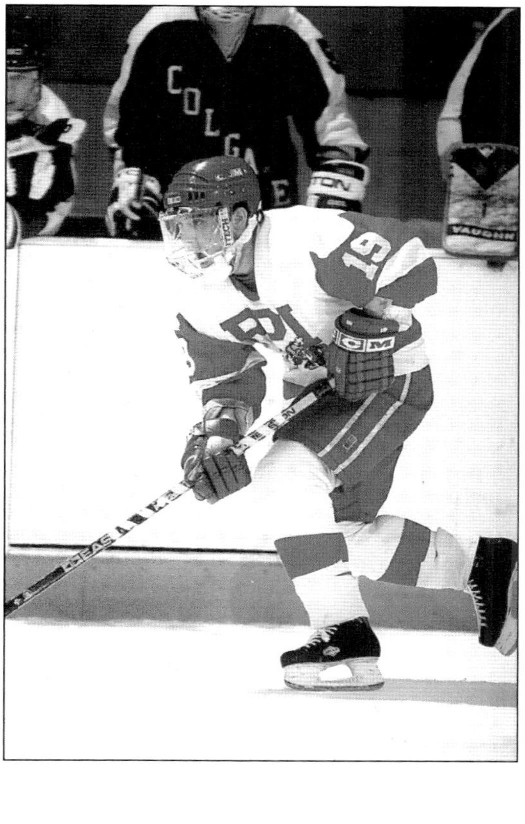

Bryan Richardson '96. A center from Pointe-Claire, Quebec, Richardson was a centerpiece of the offense for the four years he played. He finished second in team scoring his freshman and sophomore years, and he led the team his final two seasons. His 113 assists are fourth on the all-time RPI list, and he ended his career with 193 points. Richardson picked up a hat trick to help knock Union College out of the playoffs in 1994. He continued playing in the minors, mostly in the ECHL.

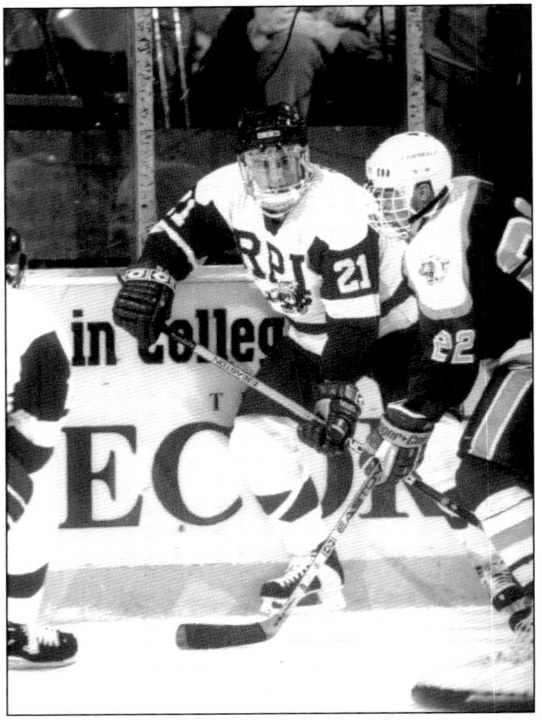

PATRICK ROCHON '96. Rochon, a defenseman, was captain of the 1995–1996 squad. He increased his offensive production during his career, and in his senior season, he had a career-high 34 points. Rochon has played most of his minor-league hockey career with the Mississippi Sea Wolves of the ECHL.

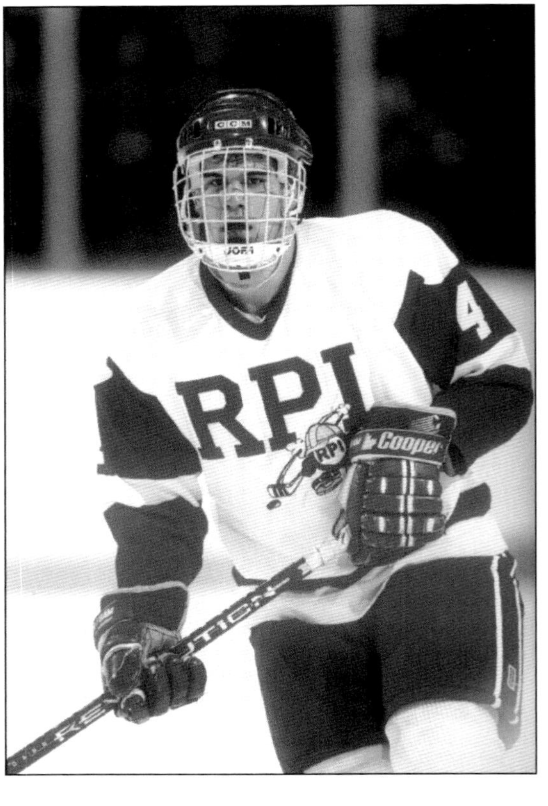

PATRICK BROWNLEE '98. Brownlee served as a two-year captain from 1996 to 1998 while playing as a stay-at-home defenseman. Under his leadership, the team returned to a winning record, after a poor showing in the 1995–1996 season. They made the ECAC semifinals in 1997, where they lost to Cornell. Brownlee continued playing hockey in the minors, most recently with the Austin Ice Bats of the CHL.

Bryan Tapper '98. Another stay-at-home defenseman, Tapper was one of a trio (along with Brownlee and Aldous) that made the Engineers difficult to score upon in the mid-1990s. He picked up two points in the losing effort against Cornell in Game 1 of the 1998 ECAC quarterfinals, one of the tightest and most interesting playoff series the Engineers have played.

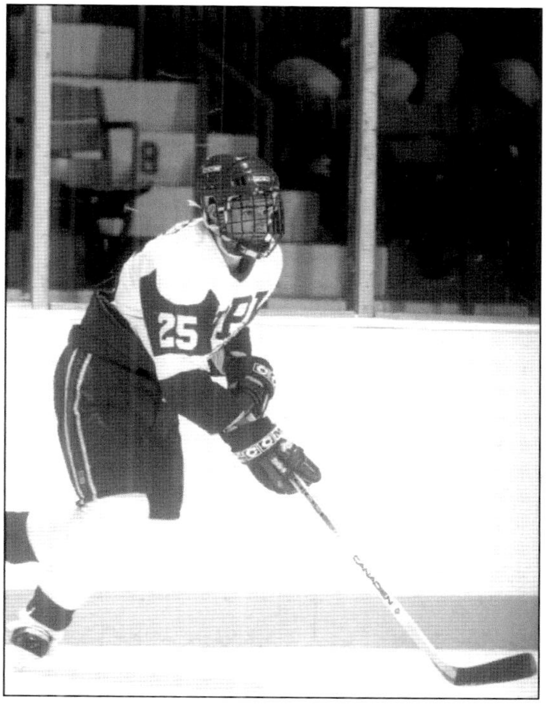

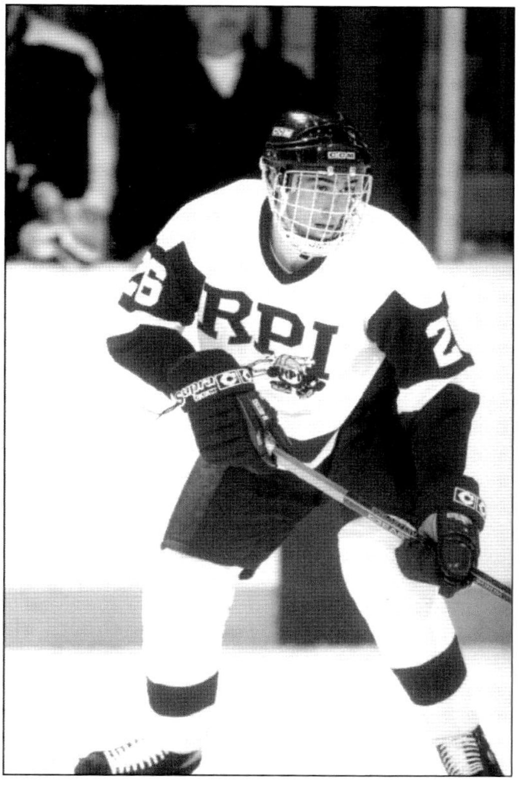

Chris Aldous '98. Aldous was a relentless defender on the strong blue-line corps that included Tapper and Brownlee. He scored the game-winning goal in 1997 at Princeton to lock the Engineers in fourth place for the ECAC Tournament. Following his college career, Aldous went on to a minor-league career in the AHL and ECHL.

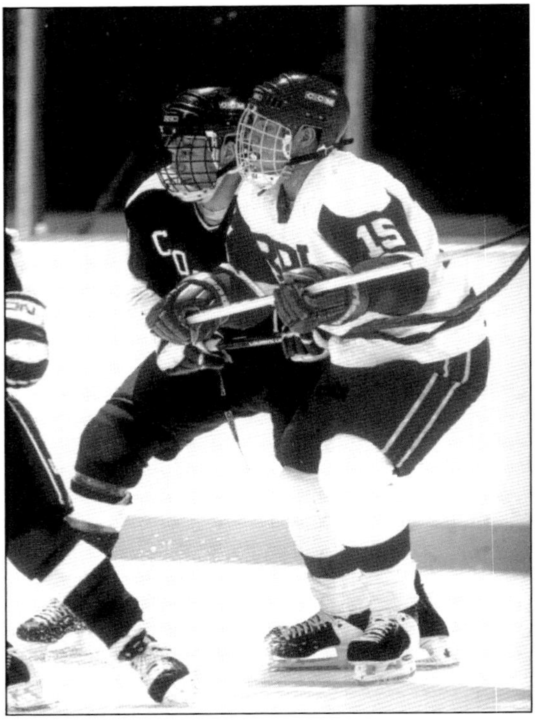

Eric Healey '98. Healey, one of the best scorers at RPI in recent times, scored 82 goals in his four seasons, with a personal best of 30 in the 1996–1997 season. RPI beat Union College in the 1997 ECAC playoffs, and Healey scored four of the six goals that knocked the Dutchmen out and advanced RPI. He was twice named to the East All-American second team in the 1996–1997 and 1997–1998 seasons. Healey played in the AHL and recovered from a horrific injury to his wrist that occurred during the 1999–2000 season.

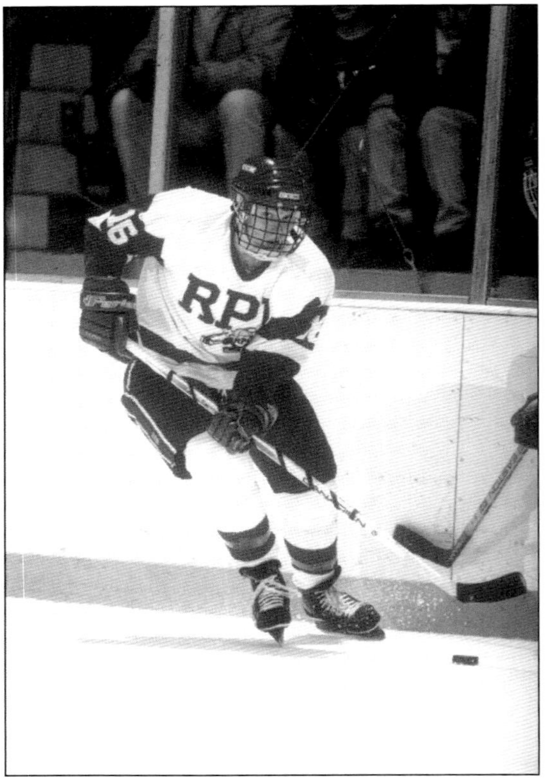

Doug Battaglia '98. Battaglia, a forward who played a solid two-way game, had his best offensive season in 1996–1997, when he scored 30 points. He scored the game-winning goal that sent Union College out of the playoffs in 1997, and then scored twice in the losing effort against Cornell in the semifinals. Battaglia had a short minor-league career with the Charlotte Checkers and Wheeling Nailers of the ECHL and the Anchorage Aces of the WCHL.

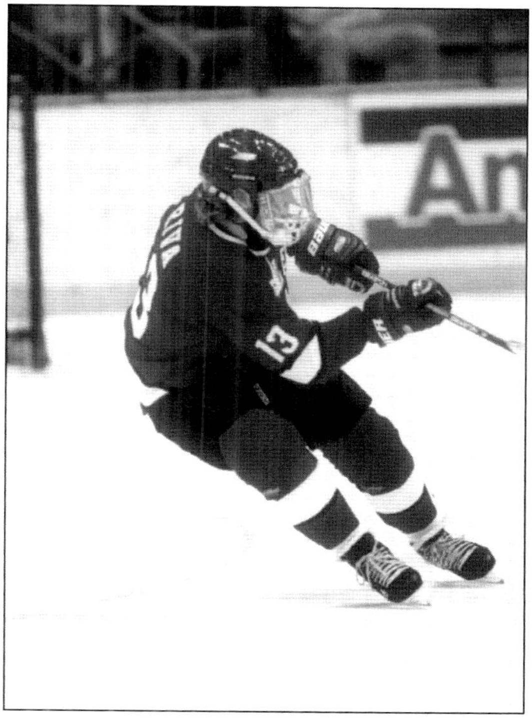

Danny Riva '99. Most have forgotten that Riva scored a disputed goal in the 1998 quarterfinals against Cornell. With the score 1-0 in Game 2, Cornell slipped the puck behind Joel Laing, and it is still debated as to whether the puck entered the goal or not. No on-ice official called a goal, so RPI recovered and Riva scored in the other direction. Riva played minor-league hockey after leaving RPI.

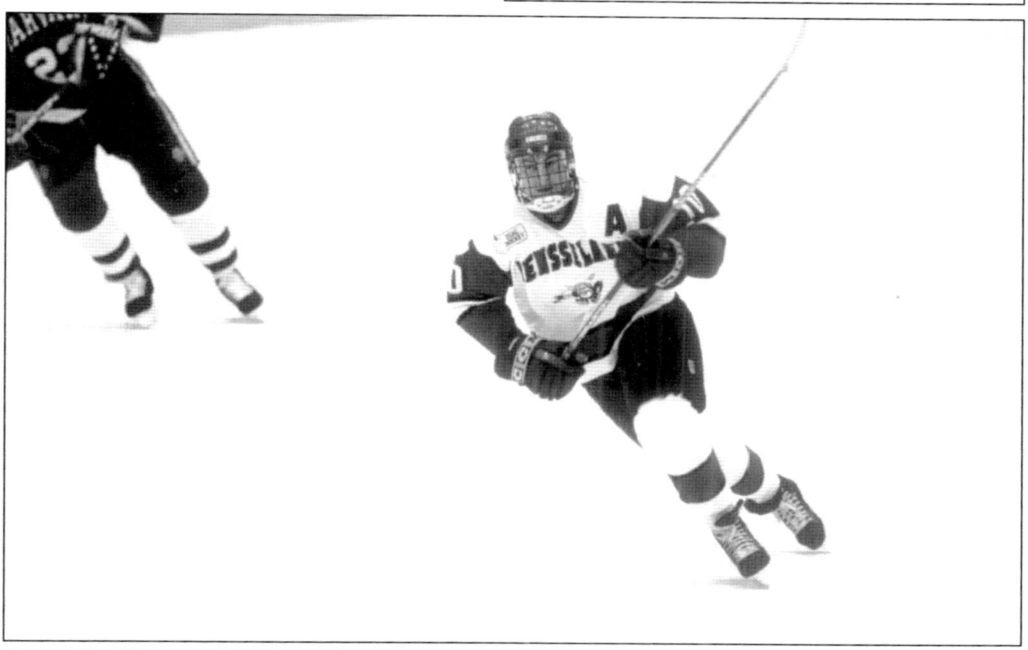

Alain St. Hilaire '99. St. Hilaire was one of the best face-off artists the Engineers have had. When the game was on the line, odds are St. Hilaire would be sent out to take the draw. He was co-captain of the 1998–1999 team and completed his career with 145 points in 128 games. St. Hilaire played in the AHL with the Philadelphia Phantoms, where he was a teammate of Neil Little '94.

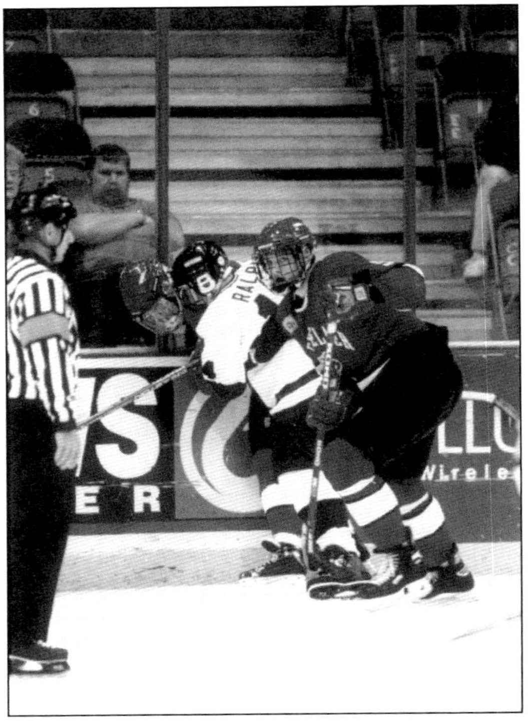

Pete Gardiner '00. Gardiner, a forward, holds the school record for most games played in a career at 144. A two-time nominee as Hockey Humanitarian of the Year, Gardiner is a member of many organizations that aid children with juvenile diabetes, a disease Gardiner suffers from himself. In his minor-league career, he has advanced to the AHL, playing for the Rochester Americans in the 2003–2004 season.

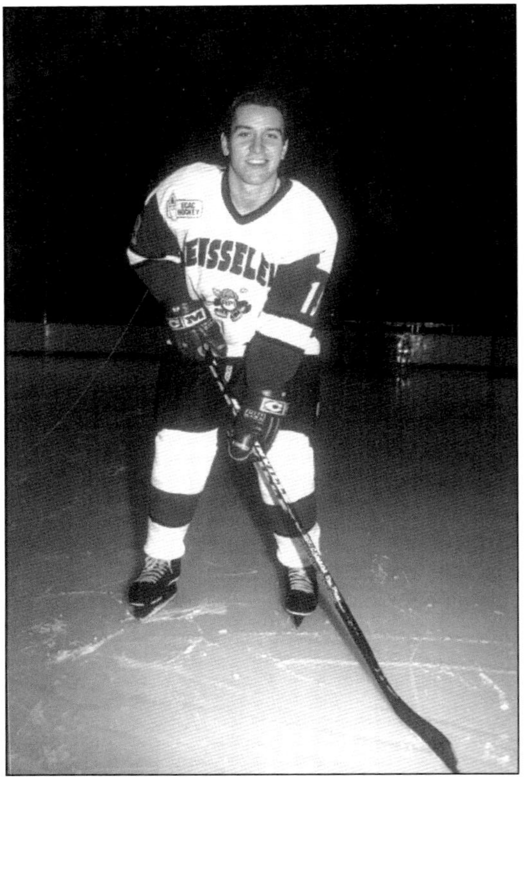

Doug Shepherd '00. Shepherd, a good two-way forward, scored the game-winning goal in Game 3 of the 1999 ECAC quarterfinals, allowing the Engineers to defeat Harvard. He improved his numbers every year; his best was 22 points his senior year. Shepherd played in the WPHL, CHL, and ACHL after college.

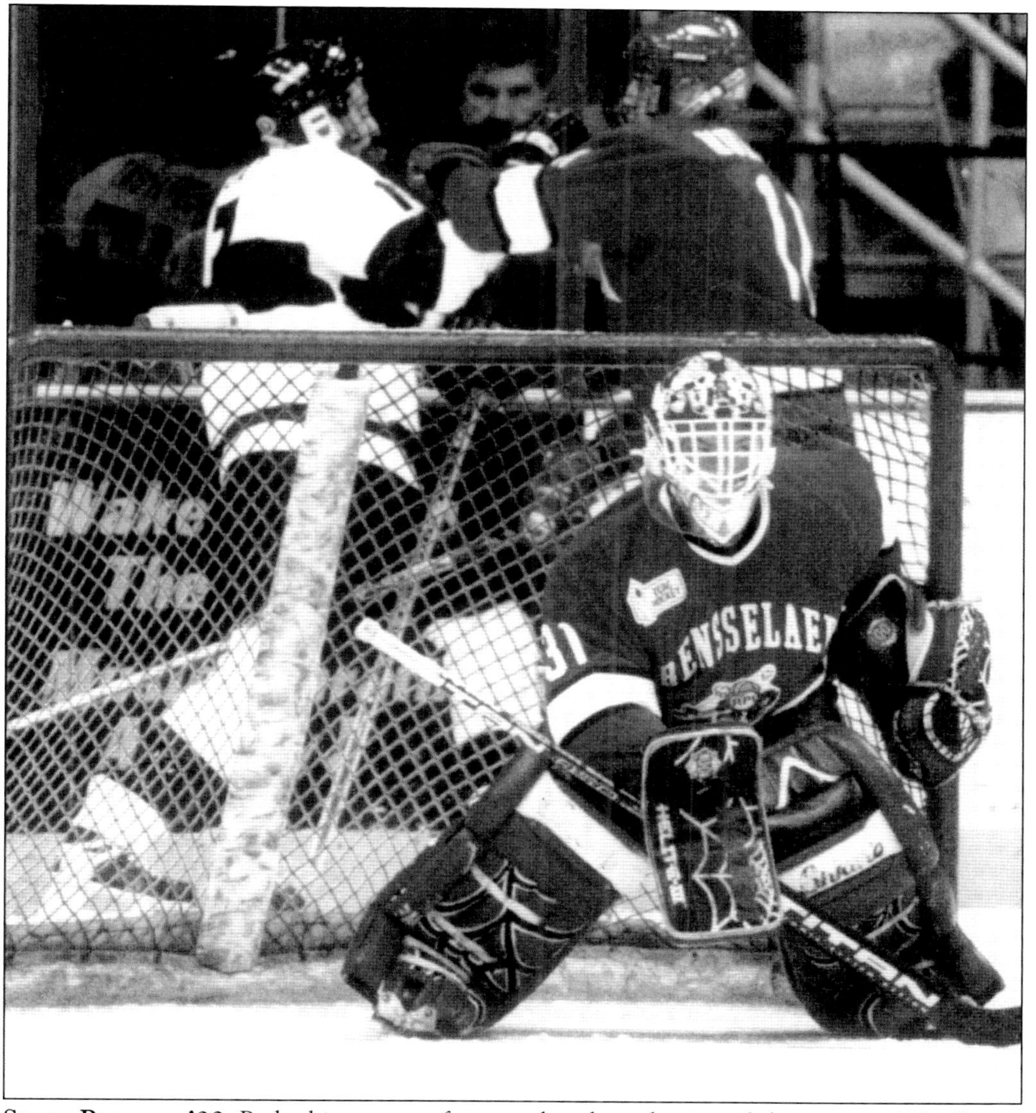

SCOTT PREKASKI '00. Prekaski was one of two goaltenders who joined the team in 1996 (Laing was the other). Both goaltenders shared time during all four years. Prekaski finished with a 31-19-6 record, with one shutout versus Colgate in February 1999. He played three games with the Richmond Renegades of the ECHL after leaving RPI in 2000.

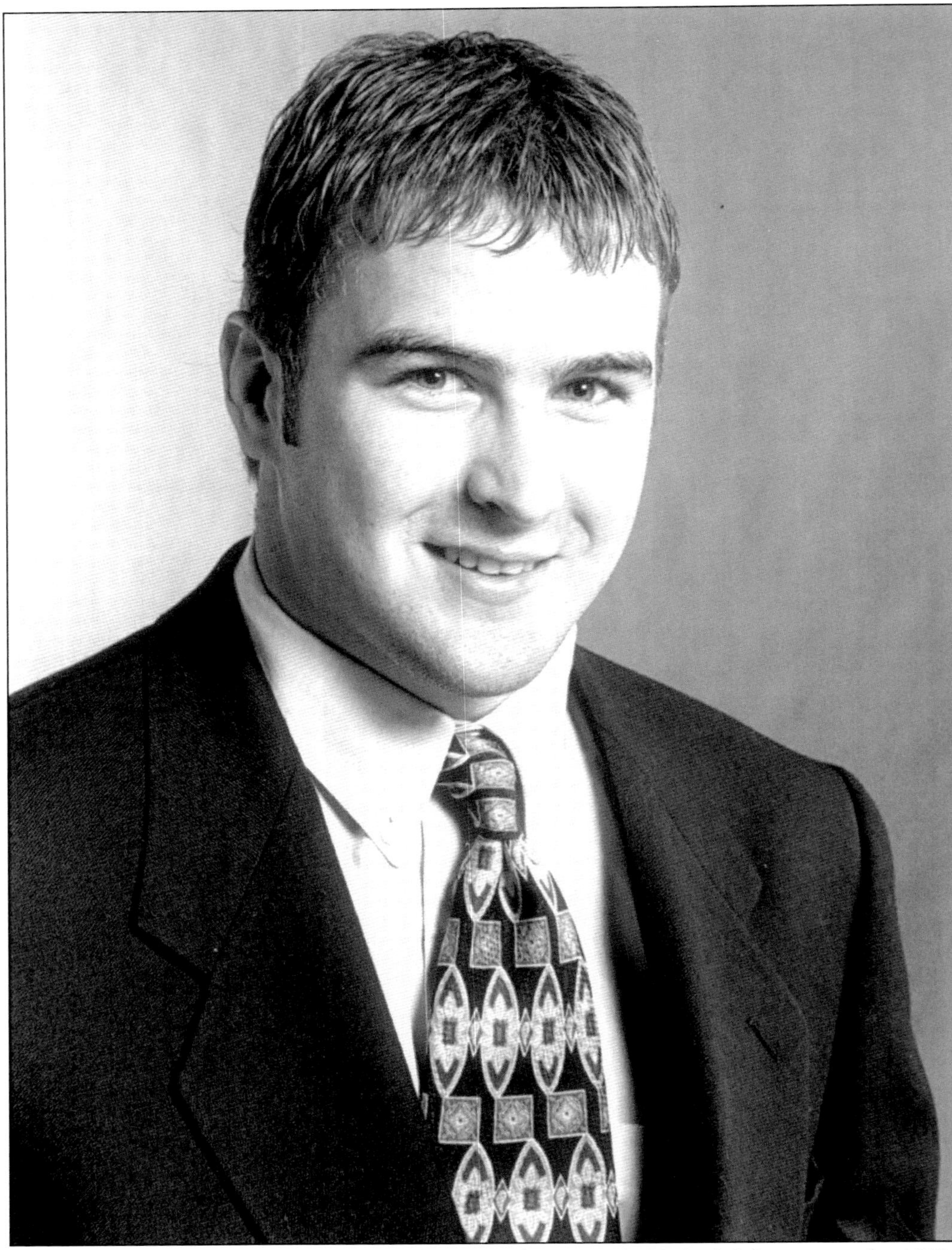

Joel Laing '00. Laing broke a number of longstanding records. He had 6 shutouts in the 1999–2000 season and 13 in his career. He finished with a 52-31-6 record, including the first RPI shutout in the playoffs in a 3-0 win against Cornell in 1998. His career save percentage of .926 is the best in school history. He was named to the East All-American first team in the 1999–2000 season and was named ECAC Goaltender of the Year that season. He has played in the minor leagues with the ECHL and AHL and in Great Britain.

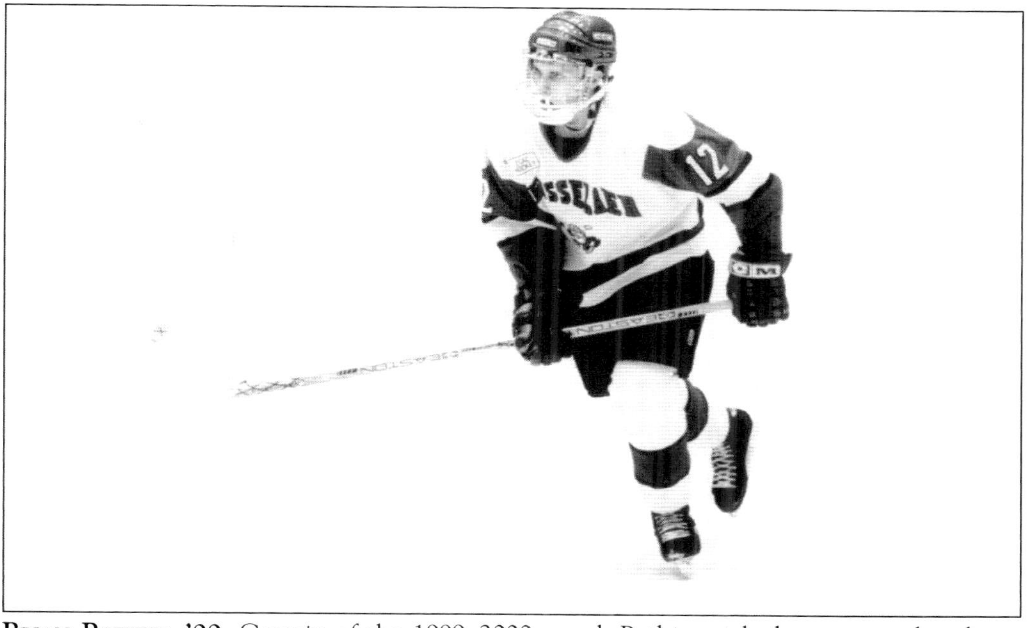

Brian Pothier '00. Captain of the 1999–2000 squad, Pothier picked up one goal and two assists in the 2000 ECAC playoffs, where RPI finished second to St. Lawrence University. He was named to the East All-American second team in the 1999–2000 season. The most successful of recent alums in the pros, Pothier spent the entire 2003–2004 season with the Ottawa Senators of the NHL.

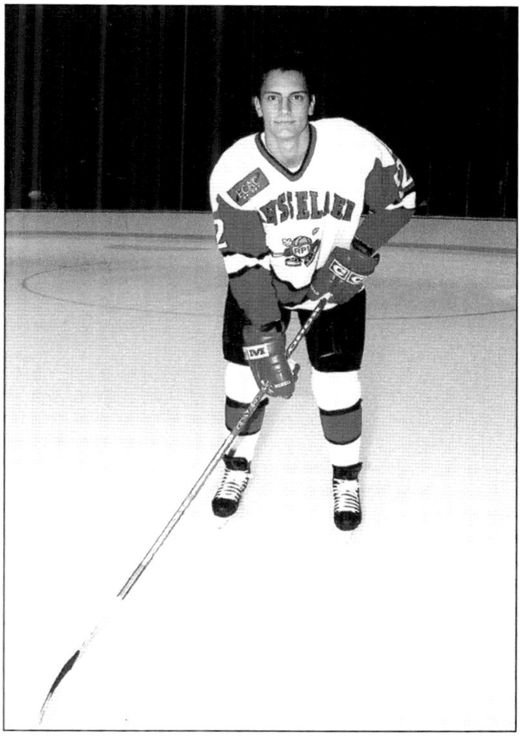

Brad Tapper '01. Brad Trapper, Bryan's younger brother, was a physical forward who scored goals and took his share of penalties. He finished his career with 65 goals and 51 assists in three seasons, after which he signed with the Atlanta Thrashers organization. He was on the East All-American second team in the 1999–2000 season. Through the 2003–2004 season, he played 71 NHL games and scored 25 points.

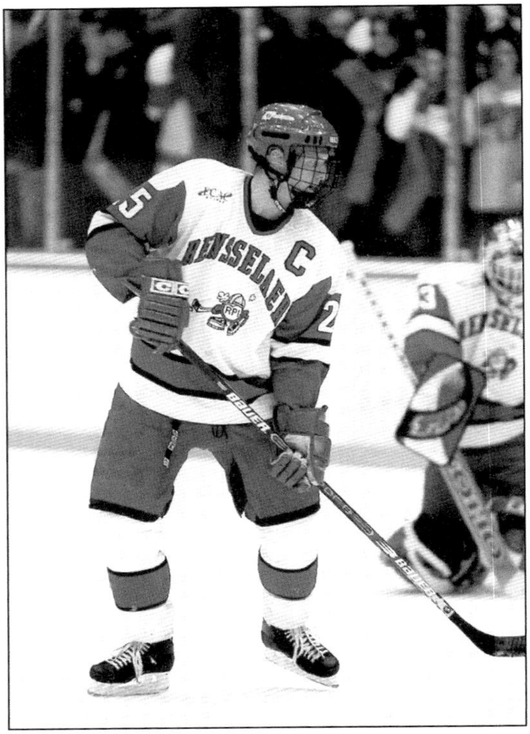

Steve Munn '02. Munn was captain during the 2000–2001 season and co-captain during the 2001–2002 season. He played a tight blue line and did not venture deep in the offensive zone, as college hockey has continued to change into a more defensive game. Munn finished his career of 140 games with 33 points and went on to play in the ECHL and AHL.

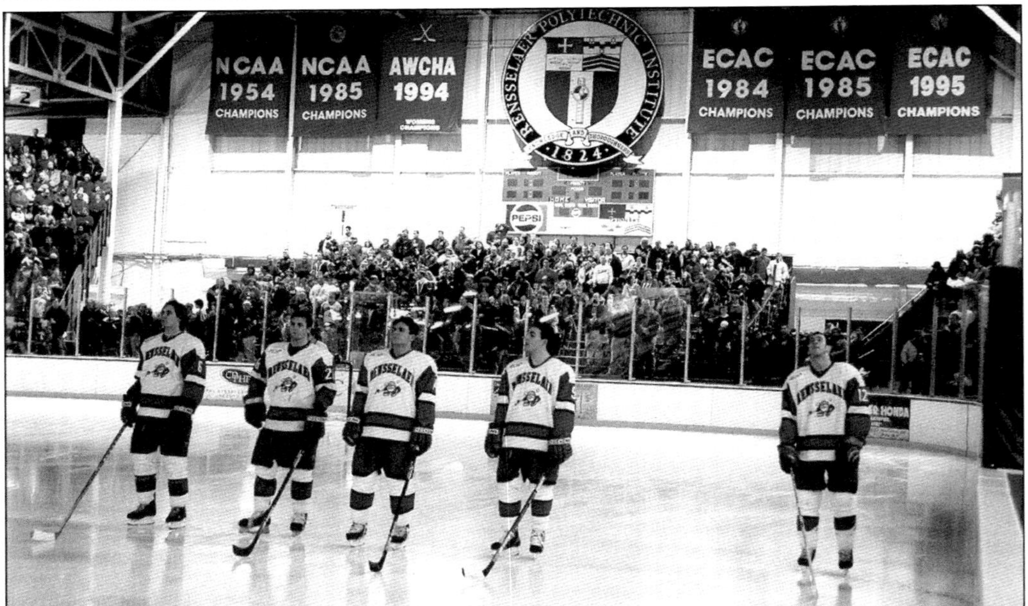

Banners. This image, taken prior to game time at the field house, shows the championship banners on display. Two banners, from 1954 and 1985, represent the NCAA Championships; three, from 1984, 1985, and 1995, are for the ECAC Tournament championships; and the American Women's College Hockey Alliance (AWCHA) 1994 banner is for the national championship won by the women's club team before it became a varsity program.

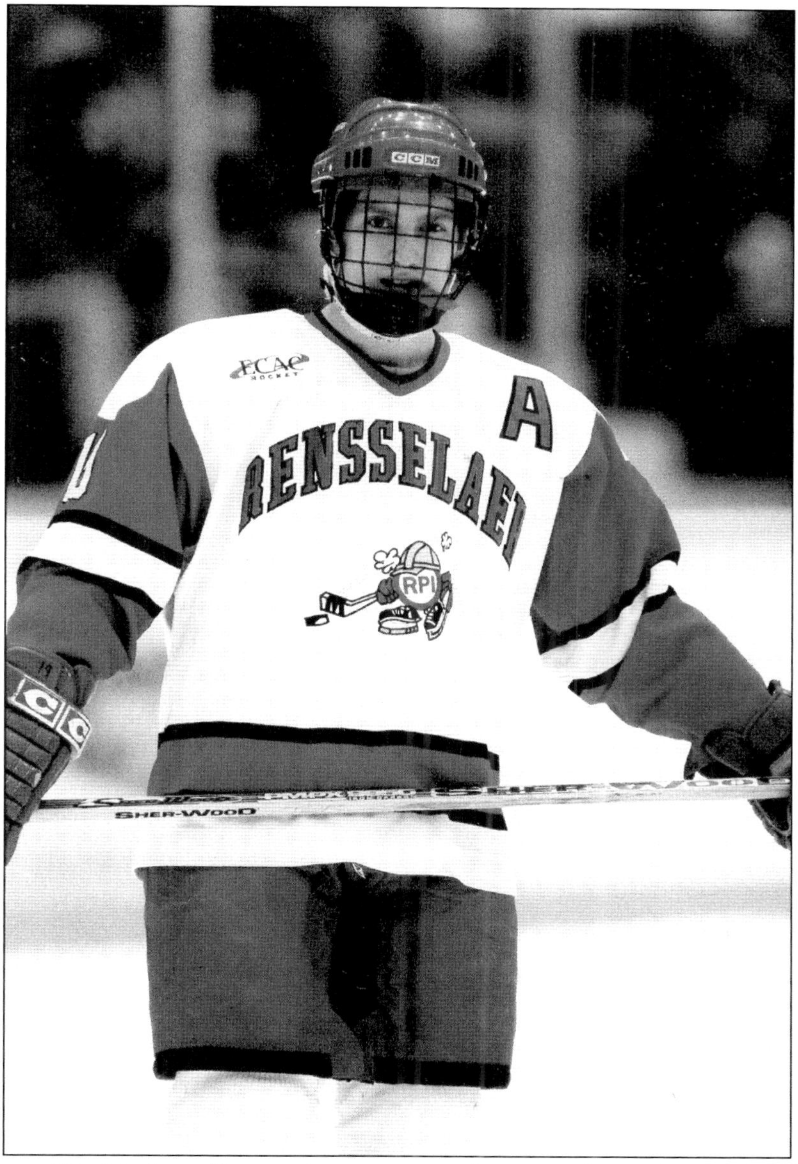

Matt Murley '02. Murley, a Troy native, grew up an Engineers fan and wanted to play for the hometown team. He came on strong his rookie season and finished second in scoring with 49 points and was named to the ECAC All-Rookie team. That off-season, he was drafted by the Pittsburgh Penguins in the second round as the 51st overall pick, the earliest any RPI player has been taken in the NHL draft. Murley followed up with a 38-point sophomore year and a 42-point junior year. He was named a co-captain his senior year and produced a 46-point season that got him named to the East All-American second team and All-ECAC first team. In the playoffs, it was his goal that tied Dartmouth College with 3:26 left that kept the Engineers alive. RPI won 2-1 but lost the semifinal game. The Engineers were forced into the consolation game, where Murley came up with a power-play goal with only 32 seconds left to defeat archrival Clarkson University 4-3. Subsequent to RPI, Murley joined the Penguins organization and played 18 games with the parent club in the 2003–2004 season.

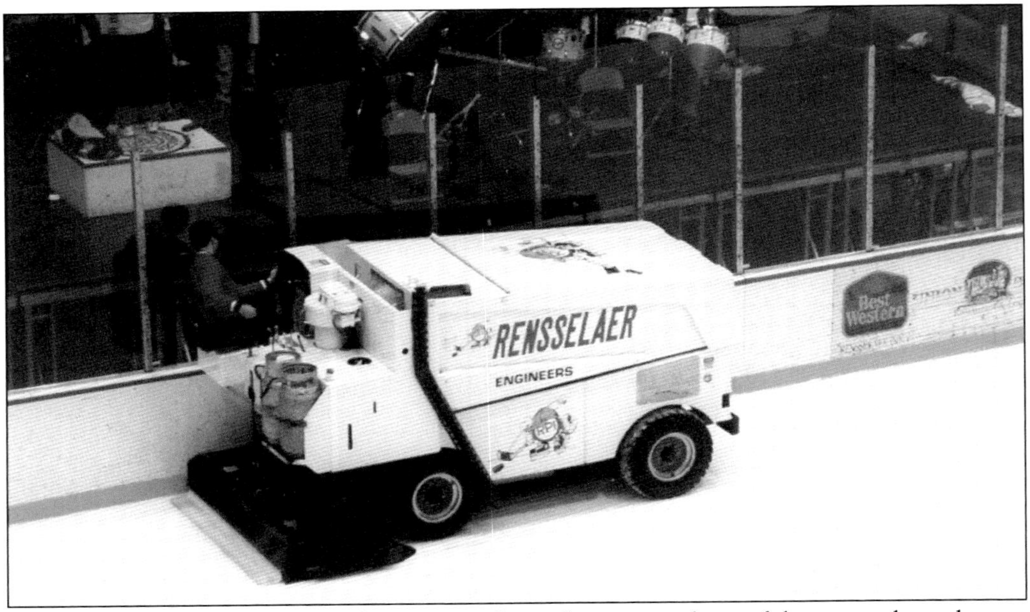

The Zamboni. The modern Zamboni ice machine cleans up in front of the stage where the pep band is stationed. The Puckman logo, the inspiration for the mascot, is pictured on the side and top of the machine. Two machines are now used to clean the ice faster and allow for promotions during the intermissions.

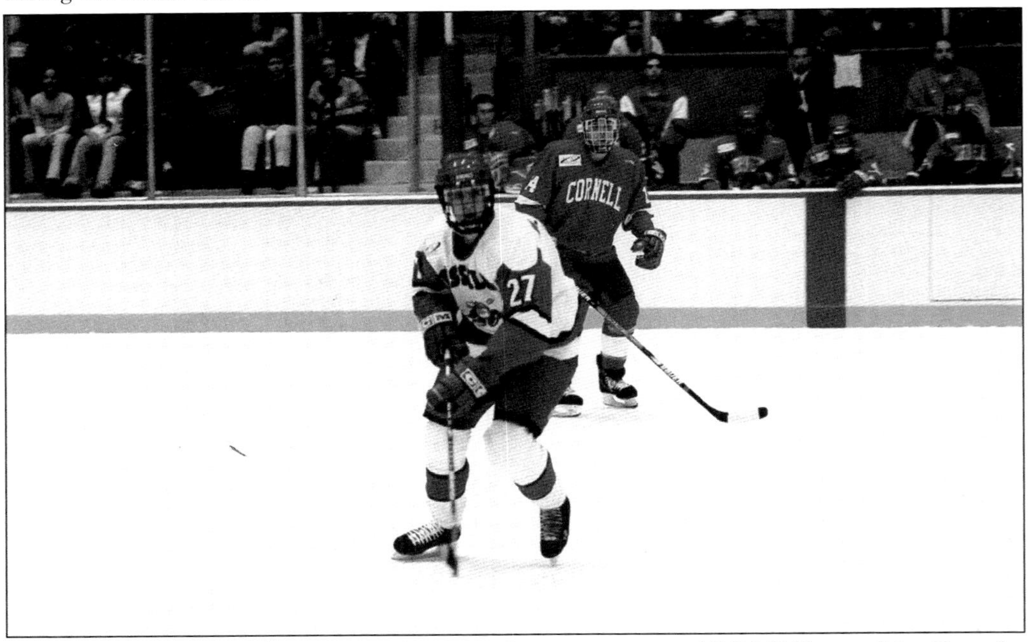

Marc Cavosie '03. In the 2001–2002 season, Cavosie was named ECAC Player of the Year, the first Engineer with that honor since Bob Brinkworth in the 1963–1964 season. He was also a first-team East All-American, and he had a career-best 50 points in 2001–2002, when RPI made it to the ECAC semifinals at Lake Placid. His older brother, Eric '02, played for RPI, and their father, Tom, was an equipment manager for the team until his sudden death in July 2003.

Nolan Graham '03. Graham took over from St. Hilaire the role as the preferred face-off man for the team. After a slow freshman year, he topped 20 points in his remaining three seasons, finishing with 77 points, 50 of them on assists. The year after he left RPI, he began playing in the ECHL.

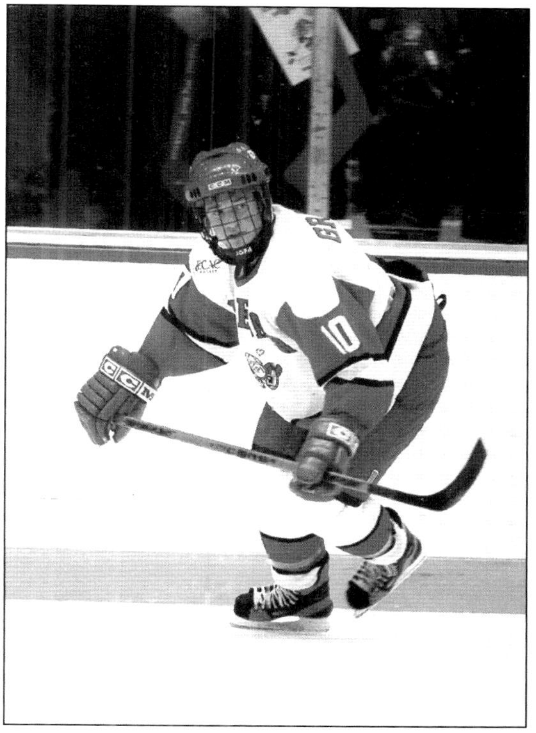

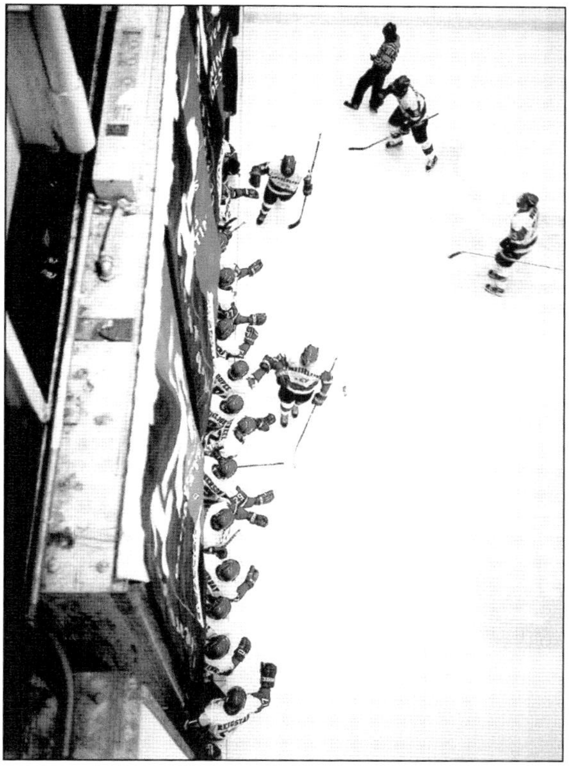

Catwalk. A view not seen by the general public, this is what it is like for broadcasters and assistant coaches to watch the ice. The field house catwalk is located about 25 feet above the ground and overhangs the ice by about two feet. It is not a location for the acrophobic, but it does offer an outstanding view of the game and makes it easy to see plays develop.

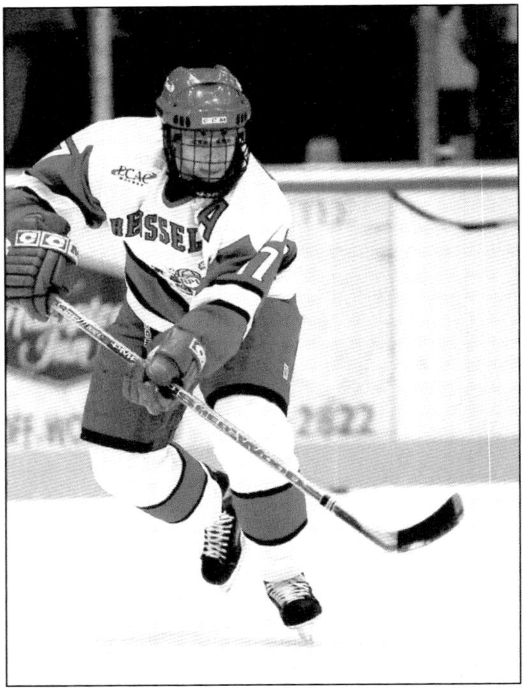

Danny Eberly '03. A defenseman and captain for the 2002–2003 team, Eberly was an eighth-round draft pick of the New York Rangers in 2000. His work on the blue line helped RPI attain some of its lowest goals-against averages in program history. As is now common among college hockey players, he continued his hockey career in the professional ranks, playing mostly for Atlantic City in the ECHL in the 2003–2004 season.

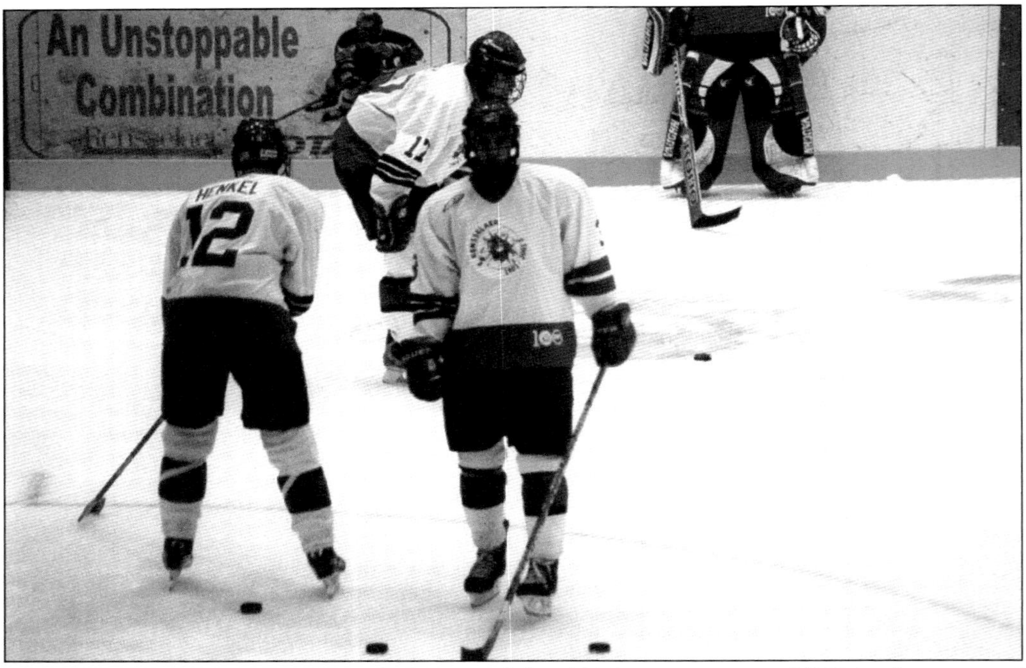

The Big Red Freakout, 2002. In honor of the 100th anniversary of RPI hockey, special jerseys were created for the celebration. Here, Jim Henkel '02 and C. J. Hanafin '05 are in pregame warmups. The 100th anniversary logo is on the front. The two stripes on the left arm represent the two national championships, and the three stripes on the right arm represent the three ECAC titles.

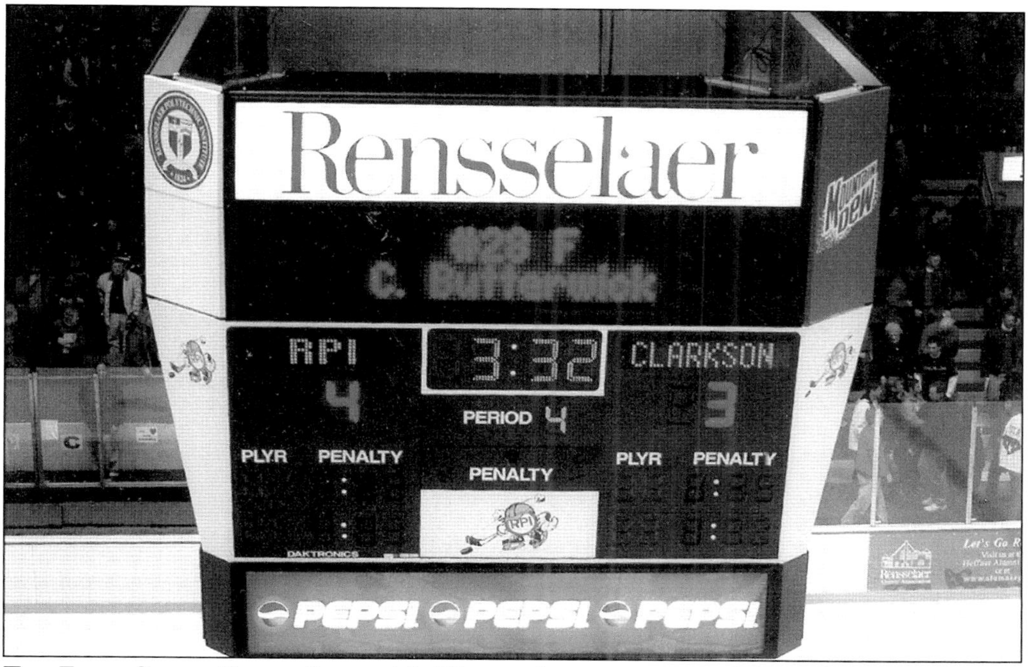

THE FINAL SCORE. Carson Butterwick '03 scored in overtime to defeat Clarkson University 4-3. The Golden Knights led 3-0 with under 13 minutes to play, but RPI roared back with two goals from Marc Cavosie, one from Jim Henkel '02, and the game winner from Butterwick. The Big Red Freakout, a tradition since 1978, is a game in the spring semester when everyone is encouraged to wear red and cheer the team on.

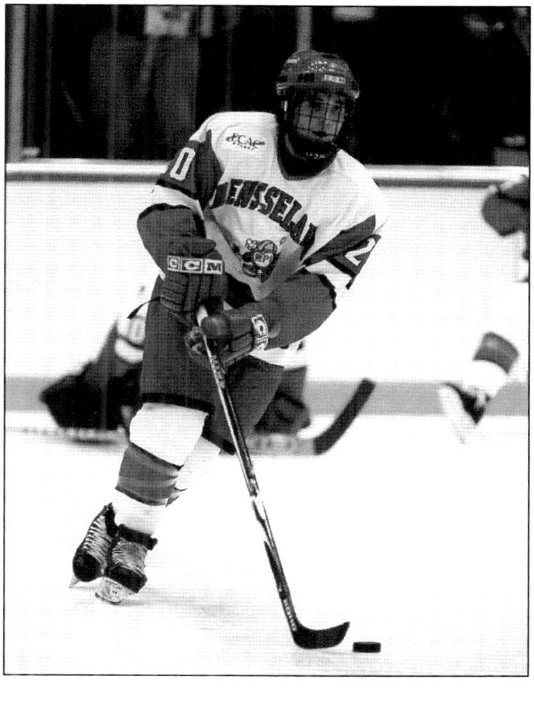

RYAN SHIELDS '04. Shields was a two-way forward who fit in well with Dan Fridgen's defensive style of hockey. He scored when it counted, and 7 of his 23 career goals either tied or won a game. Shields played well in the RPI Invitational Tournament in 2001. He assisted on the overtime game-winning goal by Chris Migliore '02 against Quinnipiac in double overtime. The next night, he scored both the tying and winning goals (the second in overtime) against the University of Massachusetts, and RPI won the tournament.

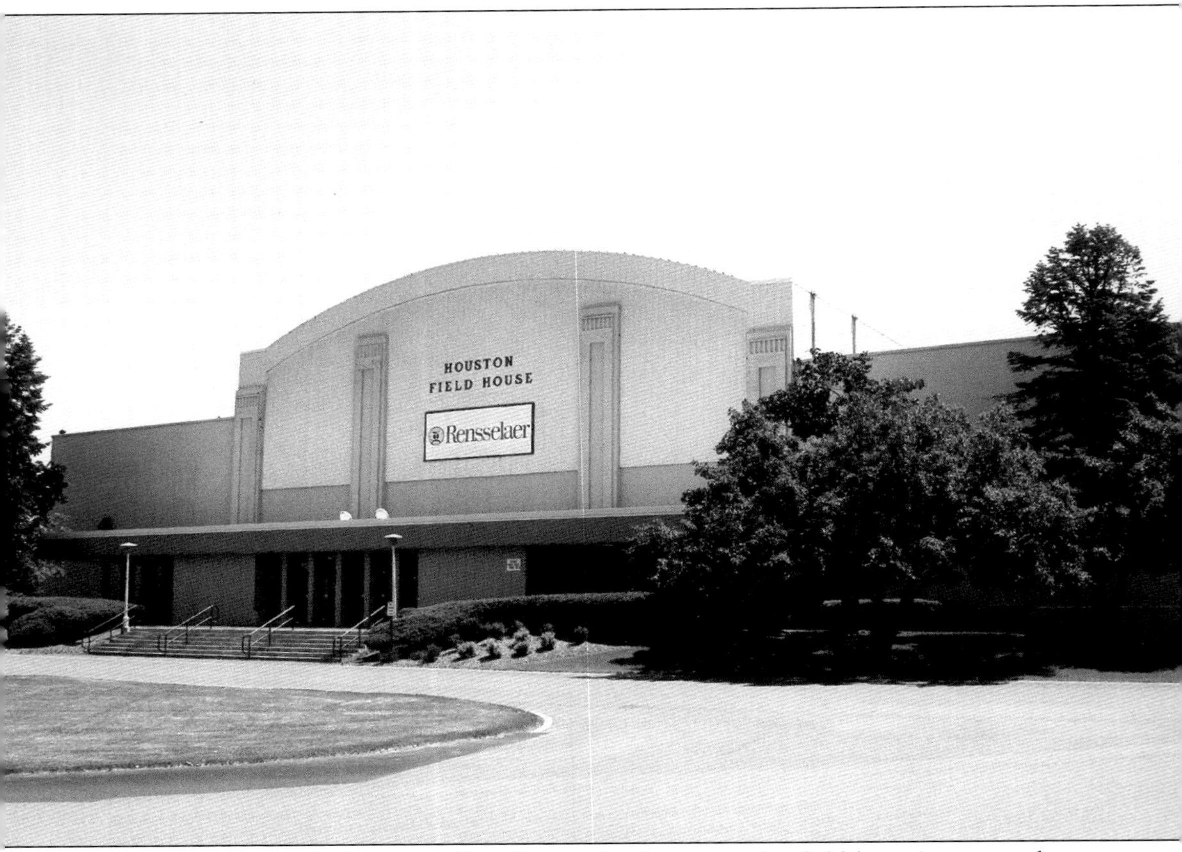

The Houston Field House, 2002. Except for the paint, the field house's exterior has not changed much since the 1960s. The noticeable difference is that it was renamed in honor of Livingston W. Houston '13. If Houston had not approved the decision to build the field house, RPI's hockey program would not exist. This is perhaps his greatest legacy to the school.

Scott Basiuk '04. Basiuk had his best scoring season as a senior and captain during the 2003–2004 season, when he picked up 26 points. This defenseman's most prominent game was at Lake Placid against Dartmouth in 2002. Just 1:28 after Matt Murley tied the game, Basiuk scored unassisted with 1:08 left and put the Engineers ahead to stay and advance.

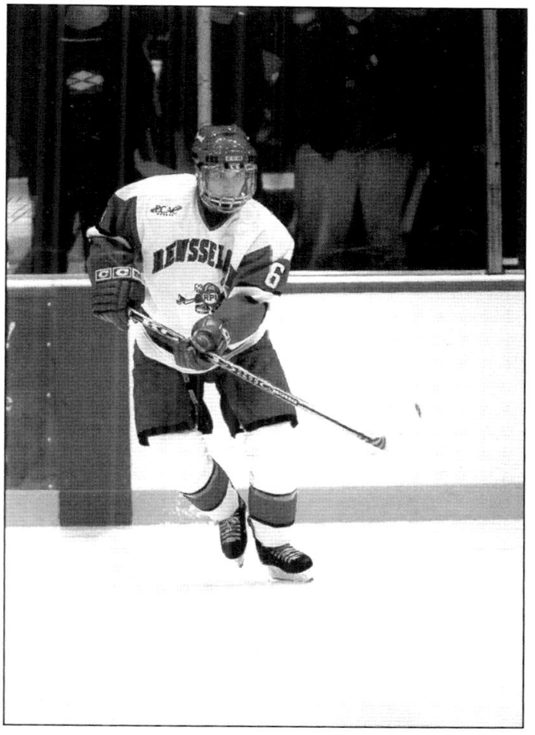

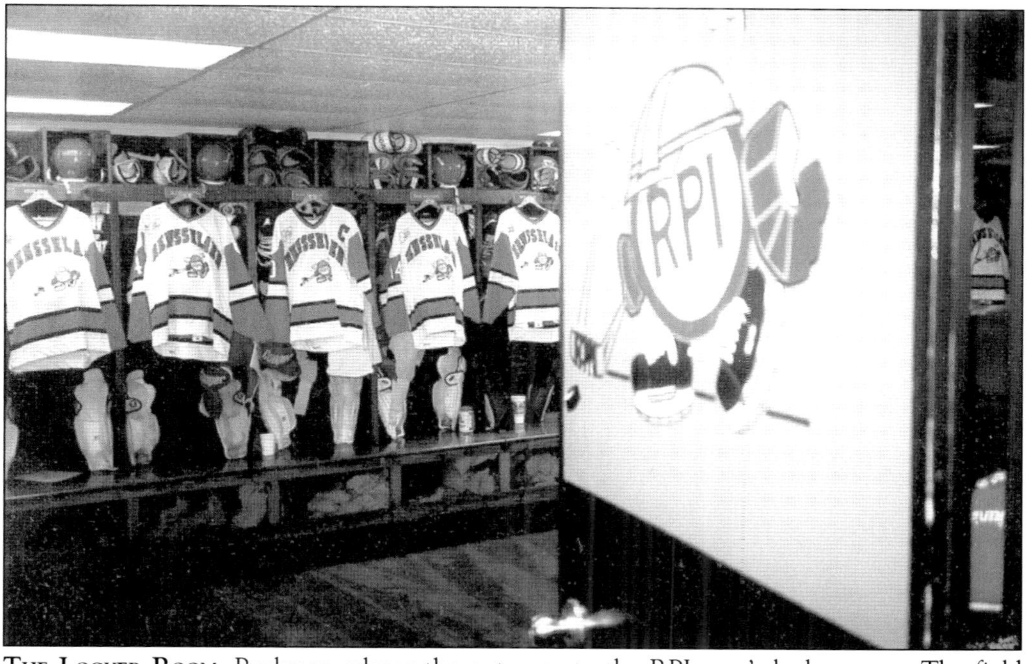

The Locker Room. Puckman adorns the entrance to the RPI men's locker room. The field house is a building of continual changes, as many improvements have been made subsequent to the major renovation in 1983. The locker room and training facilities were improved for both the men's and women's teams through the years, along with other behind-the-scenes changes.

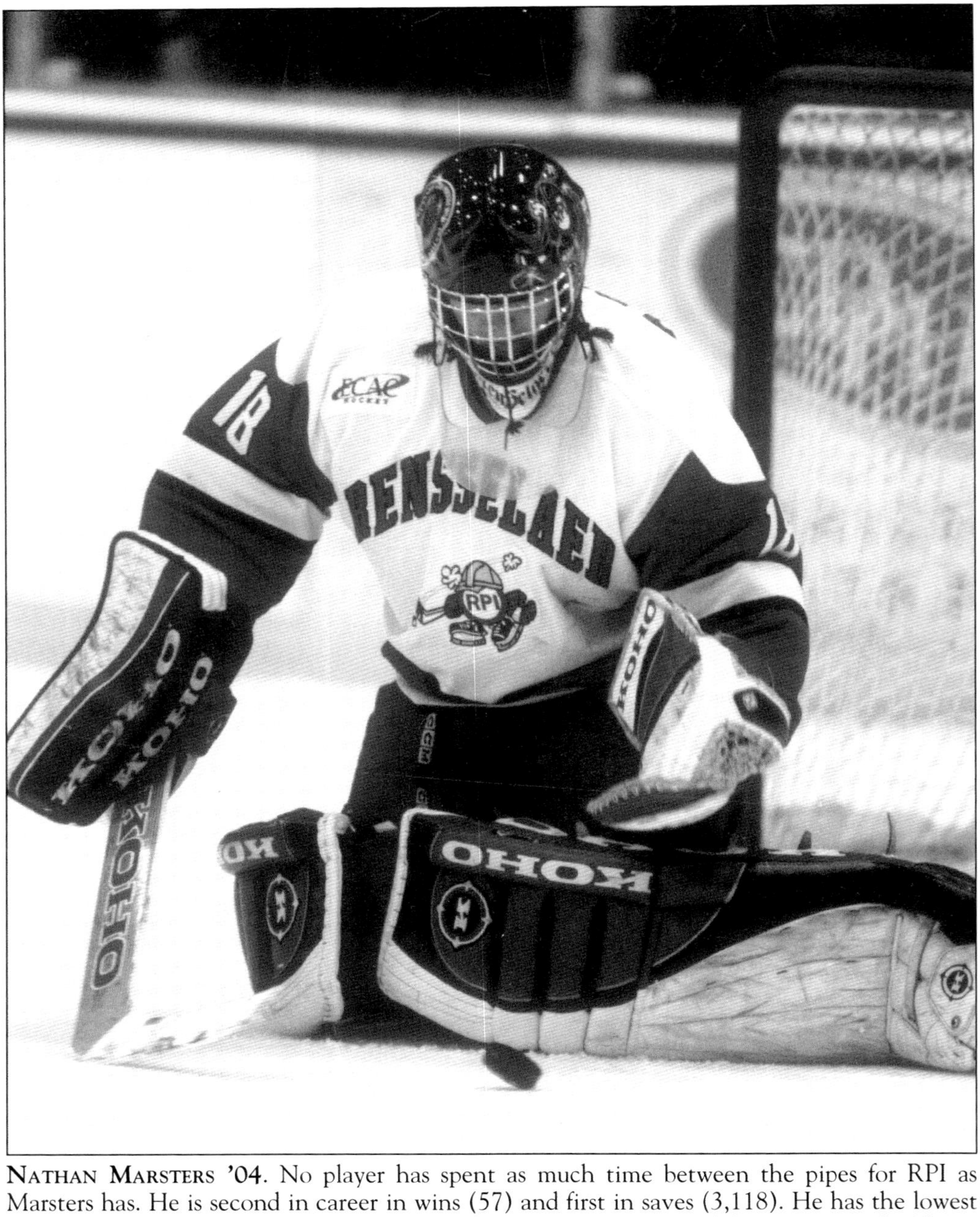

NATHAN MARSTERS '04. No player has spent as much time between the pipes for RPI as Marsters has. He is second in career in wins (57) and first in saves (3,118). He has the lowest goals-against average (2.55), the most games played in goal (115), and the most starts (107). He finished his career at RPI with a 57-50-6 record, which also makes him the goaltender with the most losses. Marsters was a member of the 2000–2001 ECAC All-Rookie team and was named to the All-ECAC second team in the 2003–2004 season, when he earned a 21-13-1 record with five shutouts. His goals-against average that year of 2.15 was the third best in school history. His heroics in net kept the Engineers in games on numerous occasions and left a huge hole to fill in the lineup. He was drafted by the Los Angeles Kings in the fifth round of the 2000 NHL draft, the 165th pick overall.

BEN BARR '04. Co-captain of the 2003–2004 team, Barr had his biggest clutch performance in the playoffs versus Union College in 2003. In the third period of Game 2, with RPI trailing by one goal, Barr scored two virtually identical shorthanded goals within a 50-second span to put the Engineers ahead to stay, and RPI advanced to the second round against Cornell.

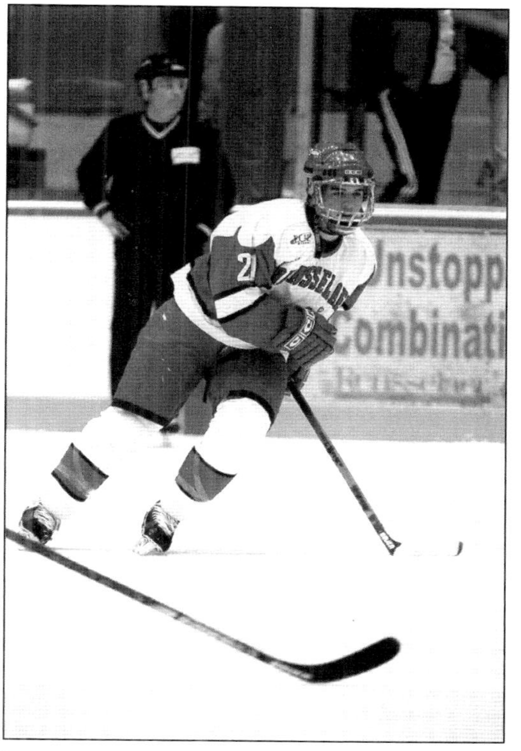

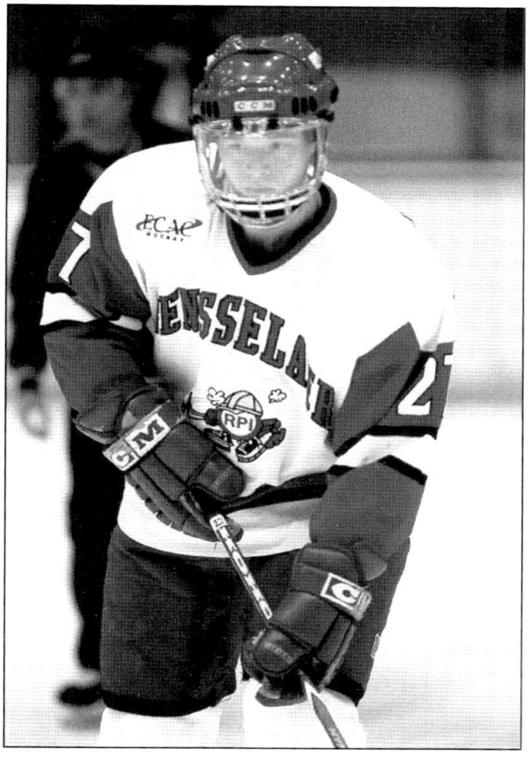

MIKAEL HAMMARSTROM '04. Hammarstrom was student from Sweden whose father played in the NHL. He was the first European native to suit up for the Engineers but the second varsity player not from either the United States or Canada. Rafael Maximo de Arozarena '17 of Mexico City played right wing against Williams College on January 8, 1916, and took that honor.

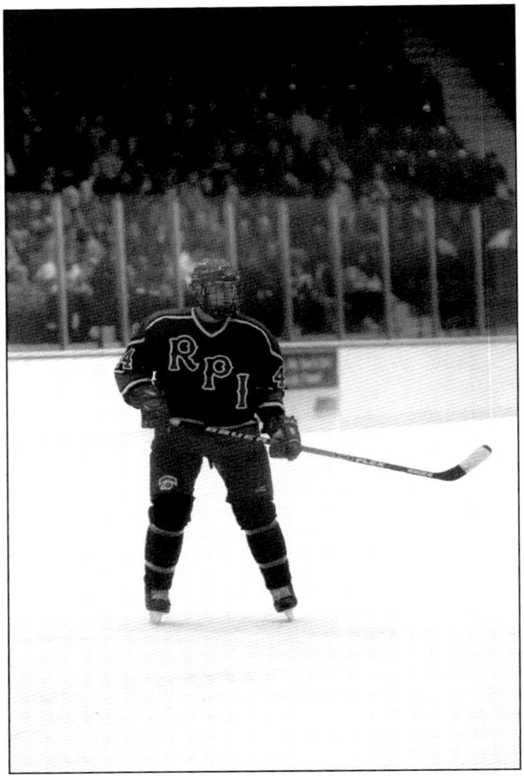

Brad Farynuk '06. A defenseman from British Columbia, Farynuk put up good offensive numbers his first two seasons. He is seen here wearing the Black Friday uniforms in 2003, the start of a new tradition whereby the crowd can bid on the actual game jerseys in an auction, and the winners receive them after the game. This popular promotion was instituted by Ken Ralph, the director of athletics.

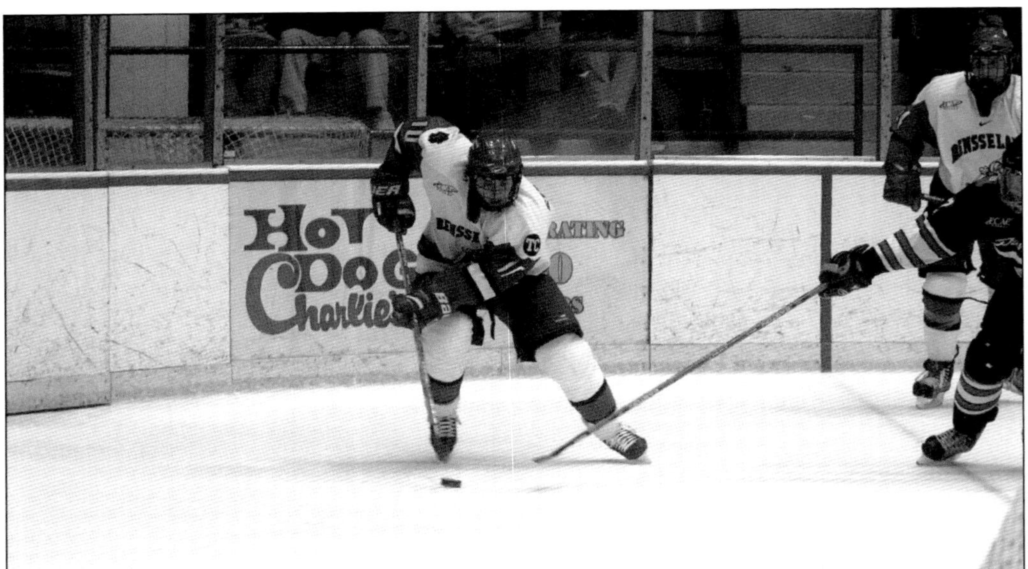

Oren Eizenman '07. Eizenman was named to the ECAC All-Rookie team his first season and led the Engineer rookies in scoring with 18 points. He took over the position as the go-to man on face-offs when the team needs a win.

Six

Women's Hockey

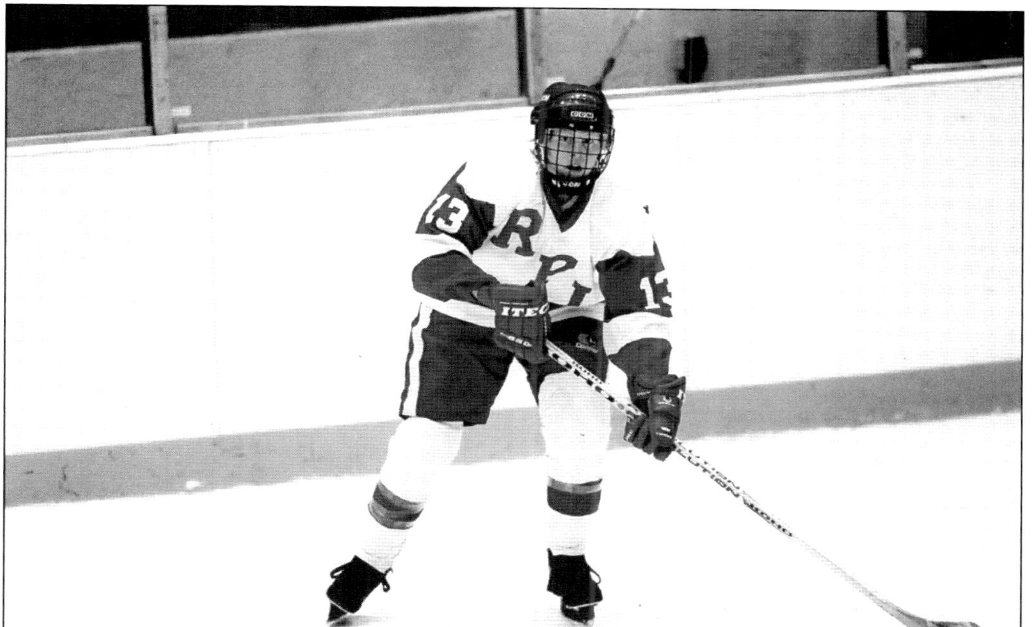

Bridget LaNoir '99. A local player from Glens Falls, LaNoir appeared right as the women's program earned varsity status. She led the team in scoring her freshman year and was named All-ECAC every season she played, making the first team in her sophomore and junior seasons and the second team in her freshman and senior seasons. After graduation, she taught at the National Sports Academy in Lake Placid before returning to RPI as an assistant hockey coach and head lacrosse coach.

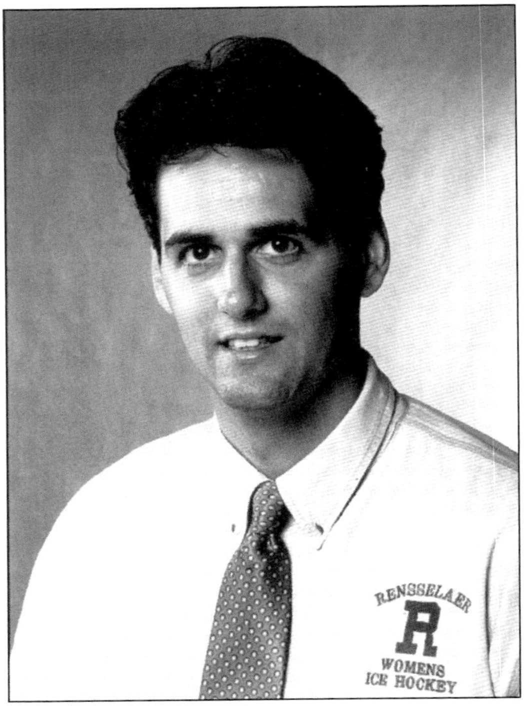

RYAN STONE '93. Stone was the coach who brought the women's team from club to varsity status. He first coached the club team in the 1992–1993 season and won the national club title in 1994. In 1995, the team went varsity, competing at the Division III level. Stone coached for the first five varsity seasons, making the playoffs in the last two, while pursuing his doctorate at RPI.

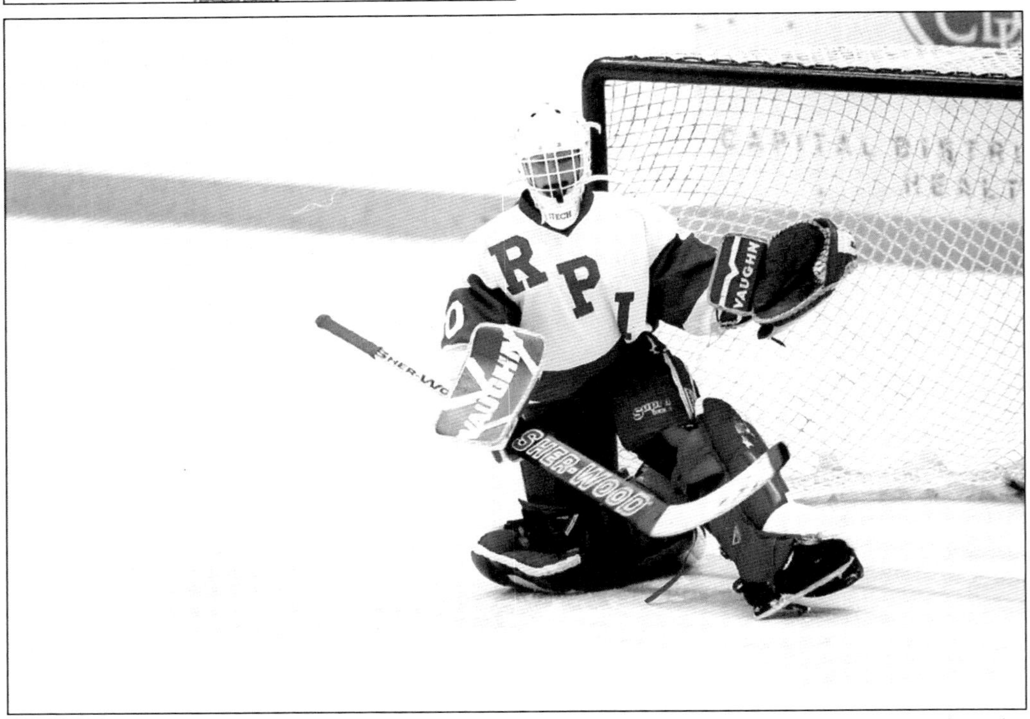

NINA LYNCH '00. A goaltender who also played field hockey and lacrosse at RPI, Lynch is the career leader in victories (32) and shutouts (10). She co-captained the team her junior and senior seasons, during which 7 of her 14 victories were shutouts.

CINDY ACROPOLIS '00. Acropolis played concurrently with Talia Acompora, and these two are the highest scoring players in team history. Acropolis holds the team records for most goals in a career (128) and a season (43 in 1996–1997). Her career total of 212 points is also the most in school history, and she had 16 hat tricks during her four years. She was named the ECAC Rookie of the Year in the 1996–1997 season and was also on the All-ECAC first team that season. She made the All-ECAC second team her sophomore and junior years. Acropolis twice scored five times in one game, against Wesleyan in 1997 and Trinity in 1999, team records as well. She was voted the team's Most Valuable Player every year she played, either solo or with Bridget LaNoir or Talia Acompora. During her high school years in Brick, New Jersey, she lettered four years while playing for the boys' team.

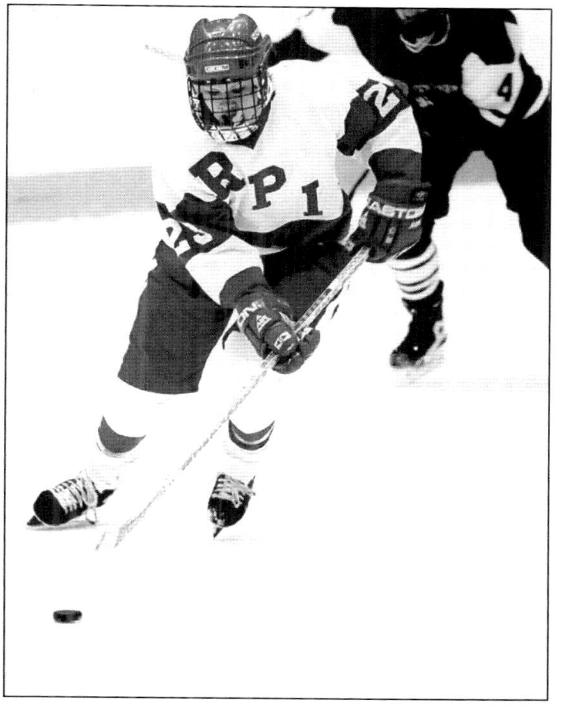

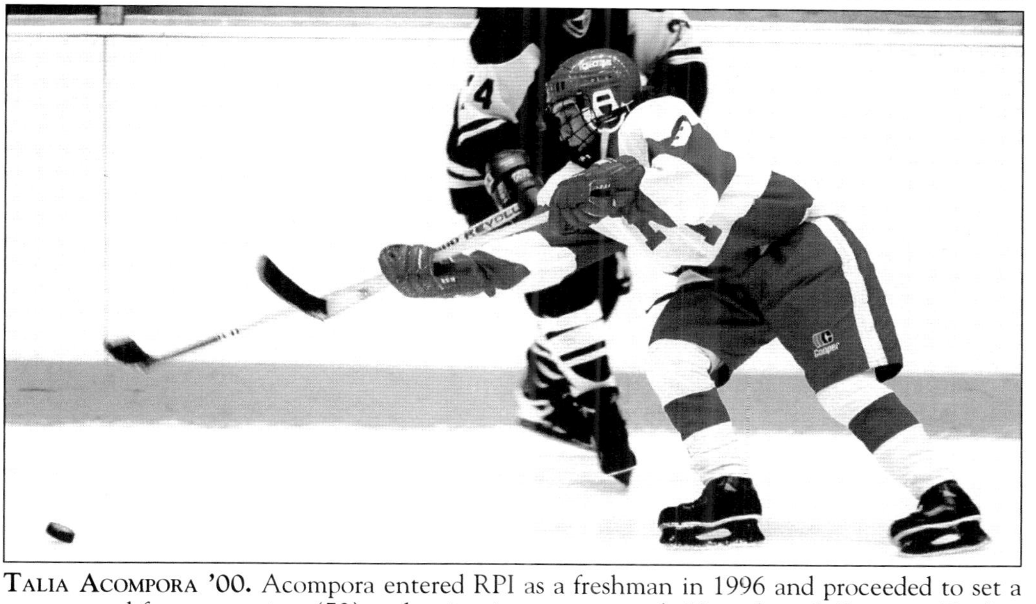

TALIA ACOMPORA '00. Acompora entered RPI as a freshman in 1996 and proceeded to set a team record for most points (73) and assists in a season, with 30 goals and 43 assists. For her efforts that year, she was voted team Rookie of the Year along with Nina Lynch. She is second on the career points list with 184 and leads in careers assists at 111. In the three seasons that Acompora, Acropolis, and LaNoir played together, the Engineers improved the goal differential from plus 9 to plus 44 and, finally, to plus 61, and they reached the playoffs for the first time in 2000, their last season. After she and Acropolis graduated in 2000, the team fell to 10th in the standings, missing their offensive output greatly.

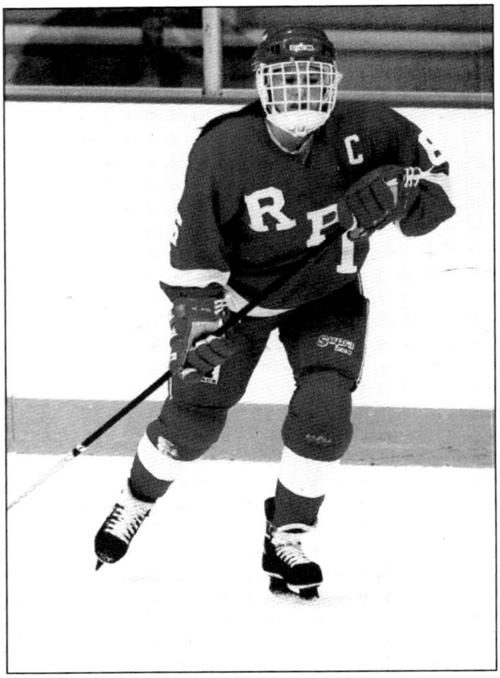

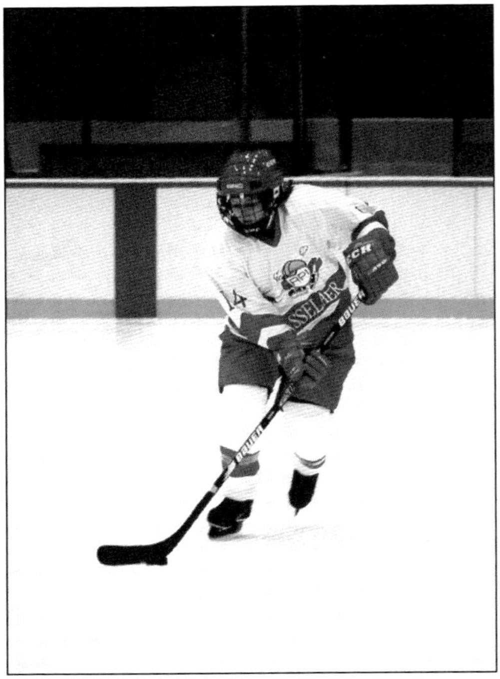

HEATHER SCAMMELL '98 AND JENNIFER SCAMMELL '02. Heather and Jennifer were the first pair of sisters who played for the varsity program, although they never played at the same time. Heather started with the team while it was still in club status and became co-captain her junior and senior seasons. Jennifer started the year after Heather graduated, in 1998. They are the daughters of Richard Scammell '69, a forward for the men's team who led RPI in scoring his junior and senior seasons. Richard finished his career with 137 points.

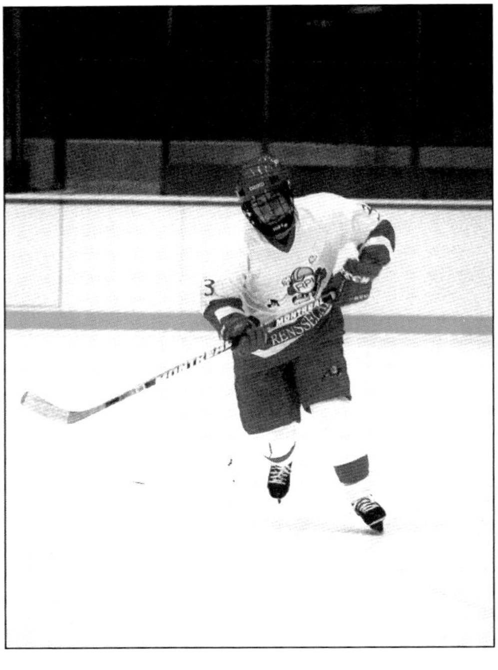

KATE ADAMS '02. Adams was a tri-captain during her senior year, her best on the squad. That year, she earned 33 points, was named ECAC East Player of the Year, and made the East All-ECAC first team. She picked up four points when RPI defeated Union College in the ECAC quarterfinals in 2002 and was named to the ECAC East All-Tournament team.

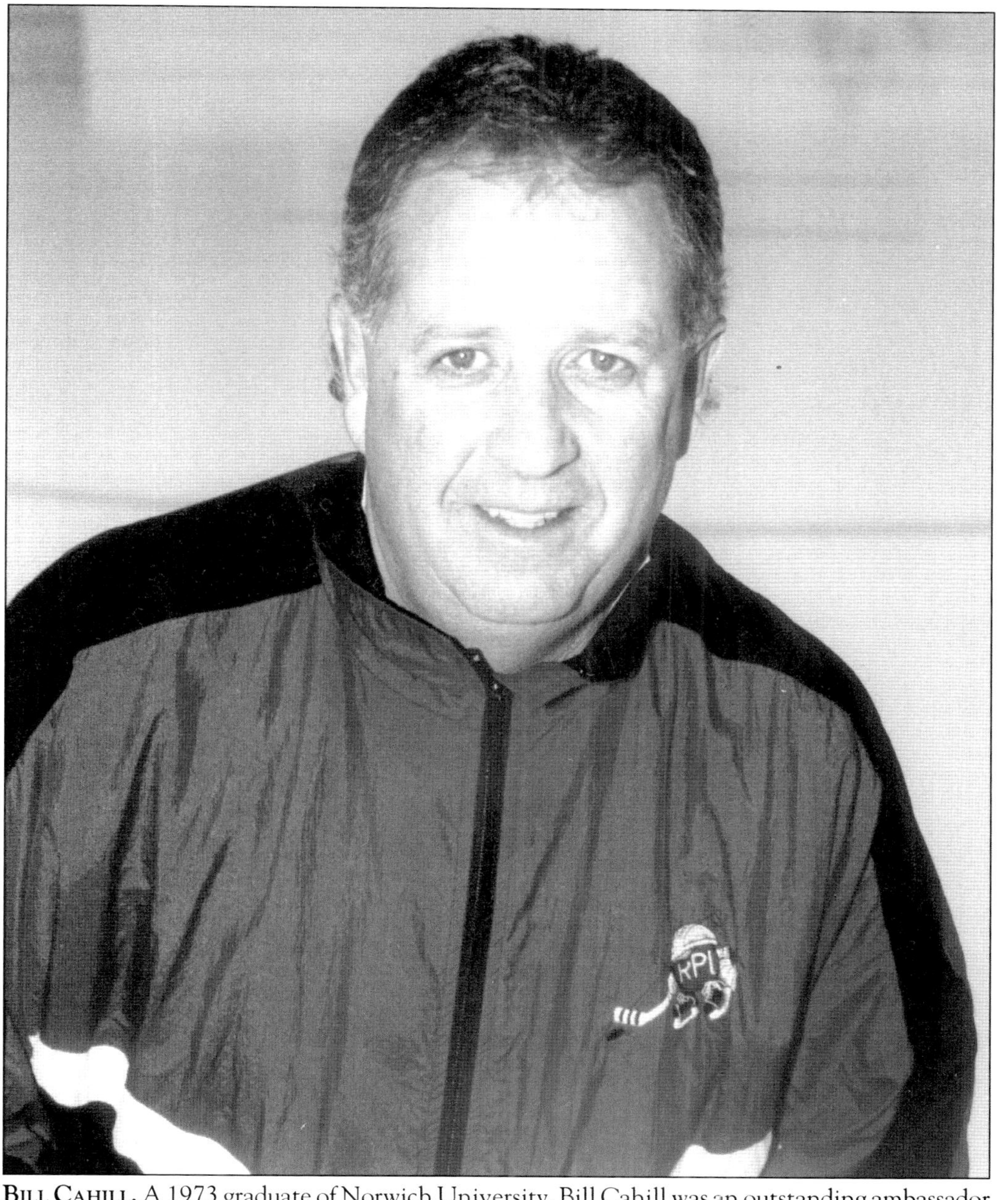

Bill Cahill. A 1973 graduate of Norwich University, Bill Cahill was an outstanding ambassador for RPI and the sport of hockey. Cahill began at RPI as an assistant to the men's team in 1988. He served as interim head coach after Addesa's resignation until Powers was hired. In 1990, he left RPI for Norwich for five seasons and was head coach there for the last three. He returned to RPI as the top assistant coach in 1995 took over the women's team after Stone's departure in 2000. He compiled a 47-28-3 record as head coach and improved the squad each year. The team finished second in both the regular season and playoffs in 2002–2003 season, earning Cahill ECAC East Coach of the Year honors. Cahill made appearances at all RPI sporting events and loved to talk with fans, which is why his sudden death in October 2003, on the eve of his fourth season as head coach, shocked and affected so many people.

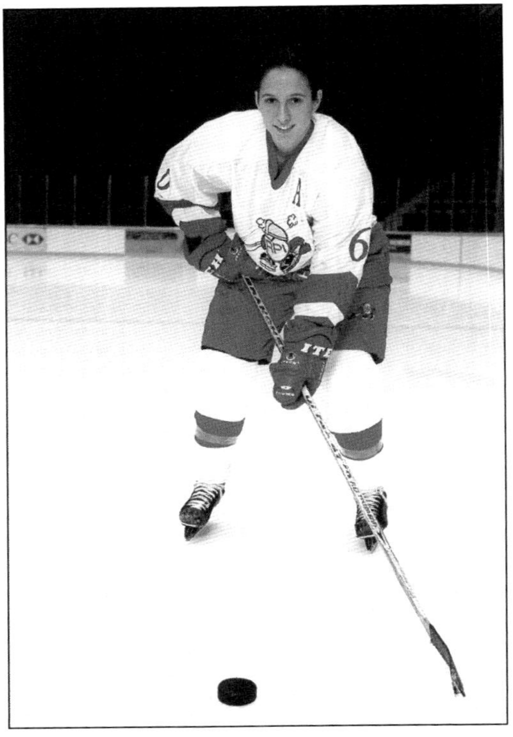

Andrea Poley '02. Named to the East All-ECAC first team her senior year, Poley led the team in scoring and picked up five points in the playoffs when RPI downed Union College and lost to Manhattanville College. She was a tri-captain that senior season, and her 110 career points are tied for fourth best. She is tied for most career games with 102.

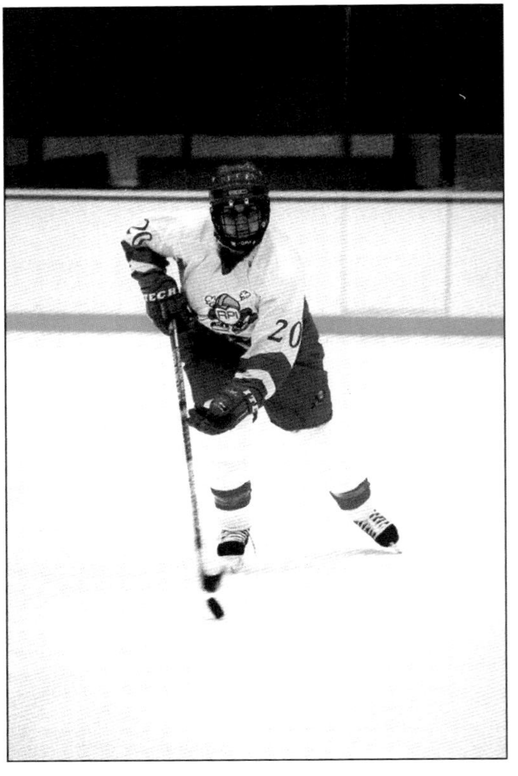

Julie Durham '02. The third tri-captain of the 2001–2002 squad, Durham had a hat trick in the playoff win over Union College, the only one ever in a playoff game. That season, she earned 30 points and was named the team's MVP. Durham shared MVP honors the previous season. Her younger sister, Paula '05, is also a hockey player.

SARA RIEL '03. Riel was an East All-ECAC second-team pick her senior year, when she co-captained the squad. She finished with 31 points in her career as a defensive player. Her stepfather, Craig Boutilier '81, played defense for the men's team and co-captained the 1980–1981 squad. This is the first instance of two generations of RPI players who captained the hockey teams.

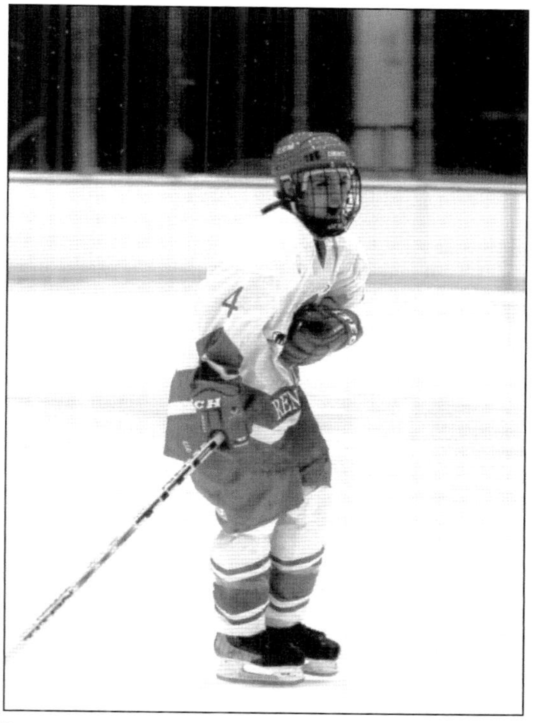

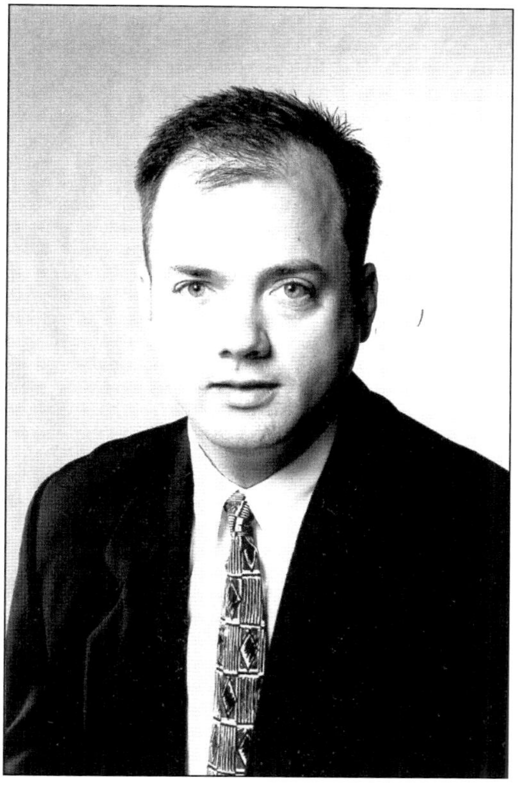

JOHN BURKE. Burke was named the third head coach of the women's team in October 2003. A native of Newton, Massachusetts, Burke played for Bowling Green State University as a goaltender, compiling a 12-14-1 record in 40 games with one shutout. He entered the coaching field after graduation, first with Worcester Academy, then as an assistant at Hamilton College, before becoming an assistant for RPI's men's team in 1995. After the death of Cahill in 2003, Burke took the reigns of the women's team. In the midst of the difficult circumstances, Burke led the team to a second consecutive second-place finish in the regular season and advanced the team to the title game of the ECAC East Tournament, where they lost to Manhattanville College in the finals 2-0.

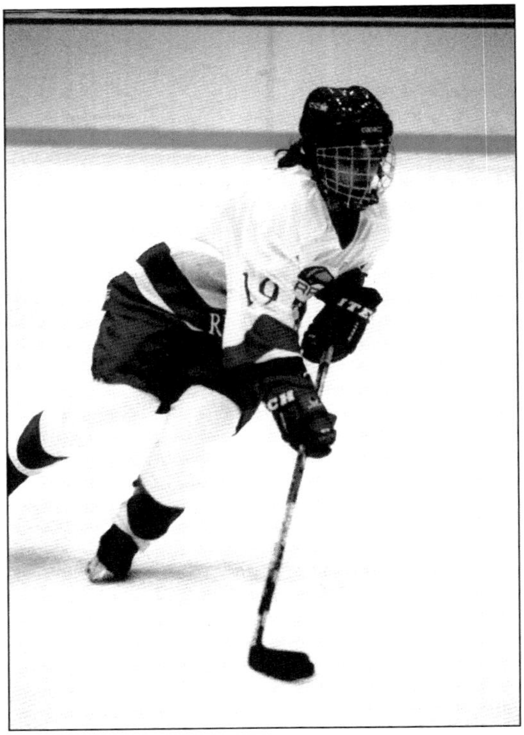

CHRISTIN SAUCA '03. Sauca was named to the East All-ECAC second team in her senior year. She was co-captain of the first team that advanced to a conference championship game, after RPI defeated Salve Regina University 11-0 and the University of Southern Maine 2-1. Sauca assisted on the lone goal in RPI's 2-1 loss in the title game to Manhattanville College in 2003.

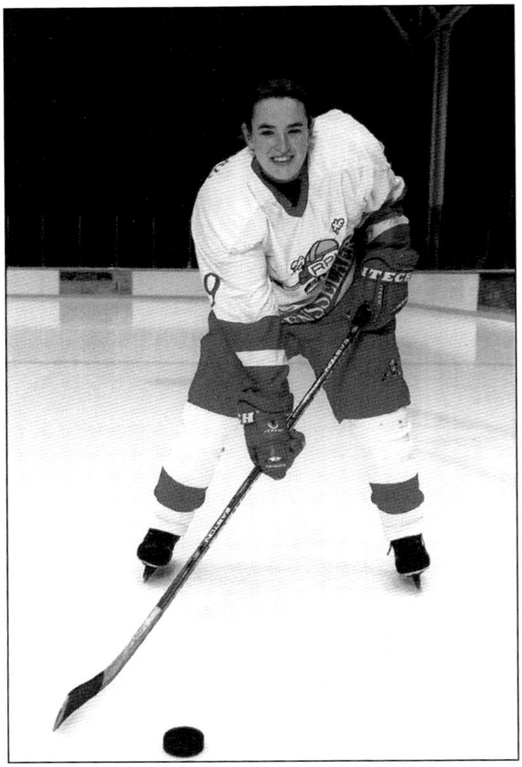

KATIE WOODWARD '04. A solid playoff performer, Woodward scored five goals and had three assists during RPI's seven playoff games from 2002 through 2004. She was named to the ECAC East All-Tournament team in 2003 because of her two-goal, three-assist performance. Woodward finished her career with 72 points in 101 games.

Julie Vallarelli '05. Vallarelli was second on the career victories list with a 30-14-2 record after only three years at the institute. She was named the ECAC East Goaltender of the Year for her performance in the 2002–2003 season, when she went 13-3-0 with five shutouts, a 2.33 goals-against average and an .899 save percentage. She was also named to the East All-ECAC first team in the 2002–2003 season and was an ECAC East All-Rookie the previous year.

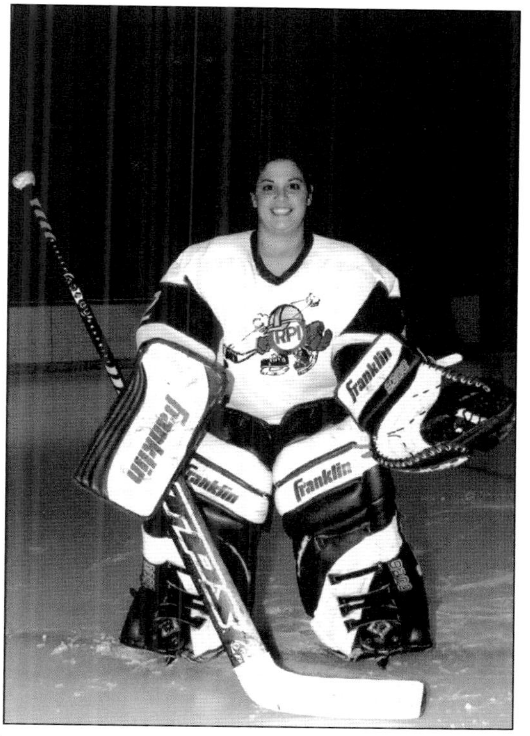

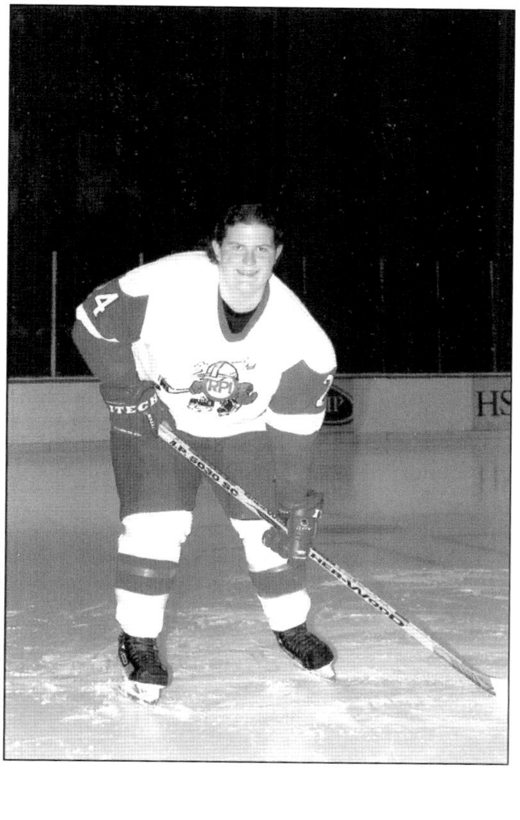

Julie Welte '06. The 2002–2003 ECAC East Rookie of the Year and member of the All-Rookie team, Welte started her career with the Engineers by leading the team with 22 goals and 33 points.

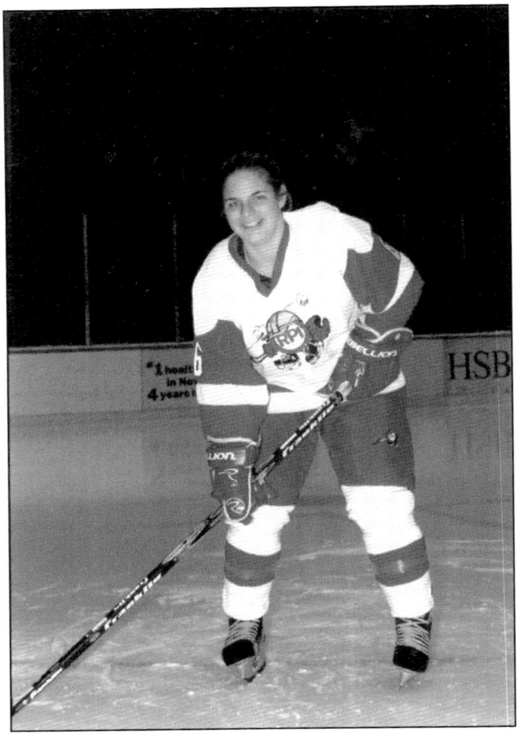

Kari Rabitin '06. Rabitin scored the game-winning goal with 6:31 left against the University of Southern Maine in the semifinals to put RPI in the 2003 ECAC East championship game. For her efforts in the postseason, she was named to the ECAC East All-Tournament team and was also on the All-Rookie team in the 2002–2003 season.

Rosina Schiff '06. Schiff earned a spot on the All-ECAC East second team in the 2003–2004 season after being named to the All-Rookie team the previous year. She has a combined record of 18-9-2 over those two seasons, with a .951 save percentage and 1.35 goals-against average. She shut out the Rochester Institute of Technology (RIT) 1-0 in January 2003, her first shutout and the first time RPI defeated RIT in regular-season play.

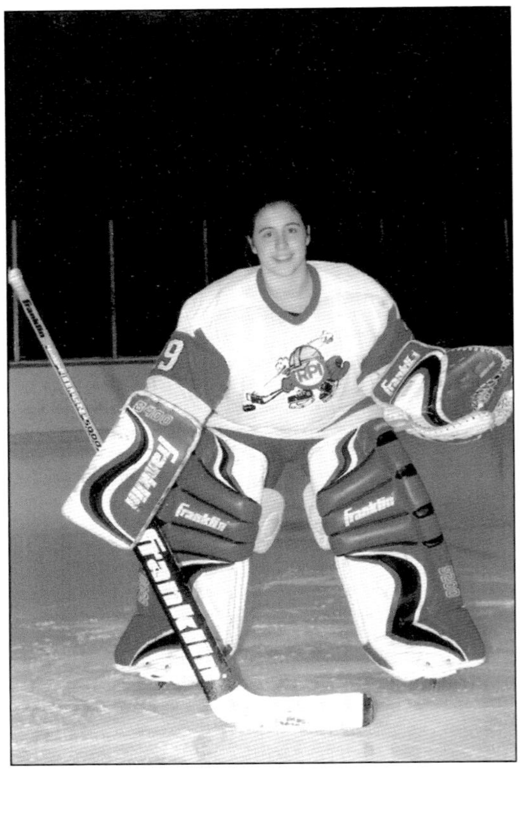